The Practice of Patriarchy

The
Practice of Patriarchy

Gender and the Politics of Household Authority
in Early Modern France

Julie Hardwick

The Pennsylvania State University Press
University Park, Pennsylvania

Library of Congress Cataloging-in-Publication Data

Hardwick, Julie, 1962–
    The practice of patriarchy : gender and the politics of household
authority in early modern France / Julie Hardwick.

        p.   cm.
    Includes bibliographical references and index.
    ISBN 0-271-01782-1 (cloth : alk. paper)
    ISBN 0-271-01783-X (pbk. : alk. paper)
    1. Family—France—Nantes—History—16th century. 2. Family
—France—Nantes—History—17th century. 3. Patriarchy—France
—Nantes—History—16 century. 4. Patriarchy—France—Nantes
—History—17th century. 5. Notaries—France—Nantes—History—
16th century. 6. Notaries—France—Nantes—History—17th century.
7. Nantes (France)—Social conditions. I. Title.
HQ624.15.N36H37   1998
306.85'0944—dc21   97-49175
                                                                              CIP

It is the policy of The Pennsylvania State University Press to use acid-free paper for
the first printing of all clothbound books. Publications on uncoated stock satisfy
the minimum requirements of American National Standard for Information Sci-
ences—Permanence of Paper for Printed Library Materials, ANSI Z39.48-1992.

Contents

Acknowledgments   vii

Introduction   ix

1   Notaries and Their Families   1

2   Notaries As Artisans of Credit, Confidence, and Political Culture   17

3   Making Marriages   51

4   Managing Households   77

5   Having and Holding: Managing Household Property   109

6   Dividing Patrimony   143

7   Kin and Friends: Networks of Daily Life   159

8   Public Life in the City   195

Conclusion   219

Bibliography   229

Index   238

Acknowledgments

Looking back with the hindsight of more than a decade, I can see that the roots of this book lie in my first year as a graduate student at Johns Hopkins. Orest Ranum organized his early modern French history seminar that year around something he called "legal culture," and I also took an anthropology seminar entitled "Gender, Kinship, and Power." Those two experiences eventually led me toward notaries and Nantes, a topic and archives that would allow me to explore how structures of authority and relations of power were mediated at a grassroots level in early modern society. From that earliest moment, Orest Ranum's encouragement and support have continued unwaveringly. For this reason and others, I am deeply appreciative of my experience at Hopkins, where the History Department's faculty, students, and seminars made it a veritable mecca for early modernists.

From the start, when Jim Collins found me an apartment in Nantes, many of my fellow early modernists—friends, conference collaborators, colleagues, and readers—have generously proffered help of every kind at every turn. I am very grateful to all of these people, who are too numerous to name individually. I am especially indebted to Claire Dolan, Donna Merwick, Laurie Nussdorfer, and Ann Wightman, who have shared their still largely unpublished works-in-progress on early modern notaries around the world with me.

Earlier versions and different forms of some of this material appeared as "Widowhood and Patriarchy in Seventeenth-Century France," *Journal of Social History* 26 (Fall 1992); and "Women Working the Law: Gender, Authority, and Legal Process in Early Modern France," *Journal of Women's History* 9 (Fall 1997).

My stays in Nantes were distinguished by the professionalism of the archival staff at the departmental and municipal archives, by the bonhomie of our landlord, Jean Cailleau, and his family, and by the friendship of my fellow archival wayfarers Didier and Isabelle Besseau.

Invaluable financial support came from a variety of institutions. My initial research and writing was funded by fellowships from the History Department at Johns Hopkins and supplemented by an Eileen Power Memorial studentship from the London School of Economics and a Bernadotte Schmitt grant from the American Historical Association. A National Endowment for the Humanities fellowship provided a year of leave, and return trips to the archives were funded by faculty grants from Gettysburg College and Texas Christian University.

I have appreciated more than I can say the friends who have (usually stoically) heard and sometimes read more about Nantes, notaries, families, and the ups and downs of professional life than they ever could have imagined. Chris Adams, Linda Hughes, Kathryne McDorman, Jim Sidbury, and Alan Shepard ceaselessly cajoled and encouraged me. Karin Wulf and Steve Lofgren have done all this and more, as we celebrated and commiserated every New Year's Eve and many days in between while this work slowly turned into a book.

Robert Olwell spent many months in France with me, and many years with early modern Nantais as our ever-present companions. He has written his own book on another early modern Atlantic community while I have been writing this one, and I cannot start to enumerate the myriad ways in which our life together has shaped this project. Our daughter, Rosie, has shared her young life with my final work on this book. She knows and cares nothing about early modern cities, and she has transformed and delighted our household with her utter insouciance.

Introduction

This book explores how structures of authority and relations of power were mediated at a grassroots level in early modern society. To approach these issues, I examine the households of the families of men who worked as notaries in a French city, Nantes, between 1560 and 1660, covering aspects of their lives from work to family to neighborhood to involvement in local politics. In seeking to reconstruct as fully as possible the strategies and agendas—large and small—of the women and men of these middling urban families, I look at the kinds of work notaries did and the ways in which they provided services for the French state and for their communities: as mediators between state and subject, between literate and oral cultures, between an increasingly commercialized economy and producers, consumers, borrowers, and lenders. I examine networks of credit and sociability, the building, management, and dispersal of family patrimony, and varieties of civic activity.

Through these lenses, I seek in particular to explore the substance and meaning that these daily interactions gave to an early modern practice of patriarchy. Early modern households were the primary sites of the daily negotiations and contestations through which concepts of gender and authority gained meaning in the lives of most working families. We think we know what patriarchy means, and the term *patriarchy* is often generically used to describe any society where men monopolize authority and where women's access to it is restricted (a framework applicable to almost any historical period). Yet focusing on reconstructing the specific forms of gender relations in one early modern community helps to recover the variety and complexity of forms that gender relations have taken.[1]

---

1. Debates over the meanings of patriarchy and its utility as an analytical concept have abounded. For a summary, see Carol Pateman, *The Sexual Contract* (Stanford, 1988), 19–38.

Gender played a crucial role in defining relations in early modern families and in shaping wider explications of power, as a central feature of daily life and as a key structure through which household, local, and royal authority were formulated. Ways of thinking about gender not only shaped the actual experiences of men and women, but also illuminated and signified relations of power of all kinds. As Elinor Accampo recently argued, historians need to think about "the influence that gender relations between ordinary men and women have on public institutions . . . and the gendered nature of any society's superstructure."[2] In early modern society, gender issues were not only domestic; they also shaped dynamics between households and larger community patterns.[3] The gendering of authority entailed boundaries and obligations as well as rights for individual men and women, for different communities, and, ultimately, for the crown.

Early modern Europeans found the familial model of a household in which authority was focused on the husband/father to be a popular concept for framing personal and political relations of authority, linking and naturalizing many forms of power. Patriarchy was not of course "invented" in the sixteenth century: the emphasis on the power of the head of the family was ancient, and its ecclesiastical sources—for example, in biblical and other early Christian texts—are well known. Nevertheless, the model of a political and social order structured by patriarchal power received new impetus in the early modern period.[4]

Rulers and members of local elites in much of the early modern West explicitly mobilized household government as a means to order social, political, and cultural organization. In Germany, Spain, and England, and in many of Europe's newly founded American colonies as well as in France, political centralization combined with religious reformations, economic uncertainties, and military struggles created a context in which household patriarchy flourished.[5] This gendered justification of the sovereign power

---

2. Elinor Accampo, "Gender Relations in the City: A Response," *French Historical Studies* 18 (Spring 1993), 56. For what has become the classic theoretical formulation of this analytical approach, see Joan Scott, "Gender: A Useful Category of Historical Analysis," *American Historical Review* 91 (December 1985).

3. For empirical studies looking at the links between gender and power in early modern communities, see Susan Amussen, *An Ordered Society: Class and Gender in Early Modern England* (London, 1988); Mary Elizabeth Perry, *Gender and Disorder in Early Modern Seville* (Princeton, 1990); Lyndal Roper, *The Holy Household: Women and Morals in Reformation Augsburg* (Oxford, 1989).

4. Alternative conceptions of the social and political order also existed. See, for instance, James R. Farr, "The Pure and Disciplined Body: Hierarchy, Morality, and Symbolism in France During the Catholic Reformation," *Journal of Interdisciplinary History* 21 (Winter 1991).

5. Work on the processes involved in the construction and meaning of early modern pa-

of the ruler had implications beyond the need for one head of each family or state. For kings asserting their sovereign power, the symbiotic relationship between husband/father and family and ruler and kingdom became a central representation of and justification for royal authority.

The place of the familial in the evolution of political rhetoric and the dynamics of state centralization in France from the 1530s onward has become clear in recent studies. Royal decrees and rhetorical tracts increasingly emphasized the supremacy of a male head of the household over his dependents as kings sought to increase their sovereign power over the families of the realm. From the last decades of the sixteenth century, the French crown and the members of its courts instituted a series of laws that enhanced men's conjugal power over women and their paternal power over children. Sarah Hanley has provocatively interpreted this aspect of the construction of the early modern state as the outcome of an alliance, a "family-state compact," between the crown and the nobility that served their mutual interests.[6]

For all the contention of the early modern period, patriarchalism had become enormously powerful by the eighteenth century. The legitimacy (or lack thereof) of male rule framed debates about sovereignty and wider discussions about public order and morality in the seventeenth and eigh-

---

triarchy outside France includes: Amussen, *An Ordered Society*; Perry, *Gender and Disorder*; Roper, *Holy Household*; Gordon Schochet, *Patriarchalism in Political Thought: The Authoritarian Family and Political Speculation and Attitudes, Especially in Seventeenth-Century England* (New York, 1975); Lawrence Stone, *Family, Sex, and Marriage in England, 1500–1800* (London, 1979). For a recent assessment of the process in European colonies, see the forum on Carole Shammas's "Anglo-American Household Government in Comparative Perspective," *William and Mary Quarterly* 52 (January 1995). See also Margaret W. Ferguson, Maureen Quilligan, and Nancy Vickers, eds., *Rewriting the Renaissance: The Discourses of Sexual Difference in Early Modern Europe* (Chicago, 1986); and Jean Delameau and Daniel Roche, eds., *Histoire des pères et paternité* (Paris, 1990).

6. Jeffrey Merrick has noted the lack of any "sizeable, systematic and searching analysis" of patriarchalism in early modern France. His articles examine some of the "meanings and uses of the family model" in elite political discourses. Sarah Hanley has traced the role of these issues in the process of state centralization. An important distinction exists in their conceptions of patriarchy: Hanley emphasizes its spousal connotations, while Merrick emphasizes its paternal aspects. See Jeffrey Merrick, "Fathers and Kings: Patriarchalism and Absolutism in Eighteenth-Century French Politics," *Studies on Voltaire and the Eighteenth Century* 308 (1993), esp. 281–82; Jeffrey Merrick, "The Cardinal and the Queen: Sexual and Political Disorders in the Mazarinades," *French Historical Studies* 18, (Spring 1994); Sarah Hanley, "Engendering the State: Family Formation and State Building in Early Modern France," *French Historical Studies* 16 (Spring 1989); Sarah Hanley, "Family and State in Early Modern France: The Marriage Pact," in Marilyn J. Boxer and Jean H. Quataert, eds., *Connecting Spheres: Women in the Western World, 1500 to the Present* (Oxford, 1987); and Sarah Hanley, "The Monarchic State in Early Modern France: Marital Regime Government and Male Right," in Adrianna Bakos, ed., *Politics, Ideology, and the Law in Early Modern Europe: Essays in Honor of J. H. M. Salmon* (Rochester, N.Y., 1994).

teenth centuries. Quarrels over "narratives of family relations" provided a primary discursive structure for the political contests of the Revolutionary era.[7]

My focus, however, is not on this level of elite political culture, but on the nature of authority as a cultural practice in daily life within families and within a local community. Although the years covered by this book, from 1560 to 1660, coincide with a tumultuous era of French history, the kinds of events that have traditionally been seen as constituting "political culture" (events such as the Wars of Religion, the growing centralization of state power, and the innumerable revolts of the seventeenth century) and whose roles in defining the nature of political authority have been the subject of extensive debate are largely absent from the political culture explored here. Available evidence suggests that these notarial families paid little attention and felt few direct effects from the political tempests that tossed above their heads.

Meanwhile, the factors (customary law, inheritance practices, the demands of raising money and marshaling resources) that fundamentally shaped the relations of gender, power, and authority in and between these households changed hardly at all in this century. The very persistence of those relations, in fact, is striking in the midst of a century that seemed so much in flux.[8] In terms of impact on daily urban life in ordinary times, the ongoing patterns of household authority were more significant than the far more visible political turmoil. For individuals, families, and local communities, household authority provided a way of viewing the world and its workings that proponents of political agendas of every kind could mobilize for their own goals.

To get a sense of how patterns of gender and authority were created within and between households, I aim to look at how notarial families worked. Families shaped and were shaped by larger political patterns as

7. For the eighteenth-century persistence of patriarchal discourses among both opponents and proponents of absolutism, see Hanley, "The Monarchic State"; Merrick, "Fathers and Kings"; and Sarah Maza, *Private Lives and Public Affairs: the Causes Célèbres of Prerevolutionary France* (Berkeley and Los Angeles, 1993). For work exploring the revolutionary crisis of patriarchy, see Lynn Hunt, *The Family Romance of the French Revolution* (Berkeley and Los Angeles, 1992), quote from xiii; and Caroline Ford, "Private Lives and Public Order in Restoration France: The Seduction of Emily Loveday," *American Historical Review* 99 (February 1994). For how ideas about gender hierarchy structured broader efforts at early modern reform and regulation, see James R. Farr, *Authority and Sexuality in Early Modern Burgundy, 1550–1730* (Oxford, 1995).

8. For an impassioned discussion of the need to focus on the persistence of gender inequality in a changing early modern world, see Judith Bennett, *Ale, Beer, and Brewsters: Women's Work in a Changing World, 1300–1600* (Oxford, 1996).

well as by a variety of other structures. They could act collectively, but they were made up of individuals who were sometimes motivated by conflicting as well as shared interests and goals, and upon whom larger structural processes had differential impacts.[9] Moreover, the responses of early modern urban men like notaries—other petty legal officials, apothecaries, surgeons, and artisan retailers—and their wives to the world around them were as critical as the great affairs of state in defining early modern political culture.[10]

I also explore the character and quality of ties between households, because these links to other households provided indispensable resources,

9. The founding work in family history, Philippe Ariès's *Centuries of Childhood* (London, 1962), provided the insight that the specific historical forms of family life are social constructs resulting from a specific configuration of forces, and not natural entities. A vast literature exists about conceptualizing family history. Many historians have pointed to the futility of confusing household structure with family form in assessing the importance of extended kin ties. In a similar fashion, historians have rejected the either/or evaluation of the quality of domestic relations by illustrating that at all times, interest and emotion have been two sides of the same coin, in family life. They have also emphasized the need to view families, collectively and as individuals, as active agents of change who initiate, adapt to, or reject larger changes in translating them to their own spheres. Moreover, the need to recognize the distinct interests and experiences of women as central players in families has been highlighted. See Miranda Chaytor, "Household and Kinship: Ryton in the Late Sixteenth and Early Seventeenth Centuries," *History Workshop* 10 (Fall 1980), esp. 26–30; Tamara Hareven, "The History of the Family and the Complexity of Social Change," *American Historical Review* 96 (February 1991), esp. 111–24; Katherine A. Lynch, "The Family and the History of Public Life," *Journal of Interdisciplinary History* 24 (Spring 1994); Rayna Rapp, Ellen Ross, and Renata Bridenthal, "Examining Family History," *Feminist Studies* 5 (Spring 1979); Louise Tilly, "Women's History and Family History: Fruitful Collaboration or Missed Connection?" *Journal of Family History* 12, nos. 1–3 (1987), esp. 307–10; and Hans Medick and David Warren Sabean, eds., *Interest and Emotion: Essays on the Study of Family and Kinship* (Cambridge, 1984).

10. The importance of this group's role in shaping French political culture has recently been emphasized, as in the assertion that *gens du bien* (men like shopkeepers and artisan masters) were the "frontier of order" in early modern French society. James B. Collins, *Classes, Estates, and Order in Early Modern Brittany* (Cambridge, 1994), 17–18. Yet we know little about the men or families situated on this fault line, with the notable exceptions of James R. Farr's *Hands of Honor: Artisans and Their World in Dijon, 1550–1650* (Ithaca, N.Y., 1988); and David Garrioch's *The Formation of the Parisian Bourgeoisie, 1690–1830* (Cambridge, Mass., 1996).

Considerable work on early modern England has recently sought to highlight the political importance of the behaviors of such middling men. See, for example, Matthew Boulton, *Neighbourhood and Society: A London Suburb in the Seventeenth Century* (Cambridge, 1987); Steve Rappaport, *World Within Worlds: Structures of Life in Sixteenth-Century London* (Cambridge, 1987); David Harris Sacks, *The Widening Gate: Bristol and the Atlantic Economy, 1450–1700* (Berkeley and Los Angeles, 1991); Linda Colley, *Britons: Forging the Nation, 1707–1837* (New Haven, Conn., 1992).

The role of similar groups in the nineteenth century in the creation of political culture and class has received great attention; see Leonore Davidoff and Catherine Hall, *Family Fortunes: Men and Women of the English Middle Class, 1780–1850* (London, 1987); and, for an American case, Mary Ryan, *Cradle of the Middle Class: The Family In Oneida County, New York, 1790–1865* (Cambridge, 1981).

not only for practical and affective purposes, but also in defining social rank and political alliances. The bonds might be based on family, gender, place of residence, religion, occupation, or myriad other foundations.[11]

Examining the personal and public lives of members of notarial families suggests how familial authority patterns were strengthened, weakened, and given specific shape. As well, it points to the broader ramifications of those patterns through the role of notarial families in building political culture. The maintenance of culturally constructed lines of authority demanded enormous individual, collective, and institutional effort and energy. Such structures of authority were continually reasserted and contested in ongoing negotiations, rather than simply imposed by law or by royal arbitrariness.[12]

Nantes was only one city in a diverse French landscape, and its notaries and their families only one of the innumerable groups that constituted early modern French society. These people and this place were in some ways exceptional—living in a highly commercialized local economy, in an urban place in a predominantly rural society, possessing literacy and above-subsistence wealth. They were residents of a region with a strong sense of its distinctive identity.

Rural notaries who worked in villages where they almost monopolized literacy were differently situated, and some evidence suggests that city notaries in the Roman law areas of southern France had quite different experiences. Variations in notarial practice also existed from place to place. In Nantes, for instance, minor officers of the city's court recorded inventories, while in Paris, notaries fought fiercely to preserve their monopoly over this lucrative job.[13] Yet without claiming that we can understand a totality of experience in this period from the lives of Nantais notarial families, this case

11. Hans Medick and David Sabean have pointed out in their *Interest and Emotion*, 20, that inter-households bonds were "of vital importance to the 'way of life' and the reproductions of life of specific classes."

12. See, for instance, revisionary interpretations of early modern state building that emphasize the role of interactions between monarch and subjects. Such studies include those of William Beik, *Absolutism and Society in Seventeenth-Century France: State Power and Provincial Aristocracy in Languedoc* (Cambridge, 1985); Albert Hamscher, *The Conseil Privé and the Parlements in the Age of Louis XIV: A Study in French Absolutism* (Philadelphia, 1987); Hanley, "Engendering the State"; and Hanley, "Family and State."

13. For insights into rural notaries, see Alain Cullomp, *La Maison du père: Famille et village en Haute-Provence aux dix-septième et dix-huitième siècles* (Paris, 1983). I thank Profs. Claire Dolan and Laurie Nussdorfer for sharing with me their unpublished work in progress on Aix and Rome regarding notaries in Roman-law cities. For Parisian notaries' efforts to ensure a notarial monopoly of inventory taking, see Monique Limon, *Les Notaires au Châtelet de Paris sous le règne de Louis XIV: Etude institutionelle et sociale* (Toulouse, 1992), 43.

study can throw light on the complex and dynamic web of people and practices that underlay early modern political culture.

That web has been reconstructed from the linkage of judicial, notarial, and parish records, and I chose Nantes in large part because of its archival richness for that purpose. Every legal instrument in which a notary or his wife or widow were involved in any capacity was recorded; not only marriage contracts and details of the sales of notarial offices, but property transactions of all kinds, whether related to inheritance, credit, leases, or sales of land. Similarly, the participation of notaries or their wives or kin in parish assemblies and any other dispute or meeting was also noted.

The civil records of local courts (especially those of the provost and the *sénéchaussée*) also provided a wealth of evidence on a variety of matters. Inventories, affairs related to guardianships, matters of public order, court depositions, and sentences all fell under the jurisdiction of these courts. Nantes is singular among French cities in having a superb set of parish registers, virtually complete since 1560. Its baptism records are particularly valuable, as they contain not only the names of the parents of the child and godparents, but also those of the other witnesses present for the ceremony. The records of the city militia, *Hôtel-Dieu*, local parishes, municipal assembly, and notarial corporation supplemented these sources. For every source except the parish registers, all extant records for 1560–1660 were examined.

I chose 1560 as the starting point for practical and historical reasons. The French king reorganized the notariat in 1560, and, with his appointment of a fixed number (forty-six) of notaries in that year, the Nantais notariat assumed the form that prevailed into the eighteenth century. Following for a century the men who worked as notaries and their families allowed me to trace the experiences of three or four generations during a critical phase of French history. Moreover, virtually no archival records of the kind used here survive in Nantes for earlier periods, and indeed the majority of the extant records (with the notable exception of parish registers) are for the post–1600 decades.

The first chapter provides some context for the notaries, families, and city who are the subjects of this book. The second chapter examines the role of notaries in their communities—their relationship to each other, to the early modern French state, to the men and women among whom they lived. Subsequent chapters examine the dynamics of the cultural production of authority in and between households. Relations within households, property-holding practices and their impacts, and other patterns of social interactions are analyzed to look at the ways in which in everyday-life authority was created and given distinctive forms in encounters with individuals and alliances that were shaped by gender and generation. The final chapter examines notarial participation in the public life of Nantes in municipal affairs, in parish organizations, and in poorhouse governance, forums in which notaries could apply their own priorities and worldviews to the wider community.

My purpose, then, is not to determine whether early modern society was better or worse for women than other historical periods, but to analyze the obligations, rights, restrictions, and opportunities that structured gender and power relations for women and for men. Family members were actors as well as subjects in historical processes, and their selection of choices played a part from a grassroots level—as did ideology and laws—in shaping the broadly patriarchal political culture of early modern France.

1

Notaries and Their Families

In the autumn of 1656, Louise Lecoq, the wife of the notary René Guilloteau, was left to deal with family, neighbors, clients, lawyers, and royal officials after her husband, accused of embezzling clients' money, fled from the city of Nantes, where they lived. The drama that engulfed the household highlighted the ways in which notaries and their families found themselves at a nexus of the processes through which early modern urban political culture was framed.

By 1656, Lecoq and Guilloteau had been married for fifteen years, and he had been working as a notary for more than thirty years. She was the daughter of a baker and had married Guilloteau not long after his first wife's death (following the birth of their tenth child) had left Guilloteau the single father of a large family. She retained the name of her birth family, as early modern women usually did. Lecoq and Guilloteau, who had seven children of their own between 1643 and 1654, lived in a household on a small street that bent around behind their parish church. Their immediate neighbors were Lecoq's sister Jeanne, who had also married a notary—Mathurin Coustans—and Guilloteau's sister Françoise, who was the wife of another notary, François Rapion. Another Guilloteau sibling, Catherine, lived in the same parish with her notary-husband, Philippe Bodin.

Little seemed out of the ordinary about the life of their household until the autumn of 1656. On the morning of 13 December, two of the city's royal officials—the provost of the local Nantais court and its royal prosecutor—arrived at Lecoq's door. Alerted by "several verbal complaints of various individuals," and by "rumors" that had been circulating about Guilloteau's "embezzlements and [about] lawsuits" pending against him, the officials had three weeks earlier sealed the locks of the armoires in and the door of Guilloteau's office (*étude*) to safeguard his notarial papers. Now they sought to inventory the papers on the grounds that the alleged embezzlements were to the "great prejudice and damage of several individuals and of the public."

"The public," they maintained, "had a profound interest" in discovering the extent of wrongdoing.[1] On this first day and on those that followed, a stream of clients and/or their lawyers (*procureurs*) also appeared. Most were looking for copies of contracts they had requested that Guilloteau make for them, often having left him money to complete the transactions in question, and for which they had received no confirmation.

The officials immediately asked Lecoq if she had seen her husband, if he had "revealed to her the state of his affairs" or if she had other acts of his besides those placed under seal. Lecoq denied knowing her husband's whereabouts or of any other notarial instruments besides those already sealed. She also denied having any keys to either the *étude* or its armoires and "did not know where they [the keys] were if her husband did not have them." She added that Guilloteau had sent her news, without telling her where he was, that made her hope he would be back in Nantes "shortly . . . when he would give satisfaction to those who had business with him."

As the provost and prosecutor finished their questions, Lecoq took the initiative. She asked to be authorized to pursue her own claims as a creditor of her husband. (Two of Guilloteau's daughters from his first marriage followed suit and also declared themselves to be his creditors.) By the time the court officials returned the next day, Lecoq had acquired a lawyer. She

1. These events and the narrative that follows were recorded by a court clerk of the Nantais provost's court in an eighty-two-page transcript. ADLA, B5694, 13 December–22 December 1656. For a fuller reconstruction of this event and its consequences, see Julie Hardwick, "Women Working the Law: Gender, Authority, and Legal Process in Early Modern France," *Journal of Women's History* 9 (October 1997).

claimed to have received a letter from Guilloteau in the intervening hours that explained that he was working out of town and that led her to hope that he would return in a week. On these grounds, she asked that the inventory be delayed. She continued to deny any knowledge of her husband's whereabouts and refused to show the court's officers the letter "because of the details in it." On this second day, she did admit to having a key to the *étude* but still denied that she knew of any other notarial acts beyond those already sealed in the armoires.

On this second day too, as on every subsequent day, Lecoq's sister-in-law Françoise was also present when the provost and prosecutor went into Guilloteau's study "at the back" of the house where he and his wife lived, to begin inventorying the papers there. They found the study full of loose papers, many "unsigned" and "for the most part eaten and spoiled by rats." Later, a locksmith called to open an armoire found its key. Lecoq professed astonishment, saying that Guilloteau usually carried the only key in his pocket and that he took it with him when he left.

As the inventory proceeded in the following days, many of the bundles of acts were found to be disorganized, with papers filed out of chronological order. Clients who had been seeking reassurance that their acts had been made could find little comfort in the chaotic conditions.

Finally, on 22 December, the officials adjourned their task for Christmas. No record survives of subsequent action in this particular case. For years Lecoq continued to deal with myriad problems, using as her notary her sister's husband Mathurin Coustans, who had kept a low profile while the provost and prosecutor were in action. Within six months Guilloteau's office of notary was sold, and he seems never to have returned, although by 1670 Lecoq was described as his widow. Guilloteau's disappearance was perhaps not surprising, given that notaries in other cities were hanged in the seventeenth century for fraud and embezzlement, the crimes of which he was accused.[2]

The experiences in 1656 of the Guilloteau-Lecoq household, whose history was so much like that of their peers, raised into sharp relief many key issues in early modern political culture that were usually muted in the course of more mundane circumstances. The state, as represented by court

2. For examples of Lecoq's difficulties and her use of Coustans as her notary, see, for instance, ADLA, 4E2/547, 24 March 1657, 28 June 1657, and 20 February 1659. For notaries being hanged, see Maurice Garsonnin, *Histoire de la communauté des notaires au Châtelet d'Orléans, 1303–1791* (Orléans, 1922), 56.

officials, perceived a "public interest" in monitoring notarial activity, and clients represented members of the community who recognized that their affairs were involved. The kin of both spouses figured prominently as resources for Lecoq. Her actions and those of her adult stepchildren as well as those of Guilloteau himself suggest the potential configurations of tensions and alliances within a household. Guilloteau's difficulties emerged out of a slippery mixing of responsibilities that he shared with many of his colleagues. All of them, with their spouses, faced the challenge of making ends meet in a changing world. Lecoq found herself as an exemplar of the competencies and disabilities of gender. While the eruption of a crisis was highly unusual, these elements were common to every household. Between the contingencies of everyday life and the dictates of families and finances and of neighbors and the state, men and women found ways to manage and order their world.

Notaries and Nantes

Notaries, in France as in large areas of the early modern West, from Italy to the newly founded European colonies, were crucial cogs, albeit at the lowest level, in the apparatus of the state and in the daily organization of people's lives.[3] In early modern societies without effective police forces or massive bureaucracies, notaries were one of the few intermediaries between state and subject.

At a grassroots level, notaries helped to build early modern states by providing key access points through which the state sought to regulate the lives of its subjects. Like many jobs in early modern France, positions as notaries were venal; that is, a man acquired the job by buying it. In 1560 the monarchy had reorganized the notariat, fixing the number of positions as royal

3. For the roles of notaries in other early modern societies, see Laurie Nussdorfer, "Writing and the Power of Speech: Notaries and Artisans in Baroque Rome," in Carla Hesse and Barbara Diefendorf, eds., *Culture and Identity in Early Modern Europe, 1500–1800: Essays in Honor of Natalie Davis* (Ann Arbor, Mich., 1993); Lauro Martines, *Lawyers and Statecraft in Renaissance Florence* (Princeton, 1968), esp. 11–61. For notaries in Europe's American colonies, see, for example, James Lockhart, *The Nahuas After the Conquest: A Social and Cultural History of the Indians of Central America, Sixteenth Through Eighteenth Centuries* (Stanford, 1992); and Donna Merwick, "The Suicide of a Notary: Language, Personal Identity, and Conquest in Colonial New York," in Ronald Hoffman, Mechal Sobel, and Fredricka J. Teute, eds., *Through a Glass Darkly: Reflections on Personal Identity in Early America* (Chapel Hill, 1997).

(as opposed to ecclesiastical or seigneurial) notaries in Nantes at any one time at forty-six. That number remained unaltered into the eighteenth century, although its justification is unclear.[4] Of the forty-six, however, only about thirty at any one time lived and worked in the city, the remainder being in the surrounding rural parishes. Although as we will see, the relationship between the state and its notaries was distant in many regards at this time, the French monarchy used notaries in various ways. All loans for more than 100 *livres* had to be registered by a notary, for example, a requirement designed to provide some safeguards on the circulation of credit.

Notaries also served their peers in early modern communities, providing protection and gateways to the legal system. Early modern people asked notaries to make public records of myriad aspects of life—loans and leases, sales and meetings, wills and marriage contracts. In some cases they did so to meet legal requirements; in all cases in legal systems such as France's, that privileged written evidence (unlike the preference in Anglo-American law for sworn oral testimony), contemporaries found the acts that notaries wrote to be crucial safeguards. The records also governed social relationships and were among the tools that reinforced personal, familial, and political authority.

Notaries' occupational skills and local knowledge allowed them to serve their communities in other ways, too, as we will see. In a period when the availability of credit and access to written materials were both increasingly important, notaries served as community credit brokers who not only made records of loans but also put borrowers and lenders together. Additionally, they served as <u>mediators between literate and oral cultures</u>.

Nantes, situated on the southern edge of Brittany at the mouth of the Loire, was already a substantial urban center in the sixteenth and seventeenth centuries. One proud resident described his town in 1647: "Its atmosphere is very temperate, the buildings beautiful, the position pleasing, its approaches delightful."[5] Others found their urban environment less at-

4. For comparison, at the same time, Tours, another Loire Valley town, had between twenty-two and twenty-seven notaries; and Bordeaux, a commercial and administrative city like Nantes, had as many as fifty-five notaries. Hervé de Larminat, "La Compagnie des notaires de Nantes, des origines a la Révolution" (thèse pour le doctorat en droit, Université de Rennes, 1955), 10; Ludovic Langlois, *La Communauté des notaires de Tours, de 1512 à 1791* (Paris, 1911); Jean Gaston, *La Communauté des notaires de Bordeaux, 1520–1791* (Bordeaux, 1913; reprinted Toulouse, 1991).

5. "Description de la Ville de Nantes au dix-septième siècle, le vingt-troisième jour de mars, en l'an MDCXXXXVI, par un habitant de la ville," in Camille Mellinet, *La Commune et la milice de Nantes,* vol. 1 (Nantes, 1841), 101.

tractive. Residents of rue des Carmes in the parish of St. Saturnin, for example, who included a number of the subjects of this book, looked out of their windows to see "all the streets dirty, bloody and stinking . . . so that the people living on the street are unhealthy and there is inclined to be an air so smelly and tainted that it often causes the plague." An adjoining street illustrated other notable aspects of urban life: it was "very narrow" and the "houses enclosed [and] there are very many people."[6]

The dual character of Nantes, both port and court, attracted large numbers of merchants and lawyers, and its population had reached about twenty-five thousand by 1600. The activities of the port and its ships, carrying cargoes along the Atlantic seaboard and across to the French West Indies, dominated the westernmost parish of St. Nicolas. The eastern parishes were home to the château of the governor of Brittany, the cathedral, and the Chambre des Comptes, a sovereign court of the kings of France. Although Rennes was the administrative capital of Brittany, Nantes rivaled it as the most prominent city of the region.[7]

Notaries and Their Families

Like Lecoq and Guilloteau, Nantais notaries' families were members of the middling ranks, a position they struggled to acquire, leave behind, or, most often, to maintain in the hundred years between 1560 and 1660.[8] Although a handful of notaries enjoyed great success and remain prominent in historical records, their visibility is misleading: most notaries (excluding the Parisian notariat, who enjoyed privileges and monopolies far beyond those of other cities) had no such luck, as evidence from every angle confirms.[9]

6. AM, DD324, c.1570, and AM, BB11, 1574, both quoted in Alain Croix, *La Bretagne aux seizième et dix-septième siecles: La Vie, la mort, la foi* (Paris, 1981), 783–84.

7. The work of Alain Croix dominates recent historiography of early modern Nantes in his *Nantes et le pays Nantais au seizième siècle: Etude démographique* (Paris, 1974) and *La Bretagne au seizième et dix-septième siècles.* For the mercantile life of the city, see also Jean Tanguy, "Le Mouvement du port de Nantes au début du dix-septième siècle" (thèse de troisième cycle, Université de Rennes, 1965). For useful information on Nantes and the province of Brittany, see James B. Collins, *Classes, Estates, and Order in Early Modern Brittany* (Cambridge, 1994). For an overview of early modern French cities, see Philip Benedict, ed., *Cities and Social Change in Early Modern France* (London, 1989), 7–68.

8. I have preferred to use "middling" throughout this book rather than the anachronistic "middle class," or the perhaps more historically accurate but overdetermined "bourgeois," not least because although "middling" is an imprecise term, so was the status of this rank.

9. Monique Limon's recent examination of the Parisian notariat in the reign of Louis XIV provides an important source for comparison between the notariat of the capital and those in

Life histories of three generations of three Nantais notarial families suggest that aspirations were often less to pursue upward social mobility than to maintain a frequently precarious hold on middling status.[10] The patterns between 1560 and 1660 of recruitment, dowry sizes, office prices, and places of residence derived from the experiences of all Nantais notaries and their families affirm this anecdotal evidence in greater detail and point to some of the strategies that middling families adopted in seeking to preserve their positions.

Mathurin Fegneux was a notary and lawyer (*procureur*) and his wife, Jeanne Parageau, was the sister of a notary. They lived in St. Laurent, one of the city's wealthiest parishes, in the last two decades of the sixteenth century. Their two daughters, Marguerite and Jeanne, married two brothers, Abel (who also became a notary) and Jean Denys (an architect), and moved to the parish of St. Donatien, just outside the city walls. The experiences of their children, in turn, showed how easily families could slide toward downward social mobility. Jeanne Denys had to sell her father's office as notary after the latter's death, to pay his debts; a couple of years later, she and her husband, Pierre Babin, repurchased it for him. They died in the 1640s, without children and in debt. Her cousins fared little better, for, at about the same time, their orphaned son Etienne Denys was apprenticed to learn the trade of his sister's husband, a master basket maker.

Pierre Liger and Marguerite Pouetard, contemporaries of Fegneux and Parageau, were peasants (*laboureurs*) who lived in the parish of Rezay, situated across from the city on the south bank of the Loire River. When Pierre

---

other towns. The Parisian notariat enjoyed the right to practice throughout the kingdom and a monopoly of work in Paris (advantages shared only by the notariat of Orléans). Her study suggests that Parisian notaries enjoyed higher status and greater promise of upward social mobility than did their peers, an expectation also indicated by the far higher price of notarial office.

Limon's suggestions as to the comparisons between the Parisian notariat and their provincial contemporaries are uncertain, shifting between suggesting the exceptional nature of the Parisian notariat and the possibility that, as with other functionaries (like members of the *parlements*), the difference was more of scale than of substance. Similarities are as striking as contrasts, in the social profiles of metropolitan and provincial notaries, suggesting that the differences were as much relative as absolute. While the higher status of the Parisian notariat in her period is clear, it had much in common with other urban notariats; the critical distinction may be less geographic and more chronological, with the evolution of the notariat into a far wealthier, more prominent, and more august institution, a transition that Limon locates in the late eighteenth century. Monique Limon, *Les Notaires au Châtelet de Paris sous le règne de Louis XIV: Etude institutionelle et sociale* (Toulouse, 1992).

10. The life histories that follow have been reconstructed from numerous sources in the ADLA and AMN. Parish registers (series GG in the AMN) and notarial records (series 4E2 in the ADLA) were particularly valuable.

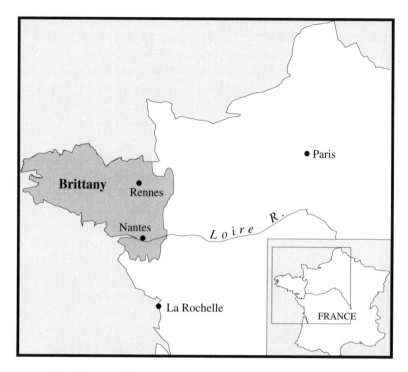

Map of Northwestern France

died his five children inherited only shacks and small pieces of land, and four of them remained as illiterate peasants in Rezay. But the eldest, also Pierre, became a clerk in a notary's *étude*. Liger's *fils* eventually moved to the commercial parish of St. Nicolas, married Françoise Locquet, the daughter of a merchant, and became a notary himself. Of their many children, only two seem to have survived to adulthood. A son, René, followed his father as a notary and married the daughter of a doctor, and a daughter, Marquise, married a surgeon. These were marriages that promised to secure the family's middling status more firmly.

Jean Charier was a notary and lawyer who lived with his wife, Jeanne Duchesne, in the parish of St. Croix for at least three decades beginning in 1580. They had ten children between 1580 and 1602, only three of whom clearly survived to adulthood. The eldest of these, Pierre, became a barrister (*avocat*), married Gratienne Bretaigne in St. Denis in 1619, lived in St. Croix until 1625, and then moved to the parish of St. Similien, just to the

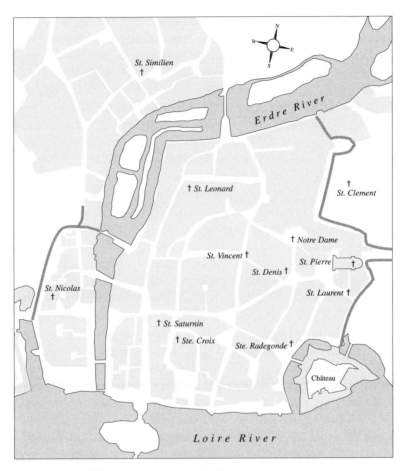

Plan of Nantes with parish churches. One other parish, St. Sebastian, lay south of the river.

west of the city walls. By the early 1630s, he was referred to, in the parish registers, at least, as *noble homme* (a courtesy title that did not connote legal nobility). Pierre's brother André married Marguerite Penifort, the daughter of a notary in St. Denis, later in the summer of 1619, and became a notary himself, living and working in St. Denis. (One other brother may have become a priest, a very common pattern.)

The apparent upward mobility of the elder son was not consistently maintained, however, in the next generation. In 1654, Pierre's son Toussaint married Jeanne Cercleux, the daughter of a man with the title of *hon-*

orable homme (used for merchants and artisans), and lived in the parish of
St. Croix working as a notary, like his grandfather. Toussaint's younger
brother François was referred to as *noble homme* in the parish register
recording his 1664 marriage. Of Toussaint's cousins (the children of André
and Penifort), Antoine married Jeanne Garnier, herself the daughter of a
notary, and worked as a notary in St. Denis; Gatienne married a notary,
René Simon; Catherine married a lawyer; and Jeanne married a barrister
in the Breton parlement.

For most notaries and their families, downward social mobility was as
likely as upward. For some families, the establishment of one son as a notary was a route out of the artisan ranks or lower, while for others it was a
step away from the ascent toward elite status that more prestigious legal careers could ultimately offer. Between these ups and downs were the experiences of most notaries and their families, like the Chariers, whose main
achievement was to ensconce themselves firmly as members of the urban
middling ranks, intent most of all on preserving the position they held.

As these three generational examples suggest, Nantais notarial families
were highly endogamous in terms of geographical origins, being overwhelmingly urban and local. The great majority of men who became notaries were born in Nantes, married Nantaises, and worked and died in the
city. Almost all of the men who were not born in the city came from no far-
ther afield than the surrounding rural parishes known as the *pays Nantais*.[11]

The social origins of Nantais notaries and their wives were also homoge-
neous: the middling urban ranks of petty legal officials and the artisanal
elite dominated, whether assessed by occupation or title (see Table 1.1).[12] A
notary's father was more likely to work as a notary than any other single occupation; if not, then to hold another minor legal position, such as that of

11. Geographic Origins of Notaries and Their Wives

	Nantes	Pays Nantais	Elsewhere	N
Notaries	76 (80%)	18 (19%)	1 (1%)	95
Wives	118 (90%)	12 (9%)	1 (1%)	131

The definition of *pays Nantais* follows the usage of Alain Croix, that is, the area in the sixteenth century included in the diocese of Nantes. Geographical origin is defined by the residence of the parents of notaries and their wives (rather than by place of marriage, which
would give an even more city-dominated result). Croix, *Nantes et le pays Nantais,* 12. For the
problems involved in assessing geographical mobility, see James B. Collins, "Geographic and
Social Mobility in Early Modern France," *Journal of Social History* 24 (Spring 1991), 565.

12. Notaries and legal professionals are overrepresented when fathers' status is considered
in terms of occupation alone. I can identify all fathers who were notaries, and professions were
specified far more commonly among men who ranked as *maîtres* than among men who were
honorables hommes.

Table 1.1. Status of the fathers of notaries and of notaries' wives

			Fathers of Notaries		
Title:	Noble Homme	Maître	Honorable Homme	Honnête Homme/Sire	No Title
Number (=101):	1	60	31	6	3
Occupation:	Notary	Other Legal Official	Merchant/ Artisan	Medical	Peasant
Number (=63):	28	22[a]	9	2	2
			Status of Fathers of Notaries' Wives		
Title:	Noble Homme	Maître	Honorable Homme	Honnête Homme/Sire	No Title
Number (=122):	3	67	43	6	3
Occupation:	Notary	Other Legal Official	Merchant/ Artisan	Medical	Peasant
Number (=72):	32	17[b]	18	5	0

[a]Including 8 lawyers (maîtres) and 1 barrister (noble homme) who were of higher status than notaries.
[b]Including 9 lawyers and 1 barrister.

court usher (*huissier*) or a bailiff (*sergent royal*), men who shared the title *maître*. The handful of city notaries who were originally from the surrounding parishes were often sons of rural legal officials. Thus notaries often came from families who were on the very lowest rungs of the legal world.

One other social group, families whose fathers were designated as *honorables hommes* (literally honorable men), frequently established some sons as notaries. This epithet covered all manner of occupations from apothecaries to merchants of various shades and often included master artisans. About a third of notaries were first-generation descendants of this group, and about as many notaries' fathers were from this diverse sector as were notaries themselves. Notaries' fathers among this group included several bakers, a miller, a herald, a haberdasher, a draper, an apothecary, and a surgeon (see Table 1.1).

Very few notaries were recruited from a broader social spectrum. None were drawn from the urban elite, and only a handful were sons of men of a higher legal rank like that of lawyers, indicating that notarial office was not considered an appropriate activity for sons of noble families, however down on their luck. Only one notary, Toussaint Charier, was the son of a barrister who was designated as a *noble homme,* and his case was exceptional, as we have seen: his father was the son, brother, brother-in-law, and uncle of notaries. Moreover, the designation of "noble man" as a title in this way designated a courtesy rather than legal status as a noble.

A small number were the sons of men whose only title was the modest *honnête homme* (a phrase for which the awkward but best English equivalent is "decent") or *sire,* but fathers who could claim no kind of epithet at all were very rare. The few notaries whose families were not city residents were largely responsible for such social diversity as did exist. Philippe Garreau, for instance, like a couple of others, came from a nearby rural parish where his father was a peasant.

The wives of notaries came from very similar families. The fathers of at least one-third, and probably half, of notaries' brides were men on the bottom rungs of the legal profession in some capacity, whether as notaries, court clerks (*greffiers*), or bailiffs. About a quarter of the women who married notaries were themselves daughters of notaries, often marrying men who had been clerks in their fathers' *études.* Another third of notaries' wives were the daughters of *honorables hommes,* men who included sundry merchants, several bakers, a draper, a candle maker, a handful of apothecaries or surgeons, and a herald. Almost none came from families of a social rank that was either higher or lower than middling.

Notaries in other provincial cities apparently shared the narrow social and geographic backgrounds of their Nantais peers. The social history of the notariat is in its infancy, but early twentieth-century studies of early modern urban notariats in the northern half of France suggest they had much in common with Nantais notaries and their families.[13] In Tours, for example, notaries were recruited heavily from within the legal community, with a few from families of petty legal officials in the surrounding *pays Touraine* and none from outside the province.

Even the Parisian notariat had a similar social topography. Monique Limon has shown that its roots too were in the notariat, or "merchant-bourgeoisie," with an almost complete absence of other officeholders and "through

13. See, for instance, Maurice Garsonnin, *Histoire de la communauté des notaires au Châtelet d'Orléans, 1303–1791* (Orleans, 1922); Jean Gaston, *La Communauté des notaires de Bordeaux, 1520–1791* (Bordeaux, 1913; reprinted Toulouse, 1991); Ludovic Langlois, *La Communauté des notaires de Tours, de 1512 à 1791* (Paris, 1911), esp. 443–66. Maurice Gresset's more recent *Gens de justice à Besançon, de la conquête par Louis XIV à la Révolution Française, 1674–1789,* 2 vols. (Paris, 1978), is also useful.

kinship . . . closely tied to . . . the merchant-bourgeoisie," while the "great majority" of the capital's notaries were Parisians by birth.[14]

The prospects of notaries and their families were not, however, static in the decades between 1560 and 1660, as shifting residential patterns, dowry levels, and the prices paid to purchase positions as notaries all point to increased pressures and socioeconomic stagnation in the seventeenth century.

Although the median dowry value of 2,000 *livres* remained constant in marriage contracts, the gap increased between the highest and lowest dowries circulating among notarial families. In the decades before 1630, the highest dowry a notary received was 3,000 *livres* and the lowest 300 *livres*, while the marriage contracts for children of notaries promised dowries of between 800 and 6,000 *livres*. After 1630, the dowries that notaries received ranged from 1,000 *livres* to 8,000 *livres*, and those of their children from 60 *livres* to 20,000 *livres*. Moreover, almost half of these dowries fell into the range of less than 1,500 *livres*, and nearly a third were more than 2,500 *livres*, with only about a quarter falling in between, in the range of the median. The growing gap seems to imply a polarization of wealth within the notariat, suggesting that, with a few notable exceptions, many notarial families were struggling to hold an increasingly insecure socioeconomic position.

The reality of reduced aspirations for many notaries and their families after about 1600 and increased risks of downward mobility is reiterated by the diverging fortunes of notaries and lawyers. Prior to 1600, men often held the offices of notary and lawyer either consecutively or, often, simultaneously. After 1600, this pattern was very exceptional; no one held both offices at the same time, and, as a rule, men who became notaries remained as such for their entire working lives.

The differing paths of the costs of various positions give one clue as to the reasons for this shift. Although the price of the office of royal notary in Nantes rose significantly between 1560 and 1660, it continued to entail far less expense than that of lawyer or any of the offices associated with the city's courts. In the 1620s, for example, a notarial office could be purchased for about 725 *livres*, only about a quarter the price of an office of lawyer, which sold for about 3,000 *livres* in the same decade (based on the prices of ten offices). At this level, the cost and no doubt status of the office of notary in a major city was more than twice that of rural notaries in the

14. Limon, *Notaires au Châtelet*, 203–15; Langlois, *Communauté des notaires de Tours*, 463–66.

surrounding parishes. However, it was far less than other legal positions, as was illustrated by the 16,000 *livres* cost of a position as barrister in the *presidial* court.

By the 1650s, the costs of all offices had significantly increased, putting many out of the reach of most middling families. Notarial offices were much more expensive, selling for about 1,650 *livres* on average (based on seventeen sales where the median value was 1,500 *livres*). Nevertheless, in the same decade, while other minor legal positions such as that of bailiff were still cheaper (800 *livres* in 1655), an office as lawyer was sold for 7,000 *livres*. And the prices of positions among the legal elite (barrister in the Chambre des Comptes, for example, which sold for 80,000 *livres*) were in a completely different league.[15]

While the ratio of the costs of purchasing the positions of notary and lawyer remained roughly steady, stagnating notarial wealth levels in the seventeenth century made the office of lawyer dearer in real terms. The increasing distance between holders of the two offices suggested that men who were merely notaries had fallen behind their lawyer peers, resulting in a loss of status as well as in financial limitations. This shift was affirmed by the reluctance of Parisian lawyers to allow their sons to become notaries even in the capital.[16]

Notarial families also moved out of the city's wealthiest parish in the seventeenth century, a significant shift given the distinctive wealth and occupation patterns of Nantais parishes, as well as of those in other early modern cities.[17] Throughout the period of this study, more than 64 percent (94 out of 146) of the notaries who lived in the city resided in the adjoining middling-rank parishes of St. Croix and St. Denis. Just under 15 percent lived across the Erdre River in the commercial parish of St. Nicolas, and about 10 percent lived in the largely artisanal parish of St. Saturnin, adjacent to St. Croix.

However, after 1600, notarial families deserted St. Laurent, the smallest and wealthiest parish in the city. More than a dozen notaries lived in St. Laurent in the late sixteenth century, but the parish included just three no-

15. Records of fifty-four sales of the office of royal notary in Nantes between 1560 and 1660 indicate a significant rise on price. Four sales between 1560 and 1600 averaged 217 *livres*, seventeen sales between 1600 and 1630 averaged 787 *livres* (with a median of 715 *livres*), thirty-three sales between 1630 and 1660 averaged 1,313 *livres* (with a median of 1,200 *livres*).

16. Limon, *Notaires au Châtelet*, 208–10.

17. For these patterns, including wealth, social homogeneity, and horizontal social orientation of Nantes city parishes, as well as their size, see Croix, *Nantes et le pays Nantais*, 206–14. Many early modern cities shared these characteristics. Benedict, *Cities and Social Change*, 13.

tarial households in the subsequent decades, apart from a couple of men who, unlike most seventeenth-century notaries, held notarial office only briefly before acceding to higher rank. Pierre Guerin, for example, purchased the office of notary in the 1620s and lived in St. Laurent, but he quickly abandoned notarial office in favor of the higher status and no doubt more lucrative financial opportunities of a position in the Breton financial court (Chambre des Comptes), the most important jurisdiction located in Nantes.[18]

Once again, notaries in other northern cities seem to have shared the travails of their Nantais colleagues. In Tours, for example, notaries also suffered a loss of stature and struggled to maintain their middling rank in the seventeenth century.[19] The reasons for this shift are complex. The economic stagnation of the seventeenth century may have reduced business for an overabundantly staffed occupation, and the more rigid social stratification that the same depression encouraged may have accentuated distinctions within the legal hierarchy.[20]

Notarial families found themselves in a situation in which upward mobility was increasingly difficult, loss of status ever more likely, and the preservation of their middling rank a matter of paramount concern. For these families, the relations of marriage and household life, the ties between households of kin, and participation in the public life of their community were key in meeting the challenges they faced. To preserve their middling rank, they needed to preserve their property and their public respectability. In pursuit of these goals, the choices that family members made in their personal and public lives created hierarchies of power and authority that provided a grassroots foundation for the patterns of urban political culture.

18. Based only on notaries who maintained an identifiable stable residence in one of the twelve city parishes.

19. Langlois suggests that the economic difficulties and modest social rank of notaries in Tours were shared by other urban notaries in northern France, if not those of Paris and the Midi. Langlois, *Notaires de Tours,* 443–60.

20. The transition between a fluid social structure in the sixteenth century and a much more rigid one in the seventeenth, due to changed economic and other conditions, has been observed in other Loire Valley towns. Marcel Couturier, *Recherches sur les structures sociales de Châteaudun, 1525–1789* (Paris, 1969); Langlois, *Notaires de Tours,* 443–57.

2

Notaries As Artisans of Credit, Confidence, and Political Culture

A sixteenth-century notarial manual, a sort of self-help book for notaries, urged that notaries be men of discretion, maturity, sound reputation and lifestyle, and upright conversation. They should talk very little and listen well. They should look their clients in the face and interrogate them seriously as to their names, status, and desires, so that the act would be as accurate as possible.[1] The sobriety and seriousness that such exhortations urged on notarial practitioners conjured up a quiet, dignified devotion to duty. Yet the Nantais archives are full of references to notaries who fell sleep while they were supposed to be working, who allegedly produced forgeries, who were involved in shouting and shoving matches in their workplaces, in bars, and in other public places.

The men who worked as notaries have become crucial conduits of our perceptions of early modern societies. The vast mountains of documents that notaries generated provide invaluable insights into the daily lives of

1. *Protocoles des notaires* (Lyon, 1601), quoted in Jean-Paul Poisson, "L'Apport des formulaires notariaux à la connaissance de la vision des notaires sur eux-mêmes et sur la société aux seizième et dix-septième siècles," in his *Notaires et société: Travaux d'histoire et de sociologies notariales* 2 (Paris, 1990), 31.

their contemporaries. The marriage contracts, wills, loans, leases, apprenticeships, and other contracts that notaries wrote have been used to trace patterns of economic practices, social relations, family strategies, religious affiliations, material culture, and political ties. Historians have mapped out the kinds of acts that notaries produced and assessed the extent to which notaries shaped the content of the documents that they drew up.[2] Yet the practices behind the acts that notaries drew up, and the roles that notaries and notarial instruments played in the process by which early modern people ordered their world, are just beginning to be recovered.

The formal function of the notarial office was to secure public confidence by guaranteeing the integrity of private transactions. In doing this, the notariat performed a service for the early modern French state, but notaries carried out the work of the state in other ways, too. Although lowly notaries were in some ways at the margins of a system of governance that had the monarch at its center, surrounded by a complicated hierarchical apparatus of law courts and lawyers of every kind, notaries were among the few representatives of the state that its subjects encountered on a daily and mundane basis. As the crown sought, for example, to regulate marriage (leading notaries to note the consent of parents in the marriage contracts of minors) and economic activity (requiring that loans of more than 100 *livres* be registered by a notary), notaries played key roles.[3] In this sense, although notaries themselves—in their way of life, socioeconomic level, and mode of working—were of modest status, they were the fingertips of royal authority.

Yet for their communities, notaries were one of the first points of access to the processes of law and government, and in this sense they were one of its centers. As such, they were also the servants of their communities, powerful both in terms of the personal knowledge that their work gave them and in terms of the public protection that their acts provided. The resort to notarized acts was deeply embedded in French society, and a legal system that relied on written evidence encouraged French subjects to seek the

2. Recent efforts include Poisson, *Notaires et société*; Margaret Darrow, *Revolution in the House: Family, Class, and Inheritance in Southern France, 1775–1824* (Princeton, 1989), 57–60; Kathryn Norberg, *Rich and Poor in Grenoble, 1600–1814* (Berkeley and Los Angeles, 1985), 123–24. Useful studies of the early modern French notariat include: Jean Gaston, *La Communauté des notaires de Bordeaux, 1520–1791* (Bordeaux, 1913; reprinted Toulouse, 1991); Ludovic Langlois, *La Communauté des notaires de Tours, de 1512 à 1791* (Paris, 1911); Monique Limon, *Les Notaires au Châtelet de Paris sous le règne de Louis XIV: Etude sociale et institutionnelle* (Toulouse, 1992).

3. François Isambert et al., eds., *Recueil général des anciennes lois françaises depuis l'an 420 jusqu'à la Révolution de 1789*, vol. 14 (Paris, 1833), 202.

protection that a notarized act offered. Clients used notaries to make public records of their personal affairs, whether borrowing or lending money, buying or renting property, making preparations for marriage or death, providing records of meetings or of arguments. However, few acts carried the legal obligation to use a notary, and none to use a particular notary, so individuals had wide discretion about which notary to use and about whether to pay a notary at all. Notaries, meanwhile, had to provide what clients wanted or see the trade go elsewhere.

Their dual roles left notaries in a gray area between state and community, having to seek business by meeting the evolving needs of their neighbors as well as fulfilling their public charge of record keeping. In practice, notaries diversified the kinds of work they did, and in doing so became entangled in many of the uncertainties that beset early modern society. For peers, notaries often seemed to pose a real threat to the very confidence they were supposed to guarantee. The tensions and challenges of early modern life underpinned the work that notaries did, but these same tensions and challenges were often elided in the acts that notaries recorded.

These ambiguities raise all kinds of questions for historians: about how notaries actually worked, about what kinds of work they did and for whom, about the character of the particular narratives in the legal instruments they left, and about the purposes that these narratives may have served for notaries, for their clients, and for the French crown. Examining these issues suggests that in a variety of ways, notaries helped to mediate the relations between state and subject, between orality and literacy, between law and commerce, between individuals and a changing economy, between gender and authority.

Attitudes Toward Notaries

The narrow responsibilities of clerkship that Antoine Furetière, an eminent seventeenth-century lexicographer, associated with the work of a notary seemed to allow little room for controversy. He defined "notary" in his *Dictionnaire Universel* as a "keeper [*officier depositaire*] of public faith, who keeps the records of contracts that parties make before him, and who delivers copies of them that are genuine and binding."[4] Yet early modern per-

---

4. Antoine Furetière, *Le Dictionnaire universel* (Paris, 1690; reprinted Paris, 1978), entry "notariat."

ceptions of the roles and attributes of notaries ranged from laudatory to condemnatory. The variety of opinions suggests the potential for complexity that notarial work involved, for the men who did it and for their clients and others.

Commentators sympathetic to the notariat liked to emphasize the significance of the office in securing social and political stability. Printed notarial handbooks, like the one cited at the start of this chapter and others, described a mode of notarial activity that served perfectly, through the objectivity, diligence, and uprightness of its practitioners, to secure the position of notaries as safeguards of public order.

The seventeenth-century author of a handbook on notaries (*La Science parfaite des notaires ou le parfait notaire*), Claude Joseph de Ferrière, observed that the notary's office was among "the most important and most necessary for the maintaining of civil society." As he explained, "The profession of notary is of an immense domain; since properly speaking, there is no affair which cannot be within its domain, nor persons who do not every day feel the necessity for it." Some years later, a commentator on the French legal system observed that "of all the offices which are necessary in a political state, it has always been held that the office of Notary was one of the most important and necessary for the maintenance of society and the commerce of men."[5]

This perspective emphasized that notaries' importance lay in their function as guarantors of public confidence, by giving "public authority" to the acts they drew up. Necessitated by human weakness and corruptibility, notaries were said to maintain civil society by endowing individual acts with the integrity and good faith that their professional personae represented.[6] The state and the individual encountered each other in the person of the notary. As state officials, notaries made public, legally binding records of the matters that ordered private life. As guarantors of the integrity of the acts, notaries had a crucial influence over the fortunes and property of the clients who entrusted their affairs to them.

Observers suggested that the repercussions for state and individual of notarial incompetence or wrongdoing were so vast that only men of the most certain probity and capacity should become notaries. De Ferrière ex-

5. Claude Joseph de Ferrière, *La Science parfaite des notaires, ou le parfait notaire* (Paris, 1681; rev. ed. Paris, 1741), 1, 8; Maurice Bernard, *Divers Observations du Droit . . . contient plusieurs notables recherches des offices des Notaires et Tabellions Royaux, Protonotaires, Secretaires du Roy, Greffiers et autres Semblables* (Bordeaux, 1717), 22.

6. Bernard explained the need for notaries: "The little faith met in human actions obliges and constrains us to employ the hand and pen of notaries." *Divers Observations,* 24.

plained that "the task of keeping the confidence of the whole world demands extraordinary qualities in he who does it."[7] Another commentator noted that only men of "complete virtue, of inviolable faithfulness" should become notaries, and added, "One cannot imagine what evils and ravages false notaries produce in a state . . . if it happens that they begin by corruption to drift from their duty and to commit frauds, they introduce total disorder and confusion in the world."[8]

The desire to trumpet the importance of notaries in these ways circulated among at least a part of the local notariat in Nantes. The notary Michel Forget, for example, wrote a "dissertation sur l'origine des notaires" in the early eighteenth century that elaborated a mythical genealogy for the notariat, giving it a nobility of spirit and ancestry.[9] Forget located the roots of notarial practice "in the first century," dating from the time of the fall of Adam and Eve. As a consequence of this, he said, human self-interest and jealousy in a society of widespread illiteracy created the need for notaries. According to Forget, therefore, notaries were "the first *officiers*" in the history of the world. He asserted that "probity has always been the essential characteristic of a notary, their acts being of such great weight that judges see them like laws." Moreover, Forget claimed, the office was so respectable that its original holders were nobles, and most of the French nobility included notaries among their ancestors.

In addition to guaranteeing the veracity of the transactions, notaries could be representatives of "public faith" in other ways. They could be called upon to serve as signifiers of public authority in a wide variety of circumstances far beyond the contracts that notarial manuals enumerated. Pierre Liger and Michel Jumeau, for example, in 1649 observed the birth of an illegitimate child and attested to the declaration of paternity that the mother had made during labor.[10]

Notaries themselves were not, however, able to translate automatically the weight of the public faith that their office embodied into respect or status for their persons. Few contemporaries seemed persuaded that their notaries merited such esteem, although all acknowledged the power that notaries' positions gave them in daily life.

7. Ferrière, *Parfait notaire*, 1.

8. Bernard, *Divers Observations*, 32. Bernard added that counterfeiters, usurers, or vicious criminals were as "pernicious to the public" as a false notary, "who by a single falsity will plunge us so quickly to legal action, that will devour the best of our property."

9. ADLA, 4E2/2101, *Repertoire des Actes de Maistre Michel Forget Notaire Royal à Nantes 1731.*

10. AMN, GG188, 25 October 1649.

Awareness of the potential, or even likelihood, of notarial wrongdoing and the havoc that resulted was widespread in early modern France. Preachers warned about notaries who altered contracts and lumped them with lawyers, officeholders, merchants, and soldiers as people who lived at the expense of others and made little positive contribution to French society.[11] Even the leader of the notarial company of Paris worried about his fellow notaries in the capital, who compromised their office by being "selfish men, hungry for property, zealous and impatient about making money, looking for it or rather hurrying towards it by every kind of means that are often opposite and contrary to the honor and dignity of our charges," or by acting "like peddlers going door-to-door offering everyone their store of know-how."[12]

An early seventeenth-century Lyonnais, Jean de Croset, published a pamphlet demanding that the king reform the notarial profession. He claimed the notariat was rife with abuses of all kinds, including the drawing up of acts that were known to be fraudulent and the altering of documents after their signing. Croset claimed that his demands had been motivated by his own "calamities and domestic misfortunes (the sad trophies and unhappy effects of a false act, and note Monseigneur, of a single variation) which resulted from the evil people in the midst of us, of our property, with so great a power."[13]

Croset complained that notaries were like "wolves in the middle of a sheepfold" who "fed on robberies and larcenies and who grew fat on depredations and domestic pillages." His characterization illustrated both the power that notaries were perceived to have over personal affairs and the consequences for public confidence of their shortcomings. Rich and poor were equally vulnerable, because any ill-wisher who had a kinsman, friend, or godparent who was a notary had a potential ally with whom they could conspire to do ill. As a result, "our property remains always at the command, and subject to the whim of the passions and wishes of the unjust and envious." Nor did Croset believe that notarial propensity for altering, suppressing, or forging documents was a matter of the past. "There is hardly a

11. Larissa Taylor, *Soldiers of Christ: Preaching in Late Medieval and Reformation France* (Oxford, 1992), 148–49.

12. Quoted in Limon, *Notaires au Châtelet,* 178.

13. Jean de Croset, *C'est la Remonstrance au Roy Pour le resoudre à oster aux faux Notaires Les Moyens qu'ils ont d'antidatter et de varier, d'altérer et de supporser les feuillets de leurs livres* (Lyons, 1610).

man who has seen so little and has so little experience of the world as to put this [idea] forward: we see quite the opposite."[14]

Charles Loyseau, Croset's contemporary, singled out two abuses in particular that he believed were very common and increasing. He observed that "bad notaries" were in the habit of either antedating many of the documents they drafted or changing the middle sheets without altering the last sheets on which signatures were recorded. Loyseau advocated closer surveillance of notarial record keeping to avoid these "wickednesses . . . and the other sorts of fraud that are invented every day." Only increased supervision would provide "greater assurance of public confidence of contracts, which consist of all our property and resources, and which cannot be certain enough amidst the shrewdness and malice of this century."[15]

The Nantais notariat itself articulated anxieties about the erosion of notarial standing through inappropriate behavior or outright fraud. Observing that a notary was "by his *état* the depository of the most precious titles of families, of their property, their fortune, and their reputation," the notariat maintained that only men who were above suspicion of temptation or corruption should be admitted to the office. This independence was missing from a man "whose poverty and indigence put him so to speak in the necessity of betraying on thousands of occasions the inviolable secret which is confided to him." The Nantais notaries added that for this reason, they had several times opposed the acceptance of such men as notaries. But their need to reassert this criterion, the lamentable state of the company's finances, and the small estates that many notaries left suggest that their objections were not always successful.[16]

The insults that Nantais residents directed against notaries on occasion suggested local hostility toward some of the notaries they knew. A frustrated female client accused Hervé Trebillard in front of a group of people of being a "thief, cheat, and insulter" in a dispute over fees in 1657, adding that he had failed to collect his notarial acts (presumably a reference to notaries' legal obligation to keep their acts in chronological order to deter fraud). On another occasion, an angry man accused Trebillard of fabrica-

14. Croset, *Remonstrance*, 75–76, 107, 164.

15. Charles Loyseau, *Les Cinq Livres du Droict*, in Claude Joly, ed., *Les Oeuvres de Maistre Charles Loyseau advocat en parlement contenans les Cinq Livres du Droict* (rev. ed., Paris, 1666), 175.

16. "Compte rendu d'assemblée des notaires," quoted in Hervé de Larminat, "La Compagnie des notaires de Nantes, des origines à la Révolution" (thèse pour le doctorat en droit, Université de Rennes, 1955), 26–27.

tion in testimony, calling him "publicly forger, which he repeated several times." An angry man confronted Louis Bretineau in his *étude,* shouting that "he had sold his own brother" (an apparent reference to one of Bretineau's specialties, arranging indentured servitude contracts for Frenchmen to go to the Caribbean) and that he was a rogue and a fool. Mathurin Goheau was at a wine sellers' one lunch time when the owner "called him a fool and a maker of false acts," which, as Goheau noted, was to his "great prejudice and dishonor." Several fellow lunchtime imbibers noted that Goheau had been accused of "reporting as real what was not."[17] The framing of insults around issues of fraud and general lack of principle replicated the allegations of Croset and Loyseau, and suggested popular ambivalence about the men who worked as notaries.

While there were certainly good and bad notaries, and the actual extent of the illegalities contemporaries alleged that early modern notaries perpetrated is unclear, the wide variety of opinions about their roles suggests the complicated place that notaries occupied in their communities. In meeting the needs of the community as well as their own, notaries were active in diverse functions besides their narrow formal role as public record makers.

Notaries and the State

Notaries did on some occasions emphasize their distinct identity and interests, mobilizing a corporate idiom that provided an important conceptual basis for envisioning the French body politic. Their aim was, of course, to emphasize that their work served the "public good."[18] Every legal instru-

17. ADLA, B5817, 10 February 1657; B6656, 26 October 1635; B6664, 17 August 1647; ADLA, B6666, 15 March 1650.

18. For discussions of the corporate nature of early modern French society, see James R. Farr, *Hands of Honor: Artisans and Their World in Dijon, 1550–1650* (Ithaca, N.Y., 1988), 13–59; Pierre Goubert, *The Ancien Regime: French Society, 1600–1750* (New York, 1969), 211–16; Roland Mousnier, *The Institutions of France Under the Absolute Monarchy, 1598–1789: Society and the State* (Chicago, 1979), 429–76. Historians have usually assigned great importance to corporate ties, arguing that early modern Frenchmen identified primarily with other members of their own *corps,* with whom they perceived common interests distinct from and possibly antagonistic to those of other *corps,* even if the latter were their socioeconomic peers. Works suggesting that corporate groups saw themselves as distinct, often competitive groups include Jonathan Dewald, *The Formation of a Provincial Nobility: The Magistrates of the Parlement of Rouen, 1499–1610*

ment that notaries subsequently drew up included an assertion of their place in the corporate order: "We, the undersigned . . . members of the forty-six royal notaries of the city of Nantes . . ." Disputes erupted periodically over who were truly among the forty-six and who were pretenders, conflicts whose resolution required each notary to show the papers of each of their predecessors from 1560. Notaries of different towns also engaged in jurisdictional skirmishes with each other over who could do what work where.[19]

Like other such corporations (*corps*), the notariat was regulated by the king, who in 1560 had set the number of royal notaries in Nantes at forty-six. In the sixteenth century, the French monarchy sought to regulate the conditions of notaries' work to try to ensure the reliability of notarial acts. Laws passed between the 1530s and 1570s required repeatedly, for example, that notaries ensured clients signed acts made for them, recorded their clients' place of residence, made copies for clients promptly, and kept their minutes in chronological order and without blank sheets.[20]

Yet the French state's control over its notaries was tenuous for much of the early modern period. Notaries bought their offices and paid a hereditary tax, but the state exercised little direct control over who entered the notariat. The crown's efforts to regularize notarial practice in the sixteenth century were not enough for the notariat's numerous critics, as we have seen. Royal regulation became much closer, however, beginning in the late seventeenth century. By then, after repeated earlier gestures toward demands for reform, the crown required, for instance, that each notary keep an index describing his acts, a measure specifically meant to reduce the possibilities of fraud.[21]

Like other *corps*, Nantais notaries governed themselves in meetings (usu-

---

(Princeton, 1980); William Sewell, *Work and Revolution in France: The Language of Labor, from the Old Regime to 1848* (Cambridge, 1980).

19. ADLA, 5E, Corporations 5, 12, 13.

20. Isambert, *Recueil général* vol. 12, 482–84, 835–39; vol. 14, 85, 251, 420–21.

21. No substantial analysis exists of the evolution of state regulation of notaries. Jean Gaston's early-twentieth-century study of the early modern notariat in Bordeaux suggests that late-seventeenth-century innovations, like the stamp tax on paper in 1673 and the introduction of the Contrôles des Actes (repertories) in 1693, after a century of discussion about the need for such a change, marked an important transition toward greater state supervision of the notariat. This conclusion is shared in studies of notaries in Tours and Paris. Gaston, *Notaires de Bordeaux*; Langlois, *Notaires de Tours*; Limon, *Notaires au Châtelet*. William Doyle's recent study of venality provides useful information about the evolving relationship between notaries and the state in the eighteenth century. See William Doyle, *Venality: The Sale of Offices in Eighteenth-Century France* (Oxford, 1996).

ally held at local ecclesiastical institutions such as the houses of the Jacobin or Dominican monastic orders) and sometimes participated together in a variety of events, secular and religious. On occasion they celebrated mass together, held dinners to celebrate the recovered health of the king, and collected dues from their members to underwrite their costs as a corporation. They expressed their identity as a group by, for instance, sending one of their number to the funeral of a fellow notary in a nearby town or by petitioning the Breton Estates to keep their number at forty-six.[22]

Notaries also sought to distinguish themselves as part of the upper echelon of the hierarchy of corporations. They, like doctors and members of the legal elites, called their corporation a company rather than describing themselves as communities, as did artisans' guilds. Similarly, Nantais notaries enjoyed privileges that they anxiously defended, such as the right granted by the king in 1575 and confirmed in 1597 to be exempt from quartering soldiers and from the charges of guardianship or tutorship.[23] Although sons and sons-in-law did sometimes become notaries, the widows or sons of notaries, unlike those of many artisans, enjoyed no protections to ensure the continuation of their families' association with the notariat after the death of the officeholder.

Although notaries were probably keen to emphasize their office holding because the holding of office was an important source of status in early modern France, their offices were among the lowliest, by official classification. Notaries were categorized with clerks, seal keepers, corn and coal carriers, and fabric measurers, rather than being included in the category of judges, barristers, financiers, and bureaucrats, who constituted France's elite.[24]

Moreover, Nantais notaries did not possess many of the characteristics of a tightly knit occupational community. Whereas the Parisian notariat met for mass and meetings every Sunday in the same chapel, the Nantais notaries, like their peers in cities such as Bordeaux, rarely gathered as a

22. Except for one act in 1650, few records of the company of notaries in Nantes survive for the period before the 1680s. The activities cited here are described in the first surviving register of the deliberations of the company (*Livre de Délibérations de messieurs Les Notaires Royaux de Nantes du nombre de 46*), dating from 1681 to 1687, and in a set of accounts for 1673–88. During this time, the secretary of the company, Mathurin Verger; its head, Pierre Lemerle; and the outgoing head, Pierre Belon, were all of a generation of notaries already active in the period of this study. ADLA, 5E, Corporations 16 and 26.

23. ADLA, 4E2/2101. The same document went on to note that "in order to mark more clearly the distinction attached to their authority," notaries were forbidden to have "bars or public gambling" in their residences.

24. For the distinctions between categories of offices (divided into *domainial*, like notaries, and *casuel*, like judges and barristers), see Mousnier, *Institutions of France*, 2, 29–30.

group.[25] The Nantes notarial assembly apparently met only sporadically, as repeated and unsuccessful efforts in the 1680s to arrange regular monthly meetings suggest. Only twenty-four meetings were recorded in the six and a half years covered by the first surviving register of deliberations. Even when meetings were held, attendance varied: between twenty and thirty of the forty-six notaries were present at most occasions, and there were many fewer at some of the meetings.[26]

The easy access to the notariat may also have undermined both any strong corporate identity or public status. Men wanting to be notaries faced easily met standards, and the company of notaries did not control its membership very actively in the ways that other corporations did. In this regard, the impact of venality of office may have been different for the notariat than for more elite groups of office holders. Although agreements for the sale of notaries' positions could be voided if the company of notaries refused to receive the buyers, reception seems in fact to have been a formality.[27] The few qualifications required for the office of notary enhanced this openness of access. Unlike artisans, who had to produce a masterpiece to be granted full membership of their corporations, or doctors or judges, who had to show university degrees and expertise in examinations, potential notaries had only to provide witnesses to attest to their five years of experience in a notary's *étude* and to their "*bonne vie, moeurs, conversation et religion catholique.*"[28]

Meanwhile, the social networks of individual notaries were marked by a conspicuous lack of other notaries if they were not kin, and by the prevalence of men of similar socioeconomic status but different formal corporate identity, such as apothecaries and master artisans. Many other potential sources of solidarity and alliance competed for notaries' time and loyalty.[29]

25. Limon's recent study of the Parisian notariat concludes, from a review of early-twentieth-century local histories of the notariat, that, as an institution, the Parisian notaries were exceptional in the strength of cohesion and discipline of their corporate identity. Limon, *Notaires au Châtelet*, 30–33. For the irregular meetings of Bordeaux notaries until the late seventeenth century, see Gaston, *Notaires de Bordeaux*, 169.

26. Between February 1681 and October 1687; ADLA, 5E, Corporations 4 and 16.

27. Of the many surviving examples of notarized sales of notarial offices in the ADLA, none note any instance where the candidate had not been received.

28. See, for example, ADLA, 5E, Corporations 43, 28 March 1664.

29. For analysis of the social networks, see Chapters 7 and 8. James Farr's study of the artisans of early modern Dijon, for example, also argued that artisan masters and journeymen there increasingly experienced solidarities across crafts that emphasized the mutual interests of horizontal social groups, rather than vertical occupational ones. See Farr, *Hands of Honor*, 59–75.

Notaries at Work

In practice, the patterns of notaries' daily lives constantly undermined both the cohesion of notaries' corporate identity and their efforts to represent themselves as more than artisans. The very variety of notaries' daily work tended to erode the authority of the notarial office, because some of the more pragmatic aspects of their activities often appeared potentially antithetical to the formal task of keeping public confidence. The work of the men who became notaries was only partly devoted to record keeping, and their lifestyles and way of working had as much in common with men like apothecaries and master artisans as with the judges or barristers of the legal elite.

Practically speaking, notaries found themselves allied with successful artisans in terms of wealth, job training, and mode of work. We have already seen that notarial wealth was far below that of the rest of the legal community, whether lawyer, barrister, or judge. Moreover, like artisans, notaries learned their work and gained access to their *corps* by practical training rather than by the university learning that lawyers and other officeholders undertook. The contracts of the adolescent boys who wanted to work as clerks in the *études* of notaries in order to become *practiciens* closely resembled those of artisans' apprentices. Clerks and apprentices both paid agreed fees and promised to stay for fixed periods, to obey their masters, and to ask permission to go out, while both master artisans and notaries promised to teach their neophytes the skills of the trade and to act in loco parentis.[30]

For clients, the atmosphere of notarial *études* may have seemed little different than that in any workshop and quite distant from the grandeur of scale of court buildings. Like artisans' workshops, *études* were usually a ground-floor room of the building where the notary and his family lived. People came in from the street and ran out again, disputes and negotiations took place, insults or even blows were traded. An anonymous man came into Louis Bretineau's *étude*, accused him of all manner of wrongdo-

---

30. See, among many examples, the typical contract between Simon Aubin and Pierre Robin. Robin arranged for his son Charles to live with Aubin for one year as "clerc pentionnaire," during which time Aubin was to "instruire . . . à son pouvoir aux affaires de tabellionage et outre le nourrir, coucher et lever," in return for a payment of 144 *livres*. ADLA, 4E2/491, [date illegible] 1629. Apprenticeship-type contracts were also used in other areas, as evidence from Aix indicates. Claire Dolan, "Le Notaire, la famille, et la ville: Aix-en-Provence dans la deuxième partie du seizième siècle." I thank Professor Dolan for sharing the manuscript of her forthcoming book with me.

ing, and pulled out a sword to strike the notary. He was restrained by a passerby who saw the uproar from the street and ran in to prevent bloodshed. Vincent Bernard pushed outside a bailiff who arrived in his *étude* to try to serve a judgment on him. When the bailiff persisted in trying to enter, he was attacked, punched, and kicked by a clerk of Bernard's who tore up the judgment and slammed the door "swearing excreably the holy name of God."[31] Confidentiality was not guaranteed either. A servant in a neighboring shop overheard a dispute in Trebillard's *étude,* as only a barrier of boards separated the two. The wives of notaries were also often present.[32] Potential clients entering a notary's place of work would not, then, be awed by their surroundings, as they might be on entering the rooms of a lawyer in a court building.

The manner in which notaries produced the acts that they wrote also suggests their proximity to the artisanal community. Notaries do not seem to have cultivated particular expertise in the law itself. The rarity of book ownership suggests that notaries were not legal scholars. Extant after-death inventories show that only one in twenty Nantais notaries possessed an extensive collection of legal works and a copy of Breton customary law, while none had a printed notarial manual. Even Parisian notaries did not, on the whole, own many books in the seventeenth century. Notaries apparently made no pretence of the kind of learning and intellectual life that distinguished members of contemporary legal elites.[33]

A handwritten notarial handbook produced in Nantes suggests how notaries actually worked and points to the essentially artisanal quality of notarial practice. Its title, "Papers to Use for [illegible] Instruction," and physical form (bound with a piece of discarded parchment) suggest its pur-

---

31. ADLA, B6664, 17 August 1647; ADLA, B6653, 28 March 1628. Other instances of uproars taking place in *études,* whether caused by the act being drawn up or by issues unrelated to the practice, include ADLA, B6122, 16 June 1617 (blows and insults exchanged between clerks); ADLA, B5817, 10 February 1657 (insults traded in dispute over charge for documents); ADLA, B6657, 12 January 1637 (blows and insults over family dispute); ADLA, B6136, 23 August 1641 (insults, blows, and the tearing up of the sentence whose delivery inspired the conflict); and ADLA, B6657, 13 January 1637 (events overheard).

32. For evidence of female presence in *études,* see Chapter 4.

33. ADLA, B5653, 11 April 1623. Limon notes the contrast between the paucity of books in Parisian notaries' inventories and the sumptuous libraries owned at the time by members of the sovereign courts. Dewald's study of the Rouen parlementaires similarly located their strong sense of corporate identity in their sense of their distinctive skills and responsibilities. Limon, *Notaires au Châtelet,* 278; Dewald, *Formation of a Provincial Nobility,* 16–69.

pose.[34] The locally specific forms and dates it included in the boiler-plate linguistic apparatus that framed all notarial acts indicate that this manual was used in a Nantais *étude* in the 1650s.

Like printed handbooks, it consisted of numerous examples of the form of documents that notaries might be required to draw up and often gave two slightly different possible formats for contracts with the same purpose, for example, marriage contracts. A multitude of very specific examples were included, such as an act for the "transfer of a surgeon's boutique," apprenticeships for boys and for girls, different kinds of leases, and so on.

The more practical and hands-on character of this locally written-up manuscript reference tool is illustrated, however, by two differences in content from typical printed guides for notaries, which, as we have seen, notaries apparently rarely actually owned. Unlike them, this local guide included samples of acts that responded to client desire for notarial recording of activities that were not strictly contractual, for example, the appropriate formats for *déclarations* and for parish assemblies. Moreover, the manuscript guide included no prescriptive comments on how to be a good notary.[35] Perhaps notaries had few books among their possessions because they and their clerks relied for reference instead on handwritten copies of manuals like this one, whose minimal monetary value gave little impetus to save them.

This manuscript manual evokes a vision of early modern notarial practice closer to that of the artisan or apothecary than to that of the prosecutor or judge. In utilizing such reference tools, notaries did little more than incorporate the wishes of their clients into legalese. Their initiative seems to have been quite limited, a limit rarely clear, because if clients did not know what they wanted, acts were not made. In 1651, for instance, Pierre Delesbeaupin recalled for a lawsuit unrelated to him that a couple of months before, two of the parties to the suit had come into his office to make an apprenticeship contract, but, "as the parties could not agree on the price or conditions," they left without making any act.[36]

---

34. ADLA, 1J288 (in very poor condition; several pages at the start of the book that may have revealed more about origin and purpose have been torn out).

35. Copies of printed notaries' handbooks are quite scarce, again suggesting that they did not circulate widely. But the prevalence of handwritten references is even harder to establish clearly, because they were of no value, and people had little incentive to save them or archives to collect them.

36. ADLA, B5814, 5 January 1651. Evidence of notarial practice in other areas also speaks to notaries as craftsmen in this regard. In Aix-en-Provence, the preliminary notes of a notary

Like their middling peers who labored alongside them in their own workshops, notaries had to compete for business, more or less overtly. They might do so in a number of ways, from helping clients get credit (a process examined later in this chapter) to making sure their services were accessible. Louis Coudret and his mother-in-law ended up in court, for instance, in a dispute over what constituted an appropriate work location for him. She had promised in his marriage contract to lease a boutique for him and had done so. Coudret, however, insisted that the space was not "suitable for carrying out the work of a royal notary," because it was too small and no notary had ever worked there. He wanted her instead to rent him an *étude* where notaries had worked for more than thirty years. Presumably, it had the attraction of being a well-known location for notarial business. An Aixois notary solicited business during a plague outbreak by walking along street inquiring if he could make wills for any of the epidemic's unfortunate victims.[37]

In fact, the amount of work that notaries produced in their "official" capacity—preparing documents—varied widely from person to person and from year to year (see Table 2.1). The yearly "productivity" of notaries ranged from the average of 78 acts a year (or six or seven a month) that Robert Poullain drew up to the 347 (twenty-nine a month) put out in the *étude* of three successive Bacheliers. Not surprisingly, Poullain's widow had to borrow money to pay for his funeral, whereas the third generation of the Bachelier family saw a son purchase a high-status position in a Nantais court.

Of course all acts had to be signed by two notaries, but only one of them kept the copy in his records. Thus, simply counting acts fails to account for the work of the other notary. Guillaume Penifort, for instance, kept no minutes after 1619, although he continued to practice until his death in 1629. Yet beginning in 1619, when his daughter married a former Penifort

---

for clients' wills exist, as well as the final form of the wills. Claire Dolan has concluded that the notary simply "translated" clients' stipulations into the usual form of wills, only adding his own content in the case of exceptional requests by the client. Dolan, "Le Notaire, la famille, et la ville."

Kristen Gager has shown how notaries in Paris drew up contracts for adoptions to meet local demand. However, her identification of such notarial work as legal mediation seems to me to give notaries too much credit in shaping the law. Kristen Elizabeth Gager, *Blood Ties and Fictive Ties: Adoption and Family Life in Early Modern France* (Princeton, 1996), 85–87.

37. ADLA, B6126, 18 February 1622. Aix example cited in Dolan, "Le Notaire, la famille, et la ville."

Table 2.1.   Levels of notarial activity[38]

Notary	Years of Records	Total Number of Acts	Single Year High	Single Year Low	Average Number of Acts	
					per Year	per Month
Hilleriteau	6	536	144	49	89	7
Bodin	10	2,350	354	102	235	20
Bonnett	47	15,002	522	125	319	26
Garnier	36	5,160	357	2	143	12
Denys	34	7,179	405	79	211	18
Poullain	5	389	104	69	78	6
Ouairy	34	1,741	95	21	50	4
Carte	28	5,323	264	33	190	16
Bachelier	42	14,561	601	164	347	29
Penifort	21	5,296	507	28	265	22
Guilloteau	10	3,153	360	276	315	26
Total	273	60,692			222	19

clerk, André Charier, Penifort co-signed almost all the minutes that Charier recorded. Similarly, the acts recorded by Guillaume Garnier appear to show a dramatic change halfway through his career. During his first eighteen years as a notary, he recorded only 240 acts, whereas he reported almost 5,000 acts in his second eighteen years. Again, though, this difference is deceptive: during those first years, Garnier consistently co-signed with Abel Denys, who recorded the acts, and the change in the number of acts that Garnier recorded coincided almost exactly with Denys's death.[39]

Nevertheless, in many early modern cities from Nantes to Geneva, there were more notaries than business to occupy them.[40] Albeit with wide individual variation, Nantais notaries only averaged recording 4 or 5 acts a

38. These figures are taken from all extant *inventaires des registres* exchanged between parties when an office was sold. The Bachelier *étude* included records from 1602 to 1644, during which Nicholas Bachelier and two of his sons, Jean and Julien, consecutively held the position, and some attenuation of activity was evident. The number of acts made a year averaged more than four hundred in the first fifteen years and more than two hundred in the last fifteen.

39. The minutes of Guillaume Penifort ended in 1619 as his son-in-law's began, and they constantly signed together from that date until Penifort's death in 1629. ADLA, 4E2/332, 6 June 1641; and ADLA, 4E2/294, 24 January 1657 for *inventaires des registres* of Abel Denys and Guillaume Garnier.

40. Barbara Roth-Lochner, "L'Evolution de l'activité notariale à Genève aux dix-septième et dix-huitième siècles," *Revue d'histoire moderne et contemporaine* 33 (January–March 1986), 98–100; Jean-Paul Poisson, "Introduction à l'étude de l'activité notariale dans la Vallée de la Loire (Orléans, Tours, Nantes) au dix-huitième siècle," in his *Notaires et société*, vol. 2, 117–40.

week (or about 220 a year), a figure that means that many notaries were significantly underemployed and undercompensated in terms of the writing up of acts. Starting in the seventeenth century, Nantais notaries complained that their offices sold for very low cost (claiming an average of only 600 to 700 *livres* in the first six decades of the century) and were "more onerous than profitable." By the eighteenth century, the notarial company in Nantes and its peers in other cities were so aware of this problem and its negative implications for the notariat that they began to petition the crown to reduce the number of notaries in each city.[41]

In Nantes, and surely in other cities, notaries responded by taking on activities other than simply drawing up legal instruments, thereby supplementing their revenues in a variety of ways. Sometimes they held more than one position. As we have seen, before 1600, men were often lawyers as well as notaries, but this particular pluralism disappeared after the turn of the century (although a handful of men were first notaries and then lawyers). Men constantly combined notarial duties with jobs that required similar record-keeping skills—acting as assistant clerks (*commis au greffe*) in the city's courts, petty tax farming, working as administrators for rural seigneurs and rural jurisdictions.[42] More exceptionally, men working as notaries also engaged in quite unrelated jobs: Jacques Hilleriteau, for example, was also designated as a merchant, and Thomas Robo doctored animals.[43]

These men also compensated for their underemployment as notaries per se by spending considerable time on business that was closely tied to their notarial occupation, though invisible in the legal instruments they drew up. Notaries may not have told their clients what to say in the acts they drew up for them, but in other ways they did much more than merely record the wishes of their clients in a legal form. The daily work of most men who held the office of notary included relatively little time devoted to preparing acts for clients, as the small number of documents produced in a month on average shows, and considerable time counting money and brokering credit to generate business.

41. ADLA, 5E, Corporations 13 (no date on document, but dates it refers to suggest it dates from the mid-1670s); ADLA, 5E, Corporations 12, 16 May and 23 September 1763, 25 February 1764.

42. Among many examples, Robert Ouairy was also a *commis au greffe*, René Bazille was *greffier* of the parish of Loroux-Bottereau and also *procureur fiscal* of a seigneurie in the parish, Jean Coupperie was the *procureur fiscal de la cour et jurisdiction du prieure* of the parish of St. Jacques.

43. For Hilleriteau's occupational designations, see, for example, ADLA, 4E2/214, 27 March 1646; ADLA, 4E2/214, 11 August 1646; and ADLA, 4E2/214, 7 January 1648. For Robo's treatment of a cow for money, see ADLA, B6114, 23 October 1598.

Brokering Credit

Notaries also provided services for their communities that emerged from their own need for business, the expertise their work gave them in the usual practices and individual circumstances of their clients, and the sundry needs of their clients in a changing early modern world. This changing world presented new challenges as well from the dictates of law and government. These functions were critical elements in notaries' perceptions of themselves, in their roles in the community, and in the attitudes of their neighbors toward them. Although the work that notaries performed for the French state and for their communities built on their association as builders of public confidence, their other activities often threatened to undermine their ability to fulfill their primary role successfully.

Making loans was one crucial nexus where the role of notaries met their own needs, those of their clients, and those of the state. The use of credit grew rapidly in early modern societies; indeed, its use became increasingly necessary for a broad cross section of early modern society. But there was widespread unease about credit and about the commercialization of the economy that credit was a part of.[44] A new form of credit, called *rentes,* developed in sixteenth-century France to allow the expansion of credit by getting around the limits on loans imposed by the Catholic prohibition of usury.[45] Moreover, the personal knowledge of individual affairs that notarial work gave to its practitioners, as well as the legal obligation that all *rentes* of more than 100 *livres* be notarized, left notaries ideally placed not only to record loans, but also to advise and arrange them.

The impact of the expansion of credit was evident in early modern notarial *études,* where, contrary perhaps to popular perception, notaries recorded many more loans and leases than wills and marriage contracts. Acts recording *rentes* became a mainstay of notarial practice beginning in the sixteenth century. In early seventeenth-century Geneva, for example, more than half the notarial acts recorded in 1625 were credit transactions. In mid-eighteenth-century Paris, almost 40 percent of notarial acts involved credit transactions.[46] Nantais practice followed a similar pattern.

44. Anxieties are examined in Jean-Christophe Agnew, *Worlds Apart: The Market and the Theatre in Anglo-American Thought, 1550–1750* (Cambridge, 1986).

45. For an account of the development of *rentes* in the sixteenth century, see Bernard Schnapper, *Les Rentes au seizième siècle: Histoire d'un instrument de crédit* (Paris, 1957).

46. For Geneva, see Roth-Lochner, "L'Evolution de l'activité notariale," 100–105. Numerous articles by Jean-Paul Poisson analyze the output of notarial practice in a number of towns

The narrative laid out in the legal instruments that recorded loans as *rentes* seemed to portray clearly the course of events leading to the making of a loan and to limit the notary's role to recording. Typically, the act read "Before us, the notaries undersigned. . . ." The two parties met, agreed on the loan, exchanged the money, and signed the contract, usually in the *étude* of the recording notary on a given date. The act declared that the parties had agreed on the transaction and met in an identified place to hand over the money, and to legalize their agreement by having the notary make a record of it.

However, in fact, Nantais notaries not only recorded credit exchanges, sometimes no doubt in the disinterested manner that the prescriptive literature of their profession described and the acts themselves implied, but also acted as brokers of local personal credit networks, actively bringing borrowers and lenders together, starting at least in the late sixteenth century.[47] People wanting to lend or borrow knew they could turn to notaries. In 1608, for example, a friend of Jean Papin's, a court clerk, gave him 300 *livres* to use toward a dowry for one of his daughters when she was ready to marry; in the meantime, the "profit" from the gift was to be used for the daughter's maintenance. Papin asked Jean Carte "to find solvent people" for a *rente*.[48]

The unexpected death of a notary revealed some of the complexities of money management that lay behind notarial credit brokering. Pierre Que-

---

and regions, but especially "L'Activité notariale à Paris en 1751," in his *Notaires et société,* 297–308. Roth-Lochner finds credit transactions declining in importance in notarial activity. From over half the transactions in 1625, acts concerning credit occupied just over a third of documents produced in 1700, and more than a quarter in 1775.

47. Recent work has pointed to the role of Parisian notaries in particular in arranging large-scale credit for the French state, from the late seventeenth century onward. In late-seventeenth-century Paris, for example, when the clergy were faced with raising a huge sum of money to pay a forced loan to the king, they turned to the Parisian notariat to secure the *rentes* that would provide part of the capital.

Monique Limon has argued that the notoriety that Parisian notaries gained as credit brokers in the later eighteenth century—a role encapsulated by the late-eighteenth-century commentator Louis-Sebastien Mercier, who observed that notaries "had become dear to the ministry because they encouraged individuals to lend their money to the king"—probably had its roots in the reign of Louis XIV.

Work now in progress by Philip Hoffman illustrates the role of notaries in the eighteenth-century Parisian credit market. Claude Michaud, "Notariat et sociologie de la rente à Paris au dix-septième siècle: L'Emprunt du clergé de 1690," *Annales E.S.C.* (November–December 1977), 1154–87; Limon, *Notaires au Châtelet,* 284; Philip Hoffman, Gilles Postel-Vinay, and Jean-Laurent Rosenthal, "Private Credit Markets in Paris, 1690–1840," *Journal of Economic History* 52 (June 1992).

48. ADLA, B5801, 16 July 1608. See also ADLA, B6141, 23 November 1650; and ADLA, B5694, 21 November 1656.

nille arrived at a house in the city in 1653 with a client, "each with a bag of money," to oversee and record the repayment of a *rente*. The notary sat down and put his bag on the table. As he opened it and some coins rolled out, he was struck with "apoplexy" and died. In the ensuing chaos, his bag of money disappeared.[49] If Quenille had survived, his records of the transaction would have been among the most mundane of notarial acts, of the kind that survive in the thousands. One act would have shown Pierre Burot (who was referred to with the courtesy title *noble homme*, an acknowledgement of his social status rather than legal nobility) borrowing money from Françoise Martineau, a sixty-year-old spinster. Another would have shown Burot repaying a loan from Jean Charete, a nobleman who was a member of one of the city's most politically powerful families.

Such documentation would have hidden the quite different events and imperatives behind the transactions, revealed only by a court case between Quenille's heirs and clients over the missing bag of money. A few days before Quenille's death, Burot and his brother-in-law had visited Jean Charete, the creditor, and asked to repay their loan. Charete agreed and asked where to collect the money. They said he should go to Quenille's, as he was their uncle. At about the same time, Quenille sent a message to Burot that he "was very angry" that Burot had not produced the 1,000 *livres* due to be repaid, as promised. However, Quenille added that "he had found" another 1,000 *livres* and said he "would have it lent to him" the following Sunday. In this message, Quenille emerged as Burot's co-signer, who guaranteed payment of the loan. Quenille had instigated the repayment because he wanted to end his own commitment.

The next Sunday, Martineau went to Burot's house to lend him the money and met Quenille there. Burot was, Martineau recalled, "in a hurry" and asked Quenille to take Martineau and the money back to Quenille's *étude* to count it. Quenille was "falling asleep" while he was counting the money, and Martineau said she would come back another time. When she returned two days later to pick up her copy of the contract, Quenille said she had not given him enough money, and she somewhat doubtfully paid him the difference. Meanwhile Charete visited Quenille, offering to lower the rate of interest on the loan rather than have it paid off. Quenille refused, saying that he wanted to be free of his commitment. It was two or

---

49. The paragraphs that follow reconstruct events described in depositions given in a law case that followed Quenille's death. It ended with Quenille's daughter and heir being ordered to repay the missing 1,000 *livres,* plus interest. See ADLA, B6142, 1 September and 7 October 1653; and ADLA, B5816, 20, 25, and 26 September, 9 and 29 October, 4 November 1653.

three days later, when Quenille and his nephew went to Charete's house to repay the principal, that Quenille died.

Quenille played multiple roles in this series of events. He was co-signer (securing a loan for Burot), negotiator of terms in his own personal affairs (demanding to be released from his guarantee and refusing an extension of the loan), banker (counting and holding the money for about four days), and credit broker (getting Martineau together with Burot). He was also the kinsman of one of the parties and the recording notary. The legal instruments that Quenille would ultimately have written to record these transactions, however, would have been silent regarding all but the last of these roles. Nor would they have admitted the absence of a second witnessing notary. The face-to-face encounters between parties that the documents would have described did not take place.

Although our knowledge of this particular series of transactions is unusual, for contemporaries it was only exceptional in its abrupt ending with Quenille's death and in the subsequent disappearance of the bag of money that the notary had brought with him. Quenille's multiple roles raised no questions for any of those involved, suggesting that contemporaries condoned notaries' acting in capacities such as credit brokering, which went far beyond their prescribed role as guarantors of the authenticity of contracts.

Nevertheless, when notaries acted as credit brokers, they in many senses endangered their claims to guarantee public confidence. Such activities left the integrity that notaries were supposed to embody open to compromise. The multiple facets of notary, banker, and credit broker resulted in a mode of practice quite distinct from that ideal promulgated in notarial handbooks and in the narrative of the legal instruments themselves.

A notary could hold money for considerable time, for instance, between when it was deposited with him and when he found a suitable borrower. What was more, the lending and borrowing parties did not necessarily—perhaps not normally—meet. All parties could at one time have been in the *étude,* but not gathered together, as the wording of the legal instrument implied. In many cases, weeks apparently passed before the transaction was completed and the paperwork delivered to all parties.

Even the co-signing notary, whose presence was implied by the opening "before us" and whose signature was meant to verify doublefold the integrity of the transaction in question, may not have been present at any point, or certainly not at all points, as the form of the document maintained. Etienne Poullain, for instance, protested to the court that the clerk of one of his fellow notaries had removed several documents from Poullain's *étude*, including one "put in Poullain's hands to sign." A young clerk in the *étude* of Hervé Trebillard noted that a dispute over payment had broken out after a lease had been made and signed, but during the time Trebillard sent someone to fetch another notary to come to add his signature.[50]

Notaries' handling of deposited money between receiving it and lending it out could call into question the ideals of notarial objectivity and disinterestedness. Apparently, for instance, the money a notary eventually handed over to a lender was not always the same money that the notary had earlier received from the borrower. When Pierre Guihaud died in 1624, he left more than 1,000 *livres* in sundry purses and chests in his *étude*, of which only 120 *livres* were identified as belonging to a specific client.[51]

Additionally, notaries sometimes lent their own money to clients or borrowed for themselves money that clients had entrusted to them. André Charier recalled being asked by a client to arrange a *rente* with a suitable person, but, having failed to find such a person, he became borrower "in his own name."[52] When other notaries appeared as borrowers, they too may have been in Charier's position. The many notaries who co-signed for lenders used the credibility of their public role to facilitate their private business as credit brokers.[53]

René Guilloteau illustrated the intertwining of banking, credit brokering, and notarial activities in ordinary notarial practice, as well as the potential for malpractice. A judge sealed his records in 1656 on the grounds of "the great prejudice and damages [suffered by] several individuals and the public."[54] The allegations were that his embezzlement of funds entrusted to him and the uncertainty as to the status of acts that clients had directed him to draw up prejudiced the public interest. Various parties de-

50. ADLA, B6122, 16 June 1617; ADLA, B5817, 10 February 1657.

51. ADLA, B5654, 20 April 1624. It is not absolutely certain that this money was held for clients, but it seems likely. The money was not included in the final total of the worth of the estate, which was valued only at just over 400 *livres*. No other extant notarial inventories show any such sums of money being kept in the *étude*, but the notarial acts that must have been present were not recorded either, presumably because such acts, not being the personal property of the notary, were not subject to valuation.

52. ADLA, B6141, 23 November 1650.

53. For an analysis of the place of notaries as borrowers, lenders, and co-signers in *rentes*, see Chapter 6.

54. The nature of Guilloteau's practice is reconstructed from a *procès-verbal* recording events and statements during the taking of an inventory of Guilloteau's notarial minutes. See ADLA, B5694, 13 to 21 December 1656.

clared their stake and came to inquire if the affairs they had put in his hand had actually been undertaken, worried, no doubt, that they had lost their money.

A series of clients sought to establish their claims. The first of these was typical of his peers. The lawyer of a nobleman demanded to know if Guilloteau had paid the 400 *livres* of principal and the small amount of interest that his client owed on a *rente*. Guilloteau had been given the money to cover this transaction two weeks earlier, but he had not yet delivered the paperwork to prove that he had done so.

The details of one client's affairs were more fully recorded, providing a revealing insight into the workings of notarial practice. Michelle Cruchet, the widow of an artisan, described how she had left "several" *rentes* with Guilloteau, asking him to find another lender to take them over. She wanted to release her capital in order to provide a dowry for her daughter.[55] But "not knowing what Guilloteau had done with the contracts, or if he had liquidated them as he promised he would," she wanted a search of his papers for her contracts to see "if any embezzlements had been made."

Cruchet explained that about four years earlier, she had inherited some money from her parents, and, "wanting to make a profit from it," she had gone to Guilloteau. He had arranged a *rente* for her that was repaid soon after, so she left the money with him to be used to buy another one. "Some time later" Guilloteau told her that he had lent the money to his sister, and he gave Cruchet a *grosse* (her copy of the contract). Guilloteau himself subsequently paid Cruchet the interest on this *rente*. At about the same time, Cruchet gave him another 1,600 *livres*, "also confidentially," to buy a *rente*, and soon afterward, Guilloteau told her that he had lent it to three men. He gave her a *grosse*, but once again he paid her the interest.

As time passed Cruchet's affairs became more complicated, although she apparently had confidence in Guilloteau, suggesting that his actions were entirely within expected bounds. Cruchet received 1,600 *livres* when another *rente* that she held was redeemed, so she brought the money to Guilloteau. He said he had loaned 500 *livres* in one contract, for which he produced a *grosse*, and 1,000 *livres* to his brothers-in-law, for which the *grosse* was delivered a year later. She gave him another 100 *livres* to supplement the remaining money in yet another *rente*, for which she received a *grosse*. When

55. It is not clear why the transcription of these events carried a much fuller account of Cruchet's claim. The regulations of *rentes* did not allow lenders to demand the repayment of their loans, so they could only liquidate their capital by finding another person willing to buy out their position as creditor.

this *rente* was repurchased, Guilloteau arranged another *rente* for her to buy. Later he told Cruchet that his sister and brothers-in-law wanted to buy back their two *rente* contracts, worth 1,400 *livres*. He said that to make the sum up to 1,600 *livres,* he would take 200 *livres* in interest still owed to Cruchet on the contracts of his kin, and lend the resulting capital to two other men.

For some reason, Cruchet's suspicions were aroused at this point. As she said, "she was obliged to inquire from Jean Bizeul, a lawyer at the presidial court, if these men were solvent." She was apparently reassured, and when another of the *rentes* that Guilloteau had arranged for her was repurchased, she again left him to find another borrower. Guilloteau then claimed that he believed he had received 600 *livres* instead of the 500 *livres* that the *rente* entailed, and that he had consequently bought on her behalf another new *rente* for 600 *livres*. Cruchet was about to leave on a trip, and, again perhaps suspicious, she went to Guilloteau's *étude* to go over with him the accounts of the money that "he had dealt with" for her, with which he claimed to have purchased *rentes*. She also wanted to get her copies of the contracts.

At that time, Guilloteau said that she owed him 92 *livres,* which was the sum he had paid to make up the difference between the 500 *livres* he had received for her from the redemption of the *rente* and the 600 *livres* he had lent on her behalf. But upon her return (in September, preceding the inventory), when she asked that all the contracts be sold to obtain cash for her daughter's dowry, Guilloteau said that he could not get the money until All Saints' Day (November 1), because "everyone was out in the country." The day before All Saints', Guilloteau promised to have the money in two weeks. In the meantime, he kept her copies of the contracts.

Hearing a few days later of his abrupt departure, she went to his house "to try to know what was owed to her or in any case" to get her contracts. Louise Lecoq, Guilloteau's wife, did not give her any "satisfaction" until Cruchet sent a lawyer who found only one of the contracts before Guilloteau's records were sealed.[56] Cruchet concluded her complaint by accusing Guilloteau of keeping her contracts "in bad faith," and by claiming that she was owed 3,800 *livres* plus interest.

Clearly Guilloteau, whether by malice, carelessness, or bad luck, had lost

---

56. Cruchet's expectation that she might do so illustrates the extent to which early modern notarial practice was part of the household mode of production. For other indications of this, see Chapter 3.

the careful balance between the banking, credit brokering, and notarizing facets of his practice. Perhaps he had simply failed to maintain an adequate reserve, so that when Cruchet demanded all her money at once, he was caught with insufficient funds in hand. He had been a notary for almost thirty years, and the active manipulation of his clients' financial affairs that was revealed in the complainants' petitions was probably more typical than not.

Although a notary's holding and management of money did not in itself ordinarily entail notarial malpractice, the varied elements of notarial practice continually raised the specter of conflicts of interest. Notaries' active roles in facilitating the agreements they recorded clashed with the objectivity that their public office was supposed to embody. Contemporary critiques of notaries, however formulated, found their context in practices that clearly raised the possibility of wrongdoing. When the parties involved in a contract never met, or the drawing up of contracts was delayed, or an act was not immediately validated by the signature of a second notary, doubts about notarial intention and integrity were easily aroused.

Jean de Croset's perception of notaries as "wolves among lambs" perhaps recognized the dangers posed to individual fortunes if the parties that notaries brought together were not solvent as much as cases of real fraud. The same activities explain the concern over the temptations that impoverished notaries could face when they were entrusted with significant sums of money.

Yet notarial credit brokering became commonplace in the sixteenth and seventeenth centuries. Indeed, it was an invaluable means of providing credit locally in early modern society, alongside the financier-dominated large-scale credit networks. Contemporaries quickly accepted this credit system, because it provided them with relatively easy access to either lenders or borrowers, in a society that had not yet developed formal institutions for the circulation of capital. Notarial practice, to some extent, evolved as a matter of practicality in a society just beginning to accommodate on a large scale to the expansion of credit in ordinary people's daily lives. People with money to lend might not know potential borrowers and vice versa, while notaries were well placed to facilitate the exchange. As well, they were in need of ways to increase their business. Clients could turn elsewhere if wrongdoing was suspected, and the banking side to notaries' activities presumably created a flexibility that helped credit brokering and generated notarial fees.

Fashioning Public Confidence and Political Culture

The differences between how loans were made and the versions of events that were recorded in notarial acts point to other aspects of the relationships between notaries, their communities, and the French state. If we consider notarial acts as both cultural texts and legal instruments, the representations contained therein illuminate some of the extralegal meanings that notarial acts embodied.

Notarial acts crafted a particular vision of textual reality for early modern men and women, as the narratives of notarial acts represented relationships and events in ways that either enhanced or elided the roles of particular groups. Notaries were in many ways artisans, who generated public confidence through the production of textual forms fostered by acceptance of key themes in early modern society, such as the impact of expanding credit, the rising importance of literacy in a traditionally oral culture, and the increasing emphasis on male heads of households as the bearers of authority.

Notarial acts were among the most common forms of the written word that early modern urban populations came into contact with, as their presence in inventories attested. Many people who did not own books or even pamphlets or chapbooks and could not read or write, as well as many who did and could, had their own copies of the notarial acts to which they had been parties—marriage contracts, wills, sharecropping agreements, loans, and so on. Notarial acts and other handwritten documents were set, like the products of print culture whose meanings have been explored in much recent work, "within a network of cultural and social practices that give it its meaning."[57]

Notarial acts perpetuated a master narrative that served the purposes not only of the state or of the notary, but also provided a usable resource for at least some of the clients. As Natalie Zemon Davis has pointed out in analyzing petitions for pardons, "Shaping choices of language, detail and order are needed to present an account that seems to both writer and reader [or client, in the notarial case] true, real, meaningful and/or explanatory."[58] Notarial acts portrayed what happened in a way that enabled all its parties to order the world in which they lived. The form of an act priv-

---

57. Roger Chartier, *The Cultural Uses of Print in Early Modern France* (Princeton, 1987), 183.

58. For this use of the concept of fictions, see Natalie Zemon Davis, *Fiction in the Archives: Pardon Tales and Their Telling in Sixteenth-Century France* (Stanford, 1987), 3–5.

ileged one version of the event that it recorded, and in doing so, it represented a particular vision of how society worked.

To return to the example of *rentes,* not only the single most frequent
form of notarial act, but perhaps the one that reached the widest spectrum
of the population, the records of loans detailed actual facts and served as
texts that helped to order the community. Although juridically, the outcome of the transaction was more important than its genesis (legally, it did
not matter how, when, or where a lender and borrower found each other),
culturally, the notarial instrument represented events in a manner that encouraged public confidence.

A complex conjuncture of cultural processes lay behind the power of
that representation and were critical in providing the meanings that early
modern communities found in notarial acts recording *rentes.* Many factors
came together in the narrative of the *rente,* including the need for notaries
themselves to stabilize—at least in appearance—their role, the notaries'
position as mediators of oral and literate cultures, the impact of the diffu-
sion of credit and a commercializing economy, and the centrality of gender
in ordering early modern visions of society.

Notaries created accounts of these *rentes* that recorded genuine financial
transactions, but that also described events in ways that both notary and
clients knew were fictitious. At their very base, *rentes* used a fiction to get
around the Catholic church's prohibition on usury. Although *rentes* were essentially loans, the language of the contracts framed the parties as buyers
and sellers of property on which rent would be paid. Moreover, in asserting
that the event took place "before us"—in the presence of two notaries—and
in assigning a date and time as well as a location, the act represented an occasion where the participants met face to face and made their agreement in
front of notaries who made a public record for the security of both parties.
In these ways, the acts elided the charging of interest, the agency of notaries
as middlemen, the time that elapsed between elements of the transaction,
and the fact that no such meeting, in fact, necessarily took place.

The assertion of the integrity of the notarial office, if not of the person of
the notary, was one critical element of notarial legal instruments. Notarial
acts positioned the notary, in his objective, disinterested role, as the main-
tainer of civil society. Each instrument drawn up opened with a bold assertion, "before us," testifying to the presence of the two notaries whose signatures were necessary to legalize the act. It located the authority of the
notaries in their membership of the company of the "forty-six royal notaries of Nantes." The names, statuses, residences, and perhaps occupa-

tions of the parties to the act were recorded. The terms of the agreement were carefully elucidated and always portrayed as a direct outcome of the active efforts of the contracting parties. The act closed with a note of the location where the transaction took place—usually the recording notary's *étude*—the date, and the signatures of all participants. The form of the act clearly asserted that the agreement had been made at a certain place, at a fixed time, in the presence of all the signatories.

The forms of the acts that notaries wrote enhanced their own official authority, as the acts raised some aspects of notarial practice to primary focus while eliding others. The opening established the notary as the voice of authority in the text, instantly asserting that notarial authority was the key to the legality of the document. The transactions in question were represented as the outcome of the direct actions of the clients, as if the notary were merely a transparent conduit of their wishes. The written account of the transaction emphasized only one aspect of a relationship between participants that was, in fact, multifaceted, serving to counteract the doubt that notaries' multiple activities as credit brokers or as petty tax farmers or as court clerks cast on their integrity as guarantors of public confidence.[59]

Moreover, notarized acts themselves became the real security for public confidence. Notaries kept the original acts as part of their private records, and these were the acts that had legal validity, while clients were given copies. Guilloteau's clients were anxious, for this reason, to find their contracts in his records. Notaries reported instances of clients attempting to tamper with the original records, as if they believed that to destroy the physical act itself would nullify the agreement. Louis Coudret, for example, recalled the actions of a woman, Françoise Moreau, who had come to his *étude*, asked for a copy of a compromise she had made with kin, and requested that the original act be read to her. She then seized it and tore it into pieces. Moreau was apparently motivated by a legal action between her and the kin.[60]

Notarial documents also had cultural values that complemented their literal uses, giving the acts an importance that went beyond the details that they recorded. They were drafted in a process that was at a nexus of oral and literate cultures, illuminating some of the tensions and possibilities

---

59. For the prominence of the notarial voice in notarial acts, see Laurie Nussdorfer, "Writing and the Power of Speech: Notaries and Artisans in Baroque Rome," in Carla Hesse and Barbara Diefendorf, eds., *Culture and Identity in Early Modern Europe, 1500–1800: Essays in Honor of Natalie Davis* (Ann Arbor, 1993).

60. ADLA, B6139, 3 May 1647.

surrounding the written word in early modern society. Notaries enjoyed fluent literacy and occupational commitment to the power of the written form, but most of their clients, as city residents, would have been familiar with the written word through contact with the plethora of printed and handwritten materials that circulated in early modern towns.[61] Nevertheless, the prevalence of the types of knowledge and interaction that characterized an oral culture still shaped written exchanges in a society where face-to-face communication continued to be of great importance in most people's daily lives.

Evidence of the continued importance of oral traditions filled notarial documents, and orality was incorporated overtly into notarial practice. The acts referred constantly to "the said" person or event, a means to orientate listeners. Notaries commonly read the legal instruments that they had written to clients, or at least were exhorted to do so in notarial handbooks and explicitly claimed to have done so on occasion, regardless of the capacity of clients to read for themselves. This practice was articulated most clearly when deeds were ratified by people who were parties to contracts that they had not originally signed, often because they lived out of the city. The acts declared that a notary had read the contract in question aloud before the ratification took place.[62]

The construction of the transaction as a unitary event, fixed in terms of time, place, and participants, similarly had meanings in the cultural and social contexts in which it was produced. Historians have recently emphasized that knowledge in the early modern period was perceived to be the result of action rather than of belief. An actual expression of an event was

61. Examples of explorations of the impact of print culture include Chartier, *Cultural Uses of Print*; Natalie Davis, "Printing and the People," in her *Society and Culture in Early Modern France* (Stanford, 1975).

62. A seventeenth-century notarial manual, for example, declared that "Notaries must read the Contracts and Acts to the Parties, before making them sign, in order that they hear if all that has been written confirms to their intentions." Notaries recording the meetings of artisans in seventeenth-century Rome similarly emphasized reading aloud their account of what had taken place. Ferrière, *Parfait Notaire*, 60; Nussdorfer, "Writing and the Power of Speech."

Notarial documents were also formulaic, repetitive, and long-winded, traits often attributed to notarial desire to increase their fees, which were calculated by length of document. Jean-Paul Poisson, for example, has suggested that it was as a means to increase fees. Cited in Orest Ranum, "Vers une histoire de l'esthétique sociale: Le Contrat de mariage du Comte de Grignan et de Marie Angélique du Puy du Fou et de Champagne," in Wolfgang Leiner and Pierre Ronzeaud, eds., *Correspondances: Mélanges offerts à Roger Duchêne* (Aix-en-Provence, 1992). These attributes also, however, reflected the transfer of the structures of oral language to written, as did the lack of punctuation and limited choice of expressions, practices discussed in Roger Chartier, *The Culture of Print: Power and the Uses of Print in Early Modern Europe* (Princeton, 1987).

crucial to give it contemporary meaning. The idea of a transaction having occurred without the participants having met was alien to a culture that was focused on face-to-face events. A notarial act was more credible, therefore, when it represented the acts that it recorded in the form of a meeting. Other genres of record in the seventeenth century, such as engraving, also conveyed the impression of a meeting, when none, in fact, took place.[63] So, although the expansion and circulation of credit, in particular, entailed a level of abstraction that often caused great anxiety in early modern society, such tensions were downplayed in the forms of notarial acts recording loans.

Notarization accentuated the authority and presence of the French state, as its requirements concerning personal decisions over marriage, estate distribution, or credit became matters of public record. Although the state required relatively few matters to be recorded before a notary (loans more than 100 *livres* probably being by far the most common example), the concerns of the crown were nevertheless recognized and legitimized in notarial acts. When the crown had ordered that parental consent be given to all marriages, for instance, it had not required that a record of this consent be made by notaries. Nevertheless, beginning in the late sixteenth century, notaries drawing up marriage contracts carefully noted that parental consent for marriages had been given, thereby reiterating at this level the enhanced familial powers of the decrees that the French crown passed.

At the same time, notarial acts gave early modern people access to the protection of the state and served as a gateway for them to the legal system. By choosing to have a notary record their transactions, French subjects were able to try to safeguard themselves in a legal system that privileged written evidence. In making their personal affairs matters of public record, they participated in constructing and affirming a particular social order.

Notarized records offered early modern people a resource that they could appropriate for their own purposes. A variety of local groups, whether artisans or parish assemblies, paid for notarized accounts of their discussions to validate their decisions, and thus they drew on the potential

---

63. David Warren Sabean, *Power in the Blood: Popular Culture and Village Discourse in Early Modern Germany* (Cambridge, 1984), chap. 6; Ranum, "Vers une histoire de l'esthétique sociale." Ranum notes a similar dynamic in a 1666 marriage contract between two great aristocrats, the Comte de Grignan and Marie du Puy du Fou. It opened by recording the ceremony "in the presence" of various great and illustrious witnesses, including the king, implying a unitary proceedings, but ended with signatures that recorded the differing locales of the witnesses. In this case, the fictional character of the event that the document purported to report was ultimately revealed, but the example again attests to the importance of the meeting in bestowing validation.

legal power of a notarized account of proceedings. Clearly such groups believed that having notaries record proceedings gave their discussions weight that accounts they drew up for themselves would lack.[64]

Individuals too could seek notarized records for their own uses. People sometimes asked notaries to provide summaries of events to be used at some later date, in case of a legal dispute. In these narratives, usually called a *procès-verbal* or *déclaration*, a notary might record the state of a residence at the beginning of a lease, providing a copy for both tenant and landlord, or he might carefully note a series of events for a client anticipating the need for written evidence. In 1652, for example, when Julien Jouneaux was embroiled in a bitter battle with his wife, he requested that Mathurin Meignen accompany him to his mother's house, where his wife was staying. He wanted his wife to return home, but she refused. All then told their side of the story, and the individuals signed the notary's account. Notaries ended such acts simply by noting that after agreeing that the act described what had happened, a copy of the narrative had been given to the parties "for their use."[65]

In these cases, members of the community themselves appropriated the authority of a notarially authored document for their own ends. The creation of these accounts often went beyond the traditional notarial acts listed in handbooks, but drew on the same cultural qualities that all notarial acts possessed. Their uses illustrated popular awareness of the mechanisms of the legal system, such as the need for written evidence, and of the resource that a notarized public record offered.

Notarial acts also embodied the legal and cultural frameworks that maintained household-based gender hierarchies: only men and widows had di-

---

64. Minutes of artisans' meetings and parishioners' meetings (called *chapitres* in Nantes) are scattered through the surviving notarial minutes. Forget's repertoire includes minutes of *chapitres* for meetings of *arquebusiers, tonneliers, cordonniers,* and *tessiers,* as well as confraternities and parishes, in the last decades of the seventeenth century. ADLA, 4E2/2101, p. 66.

These kinds of notarial activities are missing from notarial manuals, but they clearly indicate community perceptions of the enhanced value—if not guarantee of legality—of a notarial text. Evidence also exists of similar notarial records of community meetings in early modern Lyons and Rome. For a discussion of the purposes of such meetings, see Nussdorfer's "Writing and the Power of Speech"; and her "Notarial Inscription and Artisan Collectivities in Seventeenth-Century Rome," paper presented to the annual meeting of the American Historical Association, San Francisco, 1994.

65. ADLA, 4E2/1480, 28 January 1652; see, for example, the language of a local handwritten notarial *formulaire* in the 1650s: "il nous a requis la présente déclaration que luy avons délivré pour luy valloir et servir ce que de Raison," and "il nous a requis le présent acte pour luy valloir et servir ce que de Raison" (ADLA, 1J288). See also the language of a typical act: "Desquelles dires et declarations," we have made a record and given copies to the parties involved "pour leur valloir et servir."

rect access to notaries and the resources of power that they offered. This was because wives or minor daughters (women under twenty-five) were not permitted to make notarial acts, except when authorized by their husbands or their fathers, or by the legal system. The latter could occur in the case, for instance, of women whose property and/or persons were separated from their husbands. Notaries carefully noted that such authorization had been given, thereby reiterating the dependent status of wives and daughters.

While wives were normally denied independent access to the legal protections and resources that notarial acts could offer, those same acts also routinely represented relationships in ways that reiterated an equation between authority and men. Contracts for *rentes,* for example, frequently listed several male borrowers without noting that they were, in fact, brothers-in-law, and without mentioning the women who linked them (whose dowries and labor were important elements in family capital). Women's roles as links between the households of kin were elided in representations that affirmed the power of male head of households over property.

Notarial practice and the processes of cultural production in which it was embedded suggests as much about the complex web of early modern life as do the facts that notarial acts reveal. In multiple ways, notaries and the acts they drew up, in a very material and artisanal way, fashioned public confidence, credit circulation, and cultural practices in early modern France.

The artisanal characteristics of notaries' work aligned them socioeconomically and culturally with apothecaries, booksellers, and artisan retailers, rather than with the higher rungs of the legal hierarchy. This artisanality extended to the role of notaries and their acts in early modern society, for the state and for the communities they served. Like artisans, notaries physically crafted products that served their own needs and those of the people around them, not only through guaranteeing the authenticity of transactions, but through the production of textual forms that sought to elide the uncertainties and accentuate the hierarchies that were central characteristics of early modern society.

Notaries manufactured and safeguarded public confidence in the wake of the shifting realities of early modern urban life. The acts that notaries wrote served to smooth economic and cultural tensions, and to frame the lives of French subjects in terms of a household-based patriarchy. They were also credit brokers, sources of information about what was legally and socially appropriate, and mediators between oral and literate cultures. Notaries acted as conduits through which the state could reach its subjects, and those subjects could access the legal system, engage in the ever-more commercializing economy of the early modern world, and mobilize the power of the written word. In these ways, notarial acts regulated and shaped the inter-household and intra-household relationships of early modern society.

While notaries' working lives positioned them as middlemen in all these ways, the notaries also participated in ordering their communities, as men of middling socioeconomic status. They shared the values, concerns, and pressures of their peers. In their personal as well as public lives, they made decisions and exercised priorities that revealed and promoted power structures that were fundamental in early modern society. The patterns of cooperation and authority forged in and between households of which they were members were key elements in shaping urban political culture.

3

Making Marriages

Building on over a century of state intervention in the circumstances under which marriages could take place, a 1670 collection of French laws commissioned by Jean-Baptiste Colbert, as the king's chief minister, asserted the "sovereign authority" of the crown to make rules for marriages, on the grounds that marriages and the families that resulted from them were "the colonies of his state and the seminaries of his subjects." A contemporary notarial manual reiterated this perspective in defining marriage contracts as "without doubt the most important act of all those made between men, since it serves as the foundation for civil life, for family peace and for the good of the State."[1]

Widespread agreement over the broad social significance of marriage making existed because of the importance of matrimony as a moment of property transfer, and because household formation created a key unit

---

1. "Recueil de traitez sur le droit public . . . faite par ordre de Monsieur Colbert," quoted in Alain Lottin, "Vie et mort du couple: difficultés conjugales et divorces dans le nord de la France aux dix-septième et dix-huitième siècles," *Dix-septième siècle* 102, 103 (1974); Claude Joseph de Ferrière, *La Science parfaite des notaires ou le parfait notaire* (Paris, 1682; rev. ed. Paris, 1741), 251.

through which relations of gender and authority were mediated. Marriages were critical in shaping individual and familial futures in early modern communities, where power relations were fundamentally tied to the ownership, transmission, and management of property. The politics of patrimony were a cornerstone of larger power structures in general and of gender relations in particular, in the urban early modern context. Recent studies have shown how elite support of a monarchy that sought to enhance its own power and theirs by increasing parental control over marriages was driven by a desire to secure control over property.[2]

The way the patrimony of an individual household was constructed and managed had important ramifications for relations between household members and between members of different households. The building, management, and division of a household's patrimony interested multiple parties: the spouses as individuals, the couple together, two sets of parents, any siblings, and numerous other kin of various degrees. Access to and control over property affected the form and content of relations between family members, within households and between them. The practices that were developed to control and to manage property were key elements in shaping who exercised power and how that power was exercised in everyday life. As a result of property arrangements, relationships within the family evolved along with individuals' changing expectations and obligations. In these senses, property was an important element in the complex system of exchanges in which individuals, households, and kin were enmeshed. Material and affective elements of relationships were inextricably intertwined among the Nantais notarial families. As David Sabean has pointed out: "The way that property is held gives shape to feelings between family members, territorializes emotion, establishes goals and ambitions, and gives to each a sense of dependence and independence."[3]

2. See Sarah Hanley's "Engendering the State: Family Formation and State Building in Early Modern France," *French Historical Studies* 16 (Spring 1989); and her "Family and State in Early Modern France: The Marriage Pact," in Marilyn J. Boxer and Jean H. Quataert, eds., *Connecting Spheres: Women in the Western World, 1500 to the Present* (Oxford, 1987).

3. David Warren Sabean, "Young Bees in an Empty Hive: Relations Between Brothers-in-Law in a South German Village Around 1800," in Hans Medick and David Warren Sabean, eds., *Interest and Emotion: Essays on the Study of Family and Kinship* (Cambridge, 1984), 171–72. For discussions of the role of property and inheritance systems in shaping kinship patterns and gender relations, see above; and David Warren Sabean, "Aspects of Kinship Behavior and Property in Rural Western Europe Before 1800," in Jack Goody, Joan Thirsk, and E. P. Thompson, eds., *Family and Inheritance: Rural Society in Western Europe, 1200–1800* (Cambridge, 1976), 96–111; Jack Goody, introduction to Goody, Thirsk, and Thompson, *Family and Inheritance,* 1–9; Barbara Harris, "Property, Power and Personal Relations: Elite Mothers and Sons in Yorkist and Early Tudor England," *Signs* 15 (Spring 1990); Renée Hirschon, introduction to "Prop-

Patrimonial practices were the outcome of royal acts, customary law, family strategies, and individual interests; they illustrate how cultural as well as legal issues shaped property and power relations within families. Family decision making that affected property—making marriages, managing patrimony in a household, widowhood, guardianship, and the final division of an estate—revealed and contributed to the creation of authority patterns within and between families, as the possibilities and expectations integral to the construction of gender and kinship were defined.

Laws About Marriage and Inheritance

The laws regarding the transmission of property between family members included regulations about marriage and about inheritance. They were complicated by the fact that in France, as in other western countries, the legal system was a complex and often overlapping multilayered patchwork of jurisdictions and law codes where regional and even more local regulations operated alongside national ones.

Beginning in the 1560s, the French crown issued a series of decrees that articulated ever-more expressly the concern of the state to enhance paternal control over the transmission of property by regulating the conditions for marriages. New statutes required, for example, that marriages be subject to parental consent and public knowledge. They emphasized the monopoly of authority held by the head of each household in determining the management of patrimony.[4]

At the same time, however, the rules about inheritance embodied in the French customary law that prevailed in the northern half of France strongly protected the interests of heirs and tempered the increased parental control that the crown's policy on marriages espoused. The customary law of Brittany, as in most other customary-law regions, strictly limited the opportunies of parents to determine who would inherit their prop-

---

erty, Power and Gender Relations," in Renée Hirschon, ed., *Women and Property, Women As Property* (London and New York, 1984), 1; Martha Howell, "Marriage, Property, and Patriarchy: Recent Contributions to a Literature," *Feminist Studies* 13 (Spring 1987).

For historians' neglect of the interplay of "subjective and objective" aspects of family relationships, see Hans Medick and David Warren Sabean, "Interest and Emotion in Family and Kinship Studies: A Critique of Social History and Anthropology," in Medick and Sabean, *Interest and Emotion*, 9–13.

4. See Hanley, "Engendering the State," 9–10; and Hanley, "Marriage Pact."

erty and in what form. Customary law mandated strict partibility between siblings in non-noble families, regardless of sex, and gave parents little opportunity to favor one child over another or otherwise influence the succession. Testamentary bequests and other gifts between spouses were severely restricted. Parents could not limit the final interests of the children as future heirs by assigning wedding gifts as replacements for inheritances and "buying off" future claims. Under the western French system, all children had to be considered as heirs at the final division of their parental estates, and so any gifts received before that time were simply advances: they did not replace other expectations.[5]

A notable feature of French customary law was the legal protections that it offered women and children, at least in non-noble families, with regard to their access to property. The extension of property rights to daughters as well as sons, the presence of lineage property (*propres*) in the patrimony of individual households, and the rights of women to petition for separation of property and to renounce their marital property communities all contributed to women's legal rights to property. Contemporaries were even inclined to believe that as wives were legally able to renounce their stake in community property and men were not, women may have had a certain advantage, because "the wife kept all the chances for gain without running the risk of loss."[6]

Moreover, while royal legislation about marriages increasingly emphasized the distinctness of individual households with the discretion given to fathers and husbands, Breton customary-law provisions about family property envisaged households less as autonomous units and more as nodes in a

---

5. For Breton customary law, see *La Coustume de Bretagne avec les Commentaires et Observations . . . par Maître Michel Sauvageau* (Nantes, 1710). For comparisons of the differences between customary-law regimes, see Jean Yver, *Egalité entre héritiers et exclusion des enfants dotés: Essai de géographie coutumière* (Paris, 1966), 91–155; and Emmanuel Leroy Ladurie, "A System of Customary Law: Family Structures and Inheritance Customs in Sixteenth-Century France," in Robert Forster and Orest Ranum, eds., *Family and Society: Selections from the Annales Economies, Sociétés, Civilisations* (Baltimore, 1976).

For a discussion of the differences between the large discretion of parents in southern France, where Roman law prevailed, and the very limited powers allowed by customary law in northern France, see James Traer, *Marriage and the Family in Eighteenth-Century France* (Ithaca, N.Y., 1980), 40–45.

In early modern England, too, royal statute operated alongside a maze of local county and town laws. See the discussion, for example, of David Grayson Allen, *In English Ways: The Movement of Societies and the Transferral of English Local Law and Custom to Massachusetts Bay in the Seventeenth Century* (New York, 1982); and Margaret Spufford, *Contrasting Communities: English Villagers in the Sixteenth and Seventeenth Centuries* (London, 1974).

6. Quoted in Barbara Diefendorf, *Paris City Councillors in the Sixteenth Century: The Politics of Patrimony* (Princeton, 1983), 225 n. 26.

complicated web of extended familial ties. Customary-law rules about the management of family property created the possibility of kin oversight of individual households that could come into play at key moments of change in a family's patrimony.

Although these laws provided rules to structure inheritance that were critical in shaping gender relations, patterns of kinship, and alliances among these middling families, family members also had some ability to manipulate the regulations to suit their own ends. Usage was not simply the faithful reflection of law, as studies of inheritance practices in many societies have shown.[7] Family negotiations as much as legal guidelines determined the particular characters of marriage contracts. In the process, relationships were redefined as the interests of each party were worked out and laws and loopholes were manipulated to achieve whatever ends family members sought.

Nor were the interests of the whole family necessarily identical. Family concerns imposed powerful limitations on individual choices in the early modern period, but the various moments of property transmission affected household members differently, and each had their own concerns, depending on the transition in question and on members' relationship to the central actors. Prevailing patterns could represent the preferences of the most powerful individuals or alliances within families as much as the unified expression of the goals of all kin.

Proposing Marriages

Marriage choices affected the futures of the respective parents, siblings, and other kin as well as that of the marrying couple. Different family members perceived a variety of stakes and goals in prospective marriages, and

7. Warnings of the limited utility, for social historians, of studies of legal models of inheritance systems without due attention to practice include: Ralph Giesey, "Rules of Inheritance and Strategies of Mobility in Prerevolutionary France," *American Historical Review* 82 (April 1977), 272; and Sabean, "Aspects of Kinship Behavior and Property," 105–8. Few studies of early modern France have, so far, systematically examined inheritance practices and their relationship to the law.

In an early study, J.-L. Gay, *Les Effets pécuniaires du mariage en Nivernais du seizième au dix-huitième siècle* (Paris, 1953), pointed out the discrepancies between law and practice. Illuminating examples of inheritance practices as opposed to laws include: John Cole and Eric Wolf, *The Hidden Frontier: Ecology and Ethnicity in an Alpine Valley* (New York, 1974); Toby Ditz, *Property and Kinship: Inheritance in Early Connecticut, 1750–1820* (Princeton, 1986); Margaret Darrow, *Revolution in the House: Family, Class, and Inheritance in Southern France, 1775–1825* (Princeton, 1989).

the preferences and patterns expressed suggest some of the goals of marriage as well as the parameters of parental or familial control over it in nonelite families.

The cases of minors (legally defined, beginning in 1556, as men under thirty and women under twenty-five) whose fathers were dead and who, therefore, needed court permission to marry, illuminate the considerations that shaped the initial stages of family decision making. Relatives gave their opinion as to the suitability of the match, a process that indicated that young men—and perhaps women, in urban middling families, at least—were able to seek their own spouses. While kin (or parents, if they were alive, of course) retained the right of veto, arranged marriages as such were rare. Marriage proposals usually followed courtships that had been known "for some time."

When the prospect of the marriage of Mathurin Verger and Françoise Merceron arose, for example, Merceron's guardian declared that she "was sought in marriage" by Mathurin Verger and that he was seeking the opinion of her kin. Verger asserted that he sought Merceron's hand and informed his own guardian, a merchant, and other kin, asking them to find his proposal agreeable and to consent to the match.[8]

Potential brides' opinions of the proposals varied from enthusiastic to noncommittal, although the extent to which they could be sure that their views were considered is unclear. One young woman said that she "very much" wanted to marry her suitor, but nevertheless she sought the guidance of her kin; another declared the proposal agreeable to her if her kin found it "good and advantageous for her." Renée Bretineau, Julien Jouneaux's future wife, could only bring herself to say that she was "turning [to her relations] for their opinion."[9]

While young men and women were careful in these statements to present themselves as asking for permission, generally the proposals raised little debate, at least in the public context recorded in documents. The relatives present were quick to agree, "after having conferred together," that the contract should be drawn up "on the most advantageous terms possible."

Occasionally, the kin whose advice was sought did oppose proposed marriages, and their explanations for opposition suggest the kinds of issues that family members considered when one of their number married. Their reasons also hint at a hierarchy of influence among kin in determining courses of action.

Brothers or brothers-in-law (presumably on behalf of their spouses) of

8. ADLA, B5670, both dated 7 January 1651.

9. ADLA, B6374, 23 October 1636; ADLA, B6374, 13 January 1638; ADLA, B6376, 27 June 1645.

the bride were often the first to oppose a proposed match, and more distant kin usually acknowledged the primacy of sibling concerns. In the case of Julien Bachelier's niece, for example, the husband of her eldest sister protested on the grounds that the would-be groom was neither "of the status nor the property" of his sister-in-law.

In a similar argument, one of the brothers-in-law of Jeanne Girard maintained that whereas the bride was "worth 40 to 45 thousand *livres,*" the groom was "a man of no profession and son of a father who had many dubious and uncertain business dealings," so she should wait for "a more advantageous party." Two of her other siblings also expressed reluctance. One brother declared he had not wanted to be summoned to the meeting, since he had always been opposed to the bride's marrying until she was older, and another said he could not prevent the match, but did not want to give any positive advice.

[handwritten margin note: oppose cause or bride is groom is worth less]

In both cases, some more distant kin (cousins of the third or fourth degree) assented to the proposed marriage without comment. However, Julien Bachelier said he was "of the same opinion" as was the bride-to-be's brother, and three first cousins of her mother "declared they could not give their opinion since the closer kin who had previously given their opinion did not find it useful and advantageous."[10]

A focus on the potential "advantage" to be gained (or lost) from a marriage is the key to understanding how family members assessed marital prospects. The advantage lay in reputation as well as in rank and material resources. Partible inheritance practices fostered kin awareness of their common interests, and this explains the material as well as affective concern of kin to express their opinions on such decisions. Kin objected to the potential groom in the case above, for example, on the basis of his father's shortcomings as well as his own. The latter had compounded the doubts that questionable financial affairs raised about his character by remarrying a young woman "to the prejudice of his children," so that he "could have many other children."

The intangible as well as tangible aspects of a marriage were important in a society where a correlation between reputation, rank, and resources determined status. Claude Geneste, for example, pointed out to his son that his stepmother had given her "blood and her property" when he married her daughter.[11] When insults were traded, family backgrounds were

---

10. ADLA, B6374, 13 January 1638; ADLA, B7083, 29 December 1634.
11. ADLA, B7083, 29 December 1634; ADLA, B7080, 5 December 1608.

quickly invoked as individual flaws. An opponent attacking Louis Bretineau alleged that the latter had only "learned" to live as he did, and that his mother "had sold apples at the crossroads by St. Nicolas's gate." Marguerite Bernard complained that her stepson had impugned her honor and that of her family, by suggesting that she was only "the daughter of a locksmith and that her mother was only a tanner."[12]

The acute concern of siblings above all other kin as to the merits of a match lay in this complex construction of advantage or lack thereof. The threat of an ill-advised marriage was especially potent for siblings whose reputations as well as finances might be affected. Their material well-being was at risk if, for example, the groom should prove unable to return the lineage property of his spouse or compensate the others in the final accounting for premortem advances from the parental estate.

But they had more to lose, too, when marriage associations might also cause disadvantages in terms of lost reputation. More distant kin willingly acceded to matches, because to do so posed less risk to them in both senses. The assertions of some others that they would not offer opinions when closer kin had expressed opposition seem to acknowledge that siblings should have the loudest voice.

Notaries married for the first time on average at about age twenty-seven, when their brides were twenty-two or twenty-three, and they and their families (siblings and children) gave or received dowries whose average cash value was around 2,000 *livres* (see Table 3.1).[13]

These patterns affirm the middling rank of notaries and their families. Men of all social ranks tended to marry in their late twenties in early modern France, but the wives of notaries married somewhat later than elite women, urban or aristocratic, and markedly sooner than women of the lower orders, who usually did not marry until their late twenties.[14] Dowry sizes, likewise, were far smaller than those expected in contemporary elite families, but larger than those circulated among many urban workers.

---

12. ADLA, B6664, 17 August 1647; ADLA, B6817, 14 May 1614.

13. Only dowries where the cash element is clearly defined have been considered here. Dowries are useful, but not perfect, indicators of family wealth. Their total value is difficult to assess: they could include trousseau, subsidies of living costs, and other aid, as well as cash payments. Sometimes the actual value was not clearly stated, with the bride merely bringing "all her rights," especially if she was an orphan and had already come into her inheritance. The amount given was also subject to family whim rather than representing a steady proportion of patrimony. However, cash payments made up the most important element of the dowries given among these families.

14. In forty cases where the exact age of the notary at first marriage is certain, the average age was 27.2 years. In forty-nine cases where the exact age of women who married notaries as

Table 3.1.   Cash in dowries of notarial families (in *livres*)

	pre–1600			1601–1630			1631–1660		
	N	Mean	Median	N	Mean	Median	N	Mean	Median
Notaries	2	2,500	2,500	10	1,700	1,500	15	2,247	2,000
Siblings	0	—	—	4	2,150	1,900	7	2,028	2,000
Children	0	—	—	11	2,364	2,000	21	3,990	2,000
Total	2	2,500	2,500	25	2,071	2,000	43	2,755	2,000

Around 1600, barristers in the Rouen Parlement received dowries of over 5,000 *livres* on average, while the brides of its magistrates were dowried with about 27,000 *livres*, and families of the Paris City Council exchanged dowries of between 15,000 *livres* and 30,000 *livres*. Parisian notaries signaled their wealth by giving or receiving dowries that averaged 15,000 *livres* in the mid-decades of the seventeenth century and grew rapidly thereafter.

Nevertheless, the 2,000 *livres* dowries in Nantais notarial families far exceeded the dowries of 350 *livres* given on average to the daughters of Dijon master artisans in the early seventeenth century, or those of 135 *livres* that journeymen in the same city gave their daughters.[15]

With few exceptions, the children of notaries did not either acquire more elevated occupation or marry up. The husbands and wives who formed notarial households came from families, whether merchant-arti-

---

their first husbands is clear, the average age was 22.7 years. Elite women usually married around their twentieth birthday. The average age of the daughters of Paris councilors at the time of their first marriage was 19 or 20, of the daughters of Rouen *parlementaires* almost 20, and of the daughters of Florentine patricians, 19. A similar, although moderated, pattern prevailed in the Besançon legal world during the ancien régime. In *parlementaire* families, the average age of marriage for men was 29 years and six months, and for women 21 years and one month, while among the families of *huissiers*, the average age of marriage for men was 27 years and six months, and for women, 27 years and two months. Diefendorf, *Paris City Councillors*, 180; Jonathan Dewald, *The Formation of a Provincial Nobility: The Magistrates of the Parlement of Rouen, 1499–1610* (Princeton, 1980), 278; R. Burr Litchfield, "Demographic Characteristics of Florentine Patrician Families: Sixteenth to Eighteenth Centuries," *Journal of Economic History* 29 (June 1969), 199; Maurice Gresset, *Gens de justice à Besançon, de la conquête par Louis XIV à la Révolution Française, 1674–1789* (Paris, 1978), 501–2.

15. For dowry sizes among other groups (all considering cash payments alone), see Dewald, *Formation of a Provincial Nobility*, 128; Diefendorf, *Paris City Councillors*, 234; Monique Limon, *Les Notaires au Châtelet de Paris sous le règne de Louis XIV: Etude institutionelle et sociale* (Toulouse, 1992), 224–25; James R. Farr, *Hands of Honor: Artisans and Their World in Dijon, 1550–1650* (Ithaca, N.Y., 1988), 96.

sans or *petits officiers,* where sons learned their crafts by imitation as apprentices or clerks in the workshops of merchants and master artisans or in the *études* of legal practitioners. These families did not aspire to formal education or university degrees for their children. Jobs such as that of notary, apothecary, or artisan persisted. Pierre Belon, for instance, the son of a miller, became a notary and married Marguerite Daguin, the daughter of a candlemaker, whose siblings were artisans. Belon's younger brother Julien also became a notary, until debts forced him to sell his office. But their youngest brother was apprenticed to a *pâtissier,* and their two sisters married artisans. Belon and Daguin were childless, but they helped one of her nephews, Julien Lucas, become a notary, the only member of the next generation to leave the artisanal ranks. Jean Baudouin's son Pierre became a notary, but his daughter Marguerite married an artisan. She herself taught young female apprentices "how to cut cloth and all the other skills of making women's clothes."[16]

These indicators confirm that marriage was an important element in social maintenance, if not mobility, for sons or daughters in middling families. The extent of social and geographical endogamy among middling families that we have already seen suggests that marriage extended alliances within the rank to which the families already belonged, and served to differentiate them further from the rest of society.[17] In this sense, marriage was one of many means of affirming spatial and socioeconomic solidarities.

Contracting Marriages

Marriage contracts served myriad purposes: they provided a critical moment for the transmission of property between generations, they facilitated the establishment of new households by setting them up with capital and goods, and they shaped future relations within and between households by defining the terms on which property was provided. The kinds of gifts that were given, the terms on which property was given, the ways that sons and daughters were treated, all fundamentally affected future relations within and between households.

Families made marriage contracts before the wedding took place. Notaries' accounts of their agreements, which, as we have seen, can be ascribed

16. ADLA, 4E2/676, 13 August 1634; ADLA, 4E2/1194, 11 April 1651.
17. A trend to increasing solidarity among and differentiation between different sectors of French society, with marital endogamy as one of the most visible features, has also been noted among Dijon artisans in the seventeenth century. See Farr, *Hands of Honor,* 133–44.

with significant cultural resonances, if not absolute literalness, represented the event itself as well as the details of the contracts. In doing so, they recorded a version of family life that reveals the priorities and sensibilities of marriage making in urban middling families.

Serious negotiations, between families and within them, must have proceeded the formal acceptance of the contracts that such gatherings signified. Although all contracts addressed issues such as dowry payments, the proportion of the dowry entering the conjugal community, the size of the widow's dower, and the naming of guarantors, a variety of decisions and priorities determined the particular outcome in each case. Each family could add its own refinements that had significant implications for family relations and for individual circumstances. By these means, the various parties could manipulate the requirements of customary law or even circumvent its intent to suit their own goals. In their choices, family members, together and as individuals, asserted preferences that met their own concerns and set relations to property that fostered and reflected their relationships to each other.

The formal drawing up and signing of the contract usually took place in the house of the bride's parents, amid a sizeable gathering. Twelve witnesses, on average, signed the marriage contracts of royal notaries or their children.[18] These signatories included the future spouses, of course, and various "relatives and friends." A priest, who was either from the local parish or a member of one of the families, also usually attended. The formal part of the gathering concluded as the priest "engaged" the couple, those present signed the contract, and the couple "kissed as a sign of their affection."

The location of the contract signing and the character of the witnesses provided clear indications of the important roles that kin, especially from the bride's family, played in the formation of a new household. Kin involvement in marriage making revealed the cultural importance attached to kin ties beyond those of the conjugal family among urban middling families. The potential reverberations of a match made the terms of the agreement, as well as the choice of partners, matters for the consideration of kin as well as of the bridal couple and their parents.

Marriage contracts usually acknowledged the complementary role of kin, as well as testifying to the consent of parents, as royal decrees from the late sixteenth century required, by asserting that the couple promised to marry with the support of other kin or in their presence. In a typical case,

18. From seventy-three contracts. In addition, the two notaries responsible for drawing up the contract signed.

René Germond and Marie Dergonne "promised to be married together . . . with the consent and in the presence of their father and mother and other of their relations and kin signed below."[19]

Every indication points to the prominence of kin at such moments. In 1655, for example, sixteen people signed the marriage contract of Robert Rouille's daughter, in addition to the bride and groom. Twelve were identified as kin: on the groom's side, his father, two brothers-in-law, and an "*allié*"; on Rouille's side, her two brothers (one being the priest), an aunt, two male first cousins (one of whom was her guardian), and three husbands of female first cousins. Four other female signatories were not identified, except as "other close relations and friends," but their surnames suggest that they were probably two sisters of the groom and two cousins of the bride.[20] Assessing levels of kin participation from another angle points to the same prominence. Ninety percent of marriage contracts that notaries or their wives signed in a personal capacity were for people identifiable as their kin.[21]

The provisions determining the form and content of dowries balanced the interests of the new householders, their parents, and other kin. Dowries exchanged between these families were generally composed almost entirely of cash (rather than real estate or other kinds of assets). Nevertheless, each dowry was divided into two portions, between cash that was to become marital community property and cash that was to be used to purchase "inheritances"—whether real estate or offices—that were to be considered as the lineage property (*propres*) of the bride.

These middling families routinely designated a majority of the dowry as lineage property, reiterating the continued importance of the bride's kin ties—whether her parents, siblings, or other kin—in the life of the new household. Approximately two-thirds of the dowry was usually designated as lineage property among these notarial families. More than three-quarters of contracts involving either notaries or their children kept at least 60 percent of the dowry out of conjugal community property.[22] This pattern

19. ADLA, 4E2/151, 10 February 1648.

20. ADLA, 4E2/1620, 9 June 1655. The bride's parents and the groom's mother were already dead, so these usual signatories were absent, in this case.

21. In 172 of 191 marriage contracts that notaries or their wives witnessed, one spouse was identifiable as their kin. In 3 of the remaining 19, one spouse was a servant of the notarial household, and, although the relationship between the notary and his wife and the spouses is unclear in the remaining cases, some of these may also have been for marriages of kin.

22. Usually the total value of the property was only given if the bride had at least one parent still living, so only those contracts have been considered. Of forty-seven such contracts for notaries or their children, eleven had less than 60 percent of *propres* in dowries, 26 had 60–70 percent and 10 had more than 70 percent.

may have been part of a larger trend among urban middling families: in the seventeenth century, for example, Dijon artisans also increased the proportion of lineage property in their marriage contracts. Conversely, contemporary elite families in Paris assigned a similar proportion of the dowry as community property.[23] This division was crucial to future relations within and between households. The larger the proportion of the bride's dowry that became community property, the greater the financial independence of the new household, whereas the larger the share retained as lineage property, the greater the continuing interest of her kin.

Families also made provisions to support women in case of widowhood. Almost half of the marriage contracts of the notaries or their children simply observed the customary law in this regard, permitting a widow the usufruct of up to half of her husband's *propres*.[24] The remaining contracts, as a rule, promised a cash annuity to support widows, but they usually also gave women the option of taking the customary provision instead, if they preferred.

Tensions between kin interests and the independence of households were particularly acute concerning these provisions for widows. On the one hand, for heirs, the widow's customary dower was designed to conserve lineage property, while the fixed-cash dower, which freed the estate of other obligations to her, facilitated a flexibility in the use of resources that entailed the potential for loss as well as gain. On the other hand, while customary dowers left widows to enjoy the use of and income from their deceased husbands' lineage properties that were highly coveted by prospective heirs, such dowers also gave those heirs a vested interest in overseeing the widows' lifestyles, generally, and finances in particular.[25]

Ties between households were similarly accentuated by other aspects of the contracts. All signatories agreed to observe the stipulations of the contract, but in addition, the groom often called on a particular individual to guarantee observance of the terms regarding the return of the dowry and payment of the dower. If the groom's parents were still alive, they usually fulfilled this role, and widowed mothers could also provide the necessary guarantee (as in the contracts of Charles Demons and Renée Germont).

23. Parisian elites often allowed more than half the dowry to become community property, in the late sixteenth century (the earliest surviving marriage contracts for Nantais notaries date from the 1590s). There is no indication of the exact change in the proportion of *propres* in Dijon artisan families. See Diefendorf, *Paris City Councillors*, 242–43; Farr, *Hands of Honor*, 145.

24. Thirty-one of sixty-seven contracts. *La Coustume de Bretagne*, article 455.

25. See also Diefendorf, *Paris City Councillors*, 249–50.

Failing that, other kin took their place. Julien Lucas provided as his guarantors his maternal grandmother, a maternal aunt, and her husband, Pierre Belon, while Phillipe Garreau called on his stepmother and a paternal uncle.[26]

Parents could elaborate on these basic arrangements by also agreeing, in marriage contracts, to commitments that gave new households various different kinds of help, from underwriting living expenses to providing extra sources of income to offering to help set the grooms up in their future careers.

One common provision, occurring in almost a quarter of the contracts of notaries or those of their children, was for parents to subsidize the rent of the new spouses. The bride's parents almost always provided this aid when the sons-in-law were notaries, although for the children of notaries, the split was more even.[27] When Louis Coudret's daughter married in 1645, he promised to pay half the rent "of the lodgings the future spouses will occupy," for four years.[28]

In other cases, newly married couples set up their households in the residences of parents. In 1616, René Bazille's parents-in-law agreed to provide "board, bed and lodging" for the couple, "so long as they wanted to live with them in their residence." Thomas Bruneau's mother-in-law maintained the new couple and a servant of theirs in her house for four years. Simon Aubin's marriage contract provided that his wife's parents would feed, shelter, and support the new couple for three months and then provide furniture for a separate household.[29]

Usually marriage contracts specified a fixed period for such help, but sometimes such arrangements continued long after the promised period. When Jean Bonnet's daughter married Julien Rousseau in 1624, Bonnet promised to support them for a year, but when Rousseau died in 1627, after the death of his wife, he was still living with his father-in-law with almost no furniture of his own. Similarly, in 1635 Clemence Collin promised to give her daughter Clemence and her daughter's future husband, Guillaume Chapelain, use of half of the house where she lived. Nineteen years later

26. ADLA, 4E2/672, 18 June 1629; ADLA, 4E2/151, 10 February 1648; ADLA, 4E2/578, 20 November 1654; ADLA, E978, 30 May 1654.

27. Eight of thirty-four contracts where the grooms were notaries, and eleven of forty-nine contracts involving the son or daughter of a notary; seven of eight contracts, and five of eleven contracts, respectively.

28. ADLA, 4E2/465, 25 November 1645.

29. ADLA, 4E2/664, 26 January 1616; ADLA, 4E2/95, 11 February 1632; ADLA, 4E2/311, 6 October 1609.

they were still there, and Collin was sharing the other half of the house with her younger daughter, Magdelaine, and her husband, Etienne Tesnier.[30]

Provisions for residence in the same building did not necessarily entail shared accommodations, as separate households could be maintained in the multiple units into which most buildings were divided.[31] Additionally, brides' parents frequently also provided furniture, pots, and linen in varying degrees, all of which suggested the establishment of separate households.

Parents sometimes provided other forms of aid and potential advantage in the marriage contracts. Parents of both sides commonly, although not inevitably, promised to acquit their children of "board, food and maintenance" up to the day of marriage. They might also seek to reduce their children's obligations in other ways. When the daughter of Renée Coquet, the widow of Jean Bachelier, married in 1641, the groom's mother acquitted him of "his share of her dower payment." Julien Rousseau's parents stipulated that they had previously been paying 150 *livres* a year in board and lodging for their son, and that they would henceforth pay 200 *livres* "to help support the expenses" of marriage.[32]

Another frequent provision gave a couple tenancy of rural small holdings during their parents' lifetimes, returning it to the estate to be divided among all siblings when the parents died. Mathurine Pigeaud gave a son and a daughter "enjoyment" (that is, possession) of small rural properties, together with the animals on them, in their marriage contracts. Guillaume Garnier and Françoise Demons made a similar promise when their daughter married Jacques Novel. In such arrangements, the couples gained immediate access to the property's income, and immediate gain could become a permanent advantage. Garnier and Demons stipulated, like many of their peers, that the property would be returned to the estate "without report of the income" from the land and "with no report of the profits" of the animals.[33]

Grooms often received promises of material aid in pursuing their careers from both sets of parents. Grooms' parents might agree to contribute to the cost of the purchase of an office or setting up in commerce. Jacques

30. ADLA, 4E2/1668, 5 November 1624; ADLA, B5658, 17 December 1627; ADLA, 4E2/612, 11 June 1635; ADLA, B5816, 28 July 1654.

31. In only one contract did a clause providing residential arrangements for the couple articulate that parents and newlyweds would share "*pot et pain*," presumably as one household.

32. ADLA, 4E2/1697, 1 July 1641; ADLA, 4E2/668, 5 November 1624.

33. ADLA, 4E2/674, 2 July 1632; ADLA, 4E2/677, 20 November 1635; ADLA, 4E2/1366, 12 April 1654.

Rabard's father promised to pay the 1,250 *livres* that his son's notarial office cost, and Louis Lepetit's mother noted that he had already acquired his office, valued at 1,000 *livres*. Mathurin Quenille's daughter married into a merchant family who promised to give their son 5,000 *livres* to "set up his shop."[34] Brides' families also quite commonly chose to encourage the careers of new husbands by specifically assigning dowries to be used for the purchase of offices for them.

For a newly married young couple, such subsidies had obvious benefits in reducing expenses early in their marriage, but this kind of help could also provide them with longer-term advantages. In theory, provisions given "in advance of [children's] rights of succession" had to be counted at the eventual division of the parental estate, to ensure an equitable division. Yet often marriage contracts determined that a recipient was not required to report the value of this subsidy to their siblings when preparing to divide their parents' estate.

Advantaging Sons, Advantaging Daughters

One of the most important possible uses that parents could make of marriage contracts was to give gifts to children in advance of their inheritances. Advancing property was, in fact, the primary means that parents had to circumvent the strictly egalitarian principles of the customary law. Parents had few options in their selection of heirs within the guidelines of Breton customary law, and their main opportunity to favor one child over his or her siblings involved differential timing of gifts during the parents' lifetime.

The quantity and timing of the transfer of funds were crucial in an inheritance system that dictated ultimate equality of division, so a child who received a share of his or her inheritance early had the significant advantage of enjoying its benefits long before other siblings did. Moreover, income or interest derived from such gifts did not necessarily have to be reported before the final division of the estate between heirs. Parents could employ differential timing and different quantities of property advanced to get around the limitations that customary law placed on their ability to dis-

---

34. ADLA, 4E2/1027, 6 December 1643; ADLA, 4E2/179, 13 July 1656; ADLA, 4E2/1748, 5 November 1635.

perse their estate as they wished. Such practices gave them the option of favoring one child over another, or favoring sons or daughters.

First impressions suggest that middling parents often employed this strategy to differentiate between siblings. Renée Rousselet, the widow of François Bonnamy, promised to provide her daughter Marie and son-in-law Thomas Bruneau with accommodations for four years, but she had offered no such provision to her other daughter, Claude, when she married a lawyer four years earlier.[35]

On closer inspection, however, the impact and intent of the differential treatment of siblings is often difficult to assess. Sebastien Pouetard and Prudence Girard, for example, had two daughters: Isabel, who married one of Pouetard's clerks, Jean Fruneau, in 1644, and Françoise, who wed an architect eleven years later.[36] Pouetard and Girard promised to provide board and lodging in their home for Fruneau and Isabel for two years, and to help pay for a notarial office for Fruneau if it cost more than Isabel's dowry. They later did this. These provisions were not repeated for Françoise, but she received a far larger dowry (4,000 *livres* as against 1,200).

Although the differential between the dowries would eventually be compensated for when the parents' estate was divided, dowries provided ready cash, and any income that cash produced did not have to be reported later. The dowry differences were thus a potentially valuable variable, as the income on the 2,800 *livres'* difference between the two dowries could have been quite significant over a period of years.

Yet whether the complex terms and interests in the two transactions gave one sibling a greater advantage in either the long or the short term, and whether the arrangement best served the interests of all parties is debatable. In this case, Fruneau's close association with a father-in-law who pursued the same occupation probably enhanced his career, whereas the other son-in-law, as an architect, may have derived greater benefit from the immediate cash input. Moreover, Pouetard and Girard no doubt benefited from the labor of their new son-in-law as well as from that of their daughter during the years they lived together. Jean Fruneau did receive help from his in-laws to buy his office as notary in due course, and afterward he and his father-in-law co-signed for each other almost all the time.

The intents behind such arrangements are elusive, but the variations in

---

35. ADLA, 4E2/95, 11 February 1632; ADLA, 4E2/458, 31 October 1627. These two contracts are difficult to compare in other respects, since Bonnamy *père* died in between them, and, as a result, in 1632 the contract referred only to "tous droits" from her father's estate.

36. ADLA, 4E2/616, 9 January 1644; ADLA, 4E2/620, 6 February 1655.

the treatment of siblings may reflect efforts to meet the individual needs of each child, or indeed parent, rather than advantage one child over another. In the earlier example, Renée Rousselet, as a widow, may have offered her younger daughter housing in order to keep a child living with her who could help her. This issue had not been at stake in the earlier marriage of her elder daughter.

The prevalence of daughters among those favored through the underwriting of children's housing costs, and the frequency with which parents of daughters offered to help launch their sons-in-laws' careers, illustrates the complex issues involved in such actions. On the one hand, this practice facilitated greater real equality among children by compensating daughters, to some degree, for the advantages that their brothers received, such as education. On the other hand, parents no doubt benefited from the labor of married daughters who remained in the same building as a result of such provisions.

Additionally, especially in cases where the daughters married men who were or who became notaries, fathers benefited from the help of of their new sons-in-law. Although men who married notaries' daughters did not directly succeed their fathers-in-law, marriage to the daughter of a notary offered considerable advantages to both a young clerk and his father-in-law. A young man could use his bride's dowry to purchase an office, a common practice whatever the fathers-in-law's occupation, and could take advantage of the clientele and goodwill that his notarial father-in-law had built up, as the two often began to work together almost exclusively.

The marriage of André Charier and Marguerite Penifort highlighted such a process. Charier was a clerk in Guillaume Penifort's *étude* and married his daughter Marguerite in 1619. Penifort continued to work as a notary until his death a decade later, but from the time of his daughter's marriage to Charier and his subsequent acquisition of a notarial office, all Penifort's notarial minutes were saved as part of Charier's *étude,* and they constantly co-signed together. Penifort had previously always worked with his brother-in-law, Jean Carte, until the latter's death in 1617. Penifort's own son Guillaume eventually became a notary, but he was presumably too young to be a partner at the time of Carte's death and of his sister's marriage to Charier, as he was still a clerk in the mid-1620s.

Despite the possibility of using timing or differential advances to favor one or more children over the others, the powerful influence on parents of the culture of roughly equal treatment of children, girls and boys alike, in middling urban families is striking. Parents used the possibility of advancing parts of the inheritance to establish all children through dowries, offices, or other support to start a career where they could, and the advantage that any one child gained was usually relative rather than absolute.

The customary-law exclusion from the reporting of the considerable expenses associated with books and maintenance involved with "arms, studies or other vocations," which were never incurred by daughters, did favor sons.[37] Yet parents themselves did not seem to favor their sons overtly over their daughters in other ways. Middling parents could have disadvantaged daughters, by withholding the dowries and delaying the marriages that secured their futures, or by dispatching them to convents, as did families in other social ranks and at other times.[38] Although one son in these families did usually join the church, almost all daughters married in their early twenties, suggesting that little effort was made to use this most common of means of favoring sons. Moreover, in this middling milieu, the costs of dowries and those of access to the sorts of occupations that sons could aspire to were not dissimilar.[39]

Parents made remarkably little effort, on the whole, to evade the pressures for equality that were embedded in regional customary law. The desire to provide for each child seems to have been the dominant parental motive, judging from inheritance strategies that emphasized aid to all children during their lifetime, whether through dowry, assistance with accommodations, or purchase of office. Their willingness to establish each child at the appropriate time rather than sacrificing the interests of some children (by delaying their marriages, for example) in order to benefit another indicate the parents' privileging of equality over advantage.

[handwritten marginal note: equality over advantage]

37. *La Coustume de Bretagne,* article 597, lists the exemptions from reporting, which also included any income from money or property advanced.

38. Very few daughters of urban middling families entered convents, although in almost every family, one son took religious vows. Nevertheless, contracts concerning the religious profession of either sons or daughters always stressed the voluntary nature of their decisions. However formulaic such declarations may have been, they emphasized the child's choice. See, for example, ADLA, 4E2/458, 22 October 1627; and ADLA, 4E2/1688, 10 July 1634.

For families either putting daughters into convents or delaying their marriages to avoid dowry costs, see, for example, Olwyn Hufton, "Women Without Men: Widows and Spinsters in Britain and France in the Eighteenth Century," *Journal of Family History* 9 (Winter 1984); Diane Owen Hughes, "Representing the Family: Portraits and Purposes in Early Modern Italy," *Journal of Interdisciplinary History* 17 (Summer 1986).

39. Parisian customary law did allow daughters to renounce their rights to succession in return for their dowries, but apparently daughters were rarely "paid off" in this way. See Diefendorf, *Paris City Councillors,* 238–39. In contrast, the latter practice prevailed, for instance, among elites, at least in early modern England. See Randolph Trumbach, *The Rise of the Egalitarian Family: Aristocratic Kinship and Domestic Relations in Eighteenth-Century England* (New York, 1978).

These families, like their urban peers in Paris and Bordeaux, favored provision for all heirs over protection of the patrimony, in fact.[40] The notarial families' mentality favored securing the immediate needs of the family over its long-term prospects, a practice that was fully in tune with the uncertain economic and demographic prospects of all early modern families.

The priorities of urban middling families in Nantes, and apparently in other northern customary-law regions, suggest the distinctiveness of early modern family strategies. Historians have suggested that bourgeois families and their social superiors had, by the seventeenth century, adopted a long-term perspective to secure the future prestige of the family. They achieved this by careful planning to preserve the patrimony and by manipulation, especially of lineage property, to build family fortunes.[41] Yet the practice of Nantais middling families suggests that the linear orientation of middle-class behavior, which favored short-term sacrifice for longer-term benefit, was a creation of a later period; early modern middling families were quick to divide their property to secure all their children.[42]

Protecting Parents

Although most of the terms of marriage contracts perpetuated links between kin by embedding the new household in a network of ties to other households, marriage contracts also often contained agreements that sought to protect the interests of the parents. These provisions focused on clarifying and limiting the continuing obligations of parents, and on preserving their household property intact until both died, rather than allowing the customary division after the death of a spouse to proceed.

The usual practice of dividing the estate after widowhood between the

40. The egalitarian practice of urban groups in early modern Bordeaux and Paris is described in Robert Wheaton, "Affinity and Descent in Seventeenth-Century Bordeaux," in Robert Wheaton and Tamara Hareven, eds., *Family and Sexuality in French History* (Philadelphia, 1980), 121–23; and Diefendorf, *Paris City Councillors*, 264–70.

41. For this view, see Ralph Giesey, "Rules of Inheritance and Strategies of Mobility in Prerevolutionary France," *American Historical Review* 82 (April 1977); and Natalie Zemon Davis, "Ghosts, Kin and Progeny: Some Features of Family Life in Early Modern France," *Daedalus* (Spring 1977).

42. The existence of a middle-class consciousness that included longer-term planning in the nineteenth century is described by Leonore Davidoff and Catherine Hall, *Family Fortunes: Men and Women of the English Middle Class, 1780–1850* (London, 1987); and, for an American case, Mary Ryan, *Cradle of the Middle Class: The Family in Oneida County, New York, 1790–1865* (Cambridge, 1981).

surviving spouse and the other heirs could threaten the financial security
of the surviving spouse, so some parents used marriage contracts to circumvent this circumstance. When André Charier married Marguerite Penifort in 1619, her parents, Guillaume Penifort and Adrienne Legaigneux,
asserted that the couple "could not claim anything, personal property
[*meubles*] or real estate [*immeubles*]" until both parents had died. The widowed parent would continue to enjoy their daughter's share of the succession, and the parents' property would be maintained intact until they were
both dead.[43] Such efforts were also possible even after one parent died.
Catherine Guilloteau, the widow of Philippe Bodin, gave 1,000 *livres* for her
daughter's dowry. In return, Guilloteau was to enjoy for her own lifetime
her daughter's share of her father's estate, "without any account or division."[44]

Family members could also use marriage contracts as opportunities to
avert potential contention, especially over guardianship responsibilities.
Guardians were appointed when fathers died, and the frequency with
which premature death dissolved early modern families meant that many
children had guardians. The handling of the property of minor children
was a major source of tension between family members (as we shall see
later), and families often sought to avoid future conflict by firmly wrapping
up this phase and resolving the ties it entailed in marriage contracts of
wards. When Pierre Deslesbeaupin married Jacquette Anizon, for example,
her mother and stepfather acquitted her of the costs of "all and each of the
board, food and maintenance" that they had provided during her minority.
In return, "they would not be held to report to them any interest coming
from the monies and personal property [*meubles*] of the bride and revenues
from her property which interests and revenues they had compensated
with the food and support." In a common twist on this strategy, Claude
Geneste, guardian of his stepdaughter, gave 6,000 *livres* in her marriage
contract, "to be acquitted of . . . the account of the management of the
bride's goods."[45]

Again the burdens that such arrangements imposed were not necessarily
distributed evenly among inheriting siblings, raising again the issue of
whether some were treated inequitably. Marguerite Vaugour, for instance,
claimed lifetime enjoyment of one daughter's share of her father's estate in
return for an 800-*livres* dowry, but made no similar claim on a daughter

43. ADLA, 4E2/489, 10 June 1619.
44. ADLA, 4E2/495, 31 January 1651.
45. ADLA, 4E2/576, 10 December 1637; ADLA, 2E1026, 4 January 1606.

who had married three years before (when her father was still alive), nor on a son who married the following year.[46]

Nevertheless, as in other cases, apparent differences in treatment may have been the outcome of different needs, and parental awareness of the potential for dissent among siblings who felt one to be favored over the others may have ensured consensus about such treatment. Jeanne Rousseau, the widow of Lauren Guillet, followed many contemporaries in acquitting her daughter of her board and lodging in return for being herself acquitted of repaying the income that she had from her daughter's share of Guillet's estate since his death. The contract explicitly noted, however, that she did so "with the consent of her brother and sister."[47]

Forming Households

The marriage itself took place within a few days after the signing of the contract.[48] The church ceremony took place with the bride dressed in wedding clothes "suitable for her status" that her parents usually provided. A celebration followed that accounted for the other "wedding costs," which the brides' parents sometimes promised to pay in marriage contracts.[49]

The arrangements made in marriage contracts had significant consequences for household relations, not only between spouses but also between the couple and other kin, as newlyweds and their kin set about forming a new household. On the whole, the costs of setting up the new household were disproportionately subsidized by the bride's family. Husbands, as one seventeenth-century commentator has noted, contributed their "labor" and "industry," so they did not have to contribute initial capital.[50]

Subsequently, the new household's material form depended to a great extent on the dowry that the bride's parents provided. The bride's family also gave gifts of wedding clothes, as well as furniture and other household

46. ADLA, 4E2/1195, 23 November 1652; ADLA, 4E2/179, 13 July 1656.
47. ADLA, 4E2/326, 11 December 1606.
48. Both the date of contract and date of marriage are certain in only thirteen cases. The average time elapsed was twelve or thirteen days, and the median ten days.
49. The exact nature of such occasions is unclear, although Thomas Robo gave a hint, in his declaration at the accounting for his parents-in-law's estate, that he had paid a *paticier* "for the food provided for the wedding of Coupperie and his wife." ADLA, B6115, 19 February 1601. Robo and Coupperie were both married to daughters of Guillaume Leroy.
50. Ferrière, *Parfait notaire*, 243.

goods to equip the new household. A husband's family sometimes made contributions, especially if they were merchants, but these tended to take the form of money or goods to fund trade. The symbolic and material prominence of the bride's family in the construction of the new household had important ramifications, pointing to the close ties that would continue to characterize relations between the married couple and the bride's kin.

Although the inheritance that a son could expect to receive at the partition of the parental estate may have eventually compensated for the input of the bride's family (especially in view of the endogamous marriage patterns prevailing among these families), the initial emphasis stressed the importance not just of kin ties, but of bilateral kinship. Women's retention of their family name was perhaps the most obvious and permanent illustration of the ties that women retained to their birth families. Although grooms and their families were careful in other societies to offer their own gifts to counter, at least symbolically, the bride's dowry, these urban middling families usually made no such counter to the prominence of the bride's kin in the future of her household.[51]

The way in which the office of notary was often purchased certainly gave the bride's kin a stake in observing the affairs of the new household, because of their interest in the value of the office. When brides' parents dictated that dowries would buy offices for their sons-in-law, as in the marriages between Jacques Davy and Françoise Callo, Guillaume Chapelain and Clemence Coupperie, and Jean Eon and Marguerite Lucas, among others, they also determined that the office as royal notary that the dowry bought would become the lineage property of the bride. She or her family, in effect, owned the husband's office, a practice that had significant implications for the husband. Julien Belon, for example, had purchased his office of notary with his wife's dowry. When his wife, Anne Martin, died without their having any children as heirs, he was forced to use his office as security for his repayment of the *propres* of his wife to her heirs.[52]

Such cases suggest that issues of property management, which often illustrated the continued importance of kin in a new conjugal unit, were as

51. Christiane Klapisch-Zuber, for example, argued that when husbands or their families countered the dowry, at least symbolically, with gifts of their own, the inequality that the giving of the dowry symbolized was nullified, as was the superiority that an unreciprocated gift entailed. Thus, in elite Florentine families, husbands provided bridal clothes both as a counter gift and to assert their wives' integration into a new household and lineage. See Christiane Klapisch-Zuber, "The Griselda Complex: Dowry and Marriage Gifts in the Quattrocento," in her *Women, Family, and Ritual in Renaissance Italy* (Chicago, 1985), 224–25.

52. ADLA, 4E2/1718, 25 August 1624; ADLA, 4E2/612, 11 June 1635; ADLA, 4E2/1034, 20 January 1649; ADLA, 4E2/1369, 19 February 1659.

important as legal access to property. Even community property of the new spouses only became legal a year and a day after the wedding, and some of the patrimony of the new household was always reserved as lineage property, as we have seen.[53] This delay in initiating community property was premised on the expectation that in all likelihood, by the time a year and a day had passed, the new couple would have produced an heir in whom kin of both sides would be, literally, invested. The delay highlighted the contingent nature of the alliance and the importance of kin among these families.

If the death of one spouse ended the marriage prior to this time, everything the bride had brought to the new household as part of her dowry—money or real property, furniture, linen, and clothes—had to be returned to her or her heirs within a period specified in the marriage contract.[54] Additionally, if it was the bride who died, her birth family and not her husband paid for the burial.

The very considerable contribution of the bride's family to the new household, in terms of money, furniture, accommodations, and even office, may have enhanced the position of the wife within the household. Contemporaries feared that the wealth of brides undermined wifely obedience. An observer from a neighboring province in the early seventeenth century advocated limiting dowry size, "to prevent women from becoming more insolent because of the superfluity of their possessions."[55] Although, in theory, the labor and income that husbands provided more than matched women's dowries, in practice women also contributed their labor in myriad ways. Thus, dowries became key additions to the domestic economy.

Familial relations shaped and were shaped by the provisions made for marriages. The emphasis on setting up patrimony in ways that continued the interests of the wider kin group rather than fueling the independent liquidity of new households helped to perpetuate ties between households. Yet, especially in the efforts of parents to keep their marital estates intact, contractual conditions also revealed the ongoing tension between the interests of the individual households and those of the larger kin group.

53. *La Coustume de Bretagne,* article 424.

54. Marriage contracts consistently contained this provision, usually dictating that everything should be returned to the bride or her family within somewhere between six to twelve months after the death that ended the marriage.

55. Denis Godefroy, *La Coutume réformée du pays et duché de Normandie,* ff.324v. quoted in Dewald, *Formation of a Provincial Nobility,* 284.

Various parties—the conjugal family, parents, and siblings, as well as kin and future spouses—had their own stakes in the decision-making process that lay behind the contract. The particular arrangements made for the transmission of property at marriage and the patterns of interfamilial relations initiated profoundly shaped future relationships within and between the households, as they began a series of interactions that emphasized connections between households. From the start, women in these families had important roles as providers of capital and contacts, in terms of work and family. A basis was laid that shaped negotiations of authority within each household as well as between households.

4

Managing Households

The household was the fundamental block on which the rule of husbands, fathers, and kings was rhetorically and legally founded in early modern France. The household lives of middling people like notarial families suggest how the day-to-day structures of life among nonelite families shaped power relations and authority structures as realities, rather than as ideals. The conflation of personal and public authority structures around the household, writ large or small, meant that the relations of households like those of notaries helped to determine the conditions and extent of authority within households, and, in turn, in larger political structures.[1]

---

1. The significance of "household government" in early modern states has been examined in a number of recent studies, including: Susan Amussen, *An Ordered Society: Class and Gender in Early Modern England* (London, 1988); Mary Elizabeth Perry, *Gender and Disorder in Early Modern Seville* (Princeton, 1990); Lyndal Roper, *The Holy Household: Women and Morals in Reformation Augsburg* (Oxford, 1989); David Warren Sabean, *Power in the Blood: Popular Culture and Village Discourse in Early Modern Germany* (Cambridge, 1984); Carole Shammas, "Anglo-American Household Government in Comparative Perspective," *William and Mary Quarterly* 52 (January 1995). For the importance of the *ménage* in early modern French political culture, see Roland Mousnier, *The Institutions of France Under the Absolute Monarchy, 1598–1789: Society and the State* (Chicago, 1979), 84–91.

Multiple meanings of household (*ménage*) coexisted and complemented each other. The household encompassed the physical unit. It described the group of people who shared a residence: an early modern household regarded its members as a family, whether they were kin or not. The word *ménage* also implied the material contents of the household.[2]

The circumstances of the household lives of members of notarial families suggest some of their possibilities and priorities. The meanings of *ménage* for its occupants, the assembly of a specific collection of goods, the distribution of labor involved in the creation of a particular way of life, and the role of kin and other members of the local community all contributed to shaping the political economy of daily life in middling families.

Defining what constituted good or bad "*mesnagement*" became a core constituent in negotiating men's and women's status and in self-definition in middling families. They brought their perceptions not only to internal ordering of their households, but to providing parameters for relations between kin, between households in their family, and between their personal and public lives.

A Material Environment

The structures of everyday life associated with the *ménage* reflected the choices and limitations that members of notarial families faced in early modern France. A household's material forms, in terms of its membership and its physical contents, were the outcome of the practical exigencies of early modern urban life as well as of the preferences of middling urban families.[3]

Smallness was the most striking spatial characteristic of notarial *ménages* (see Table 4.1). They generally comprised only two or three rooms, a pattern that corroborated their middling rank.

2. The early modern author of *Les Maux de marriage* neatly encapsulated this ambiguity: "Or ça pour entrer en mesnaige, Il faut achepter du mesnaige." Quoted in Henry Havard, *Dictionnaire de l'ameublement et de la décoration depuis le treizième siècle jusqu'à nos jours* (Paris, 1894), 794. For *ménage* as a synonym for family, see Jean-Louis Flandrin, *Familles: Parenté, maison, sexualité dans l'ancienne société* (rev. ed. Paris, 1984), 10–11.

3. Studies exploring the relationship between the physical environment of households and social relationships include: Richard Goldthwaite, "The Florentine Palace As Domestic Architecture," *American Historical Review* 77 (October 1972); Michele Baulant, "Niveaux de vie paysanne autour de Meaux en 1700 et 1750," *Annales E.S.C.* 30 (May–June 1975); Daniel Roche, *Le Peuple de Paris: Essai sur la culture populaire au dix-huitième siècle* (Paris, 1981); Kristen B. Neuschel, "Noble Households in the Sixteenth Century: Material Settings and Human Communities," *French Historical Studies* 15 (Fall 1988).

Table 4.1.   Rooms in notarial residences[4]

Number of rooms	1	2–3	4 or more	N
Counting *étude*	2	30	15	47
Excluding *étude*	5	37	5	47

This same size was the most common among Parisian households in the seventeenth and eighteenth centuries. These small-scale residences were far removed from the great houses of urban elites, and provided less space than the four or more rooms that typified the households of well-off Parisian merchants, barristers, and the wealthiest artisans. Meanwhile, Parisian notaries, with six to ten rooms, enjoyed much grander accommodations than those of their provincial counterparts, another sign of the privileged status of the capital's notariat.[5]

Even with only two or three rooms, many notarial households were spread over at least two levels, linked by communal areas. These vertically fragmented personal living spaces were connected by public staircases and galleries. The buildings that contained the households were usually divided into at least two or three units, all sharing common staircases, galleries, yards, wells, and latrines. Some arrangements involved still closer quarters. René Grelier, for instance, could only reach his rooms by going through those of Françoise Guilloteau.[6]

In such circumscribed living areas, spatial specialization was almost unknown.[7] With the exception of the *études* where notaries worked, few rooms could claim any specific function. Inventories almost never used any more specific term than the multipurpose *chambre* (room), suggesting that working, eating, sleeping, and all other activities took place in the same spaces. Even some of the *études,* which were usually in the building in which the no-

4. Using data from inventories and leases, I have counted cabinets and antechambers as rooms here, following Annik Pardailhé-Galabrun, *La Naissance de l'intime: 3,000 foyers parisiens, dix-septième–dix-huitième siècles* (Paris, 1988), 234.

5. Roche, *Peuple de Paris*, 119; Pardailhé-Galabrun, *Naissance de l'intime*, 238–40; Monique Limon, *Les Notaires au Châtelet de Paris sous le règne de Louis XIV: Etude institutionelle et sociale* (Toulouse, 1992), 261. These Parisian notarial households were similar in size to those of doctors. See Françoise Lehoux, *Le Cadre de vie des médecins parisiens aux seizième et dix-septième siècles* (Paris, 1976), 146.

6. For diagrams of similar floor plans, see Madelaine Jurgens and Pierre Coupperie, "Le Logement à Paris aux seizième et dix-septième siècles," *Annales E.S.C.* 17 (May–June 1962), 489; ADLA, 4E2/1024, July 1641.

7. Much of the discussion that follows is based on analyses of household inventories taken after the deaths of spouses. Inventories usually took the form of a room-by-room description of the major pieces of furniture, followed by accounts, by category, of other property. *Inven-*

tary's family lived, seemed to have served as domestic as well as work space at least part of the time, expanding the available living area. The presence of a spinning wheel in Guillaume Jahanneau's *étude* points to a flexible usage of this space.[8]

The physical condition of the households was often poor, with broken or missing windows, floor planks, and locks, or worse. Jeanne Duvau, Mathurin Carte's widow, attempted to force her landlord to make repairs by court order. She claimed that the "building is ready to fall down and the latrines have collapsed [into] the cellar . . . it rains in the building and on the furniture . . . the building is so old, ruined and decrepit" as to be uninhabitable. Nevertheless, her family had lived there for years since Carte had signed the original lease.[9]

A typical notarial household had fireplaces both in the room used for cooking and in the main room.[10] Although no room was usually designated

---

taires après décès were only required in specific circumstances. For occasions requiring the drawing up of an inventory, see Pardailhé-Galabrun, *Naissance de l'intime*, 27.

Inventories as guides to material culture require some caveats. They reflect the perspective of the taker (in Nantes, an official of the local court, who might also be a notary) and perhaps the views of kin and heirs. The specific arrangements of objects listed were rarely mentioned, the overall value of the goods inventoried was often underestimated, and the extent of fraud is unclear. Inventories regularly omitted some items: children's clothing, often adult wardrobes, food and heating supplies, religious objects, and objects of minimal value, especially those used for household chores, like brooms. Likely omissions and undervaluations are discussed in Pardailhé-Galabrun, *Naissance de l'intime*, 31–32, 120–21; Baulant, "Niveaux de vie," 505–7; Roche, *Peuple de Paris*, 59–62.

Inventory omissions are sometimes difficult to interpret. A Parisian study suggested, for instance, that the lack of reserves of tallow or candles in inventories indicates that these items were bought on a daily basis. However, in a 1592 assessment of provisions in Nantes, many households had considerable reserves of tallow, described as "sufficient for one year," or as specific quantities that averaged just over 23 *livres*. These provisions do not point to the buying of supplies on a daily basis. Pardailhé-Galabrun, *Naissance de l'intime*, 347; AMN, EE30, 13 January 1592.

The issue of fraud or distortion is equally problematic. Daniel Roche argued that the sealing of doors and locks before the evaluation took place, the code of ethics guiding the officials, and the self-interest of heirs all guaranteed accuracy. Nevertheless, occasionally property was removed before it was inventoried. In 1660, for example, in a suit between Nicolas Jourdanot's kin and his widow, Jeanne Bellanger, various witnesses testified that Bellanger had wanted to put several items, including a feather mattress, bolster, two or three sheets, and a "complete outfit for [a] man . . . somewhere" to keep them out of the inventory. Several deponents also suggested that she had hidden a considerable sum of money, amounting to 600 or 700 *livres*. A visitor to the house soon after Jourdanot's death recalled seeing broken seals on a coffer and cabinet that Bellanger claimed one of her children had broken, suggesting that the widow had, apparently, evaded the security that the application of seals to all chests and other locks seemed to offer. Roche, *Peuple de Paris*, 61; ADLA, B5818, 10 December 1660.

8. ADLA, B5660, 14 July 1628.

9. ADLA, B6139, 5 February 1646.

10. I have gauged the number of fireplaces by the number of andirons. Nineteen of the

specifically as the kitchen, one room with a hearth contained a variety of pot hooks, spits, and cooking pots, and large water containers. This room usually also had a table, a couple of chairs and beds, and storage chests or armoires.

A large, high bedstead dominated the main room, which often also contained a smaller trundle bed that could be pushed aside during the day. Most main rooms also included a table, numerous chairs, and storage units. Large trunks were filled with linen and clothes, and smaller ones with money, records like marriage contracts, and *rentes* and other valuables. Most families had an armoire or buffet on which to display prized possessions.

The principal bed, enclosed by a canopy and curtains and often reached by stepping up from a surrounding wooden platform, demonstrated wealth and personal taste as well as providing warmth. Bedding formed a very important portion of the overall value of household goods, just over 20 percent, as in other early modern communities.[11] Red and green were the most popular colors for bed covers. Nicolas Jourdanot and Jeanne Bellanger's bed had a canopy of red serge with silk fringes and a red blanket, with a combined worth of 40 *livres*. This was more than 10 percent of the entire value of their goods. The bed of Thomas Chauveau and Jeanne Duvau had a green serge canopy decorated with trim and a fringe of silk and wool, and a matching firescreen.[12]

Notarial families had few items that might be described as luxuries. Most households did have two or three pictures in their main rooms, whose subjects were predominantly religious, although there were some royal portraits. Other themes were almost entirely absent. Michel Coupperie alone had portraits, one of his first wife and an unmounted portrait of himself.[13] A small mirror often hung alongside these pictures. All the households had considerable quantities of pewter, weighing about seventy-six pounds, on average. The custom of assessing pewter's value by weight rather than by

twenty-one notarial inventories included andirons. The exceptions were Thomas Robo, who died in poverty, and Julien Rousseau, who lived in the household of Jean Bonnet, his father-in-law. Seven inventories included one pair of andirons; ten had two pairs, and two others had three pairs.

11. Throughout this chapter, I have analyzed the inventories using the categories established by Michele Baulant, "Niveaux de vie," 509. Bedding was 21.8 percent of the value of twenty inventories (excluding the inventory of Thomas Robo, whose estate was valued at only 38 *livres* and 17 *sous*, 84.6 percent of which was bedding). This proportion fits the pattern observed in Parisian inventories in the seventeenth and eighteenth centuries, where bedding averaged between 15 and 30 percent of the value of estates, and it occupied a greater part of wealth as fortunes decreased. Pardailhé-Galabrun, *Naissance de l'intime*, 282–83.

12. ADLA, B5696, 4 November 1658; ADLA, 5672, 8 June 1638.

13. ADLA, B5804, 22 April 1619.

item suggests that it had intrinsic value as well as being useful. Most families had a few silver pieces that, like pewter, were sources of investment, utility, and status.

Like other nonelite families, these households did not usually own books, despite notaries' occupational reliance on literacy. Only Charles Germond had any books, and, by the standards of his contemporaries, he was quite a bibliophile. He collected forty-four volumes on various subjects, including a bible in French and a copy of the customary law of Brittany, along with a variety of historical texts. As a rule, though, these families had little pretense to intellectual life, and even books pertaining to notaries' work were noticeably lacking.[14]

The main room was crowded, as the *chambre* of Guillaume Jahanneau and Perrine Clement illustrated. It included a big canopied bed, a trundle bed, a table, a buffet, sixteen varied seats, and two four-and-a-half-foot-long benches. They also had a variety of storage pieces: two trunks on stands—a big one that was four and a half feet long and a smaller one that was only one foot in length—two big chests with rounded tops that were four feet and three and a half feet long respectively, and a small square box covered with black leather. Their household had a lot of pewter—about eighty-six pounds' worth—as well as a few pieces of silver, including a small salt pot, two cups, and three spoons, and a pitcher worth 65 *livres*. No other item came near this pitcher in value, so it may have taken pride of place on the buffet.[15]

Whether the few rooms distinguished as *cabinets* or *antichambres* were reserved for a purpose, as they were in more elaborate residences, or if, as with *études*, the name was at least partially misleading is not clear. Such rooms seem to have been smaller (to judge by the small number of items they contained) rather than functionally more specific. In only one case was an *antichambre* designated as "serving as [a] kitchen," hinting at an effort to separate this activity from living and sleeping areas.

Although rooms were crowded, the particular arrangement of space and the selection of objects reflected the choices of the notarial families, or at least certain members of them, as well as the dictates of the conditions of urban life. Middling families shaped their domestic environment in ways that suited the diverse needs of daily living and their personal preferences. Despite the cramped quarters, household members were concerned with

---

14. ADLA, B5653, 11 April 1623. For patterns of book ownership in various social groups, see, for instance, Pardailhé-Galabrun, *Naissance de l'intime*, 403–19.

15. ADLA, B5660, 14 July 1628.

appearances as well as practicality. Nicolas Jourdanot and Jeanne Bellanger, for example, had six folding chairs and six others, all upholstered with red serge that matched the canopy of their bed.[16]

The styles of tables and chairs allowed for flexible utilization of the living area. Many tables were simply supported by trestles. They were probably taken down and placed against a wall, as a rule, except at mealtimes. Other tables often retained an element of mutability, having extension leaves at one or both ends. Benches were still used sporadically, but more flexible seating was gaining the upper hand, and folding chairs were common. Of the eighteen seats in the lower room of Michel Coupperie and Clemence Collin's home, the chair "serving as table and chair" was the only substantial one. Nine small wooden stools could be used while spinning or cooking, as well as around the table. Three stools with square upholstered seats were easy to move. Two chairs (*caquetoires*) with low backs and no arms could accommodate large skirts and were of a style often used by women. Two other chairs, described merely as being "narrow behind," were presumably also simple, light, and suitable for pulling up to talk, or around the table to eat.[17]

Household members also modified their space more permanently. Some areas, probably smaller still, were given over to particular needs. Sometimes the main room included one part designated as an *étude,* even where another *étude* was also listed separately, as in the inventory of Guillaume Jahanneau. In other cases, the differentiation provided some personal space for a member of the household. Pierre Liger had constructed a "small cabinet enclosed with planks" that included a window, where his wife's aunt slept.[18]

All these efforts to manipulate and maximize living areas illuminate the efforts that early modern families of modest means could make to shape their living environments in ways that made the few resources available to them more responsive to their needs. They correspond to, but predate, the patterns identified for nonelite groups in the eighteenth century.[19] The choices and circumstances also hint, however, at patterns of relations in individual households and between the households.

16. ADLA, B5696, 4 November 1658.

17. ADLA, B5804, 11 March 1619. For *caquetoires,* see Havard, *Ameublement,* 651.

18. ADLA, 4E2/488, 4 November 1610; ADLA, B5660, 28 June 1628; ADLA, 4E2/1471, 20 July 1652.

19. Roche, *Peuple de Paris,* 120–21; Pardailhé-Galabrun, *Naissance de l'intime,* 267–70.

Ménage and *Mesnagement*

Within households, the working out of patterns of authority and location of power involved potential contests and alliances, not only between husband and wives, but also between parents and children, conjugal family and kin, masters or mistresses and servants or clerks, as well as between and across gender and generational lines. In dealing with these issues, middling families mobilized values and standards that they constantly used to measure their own behaviors and those of others in their community. They used the term *mesnagement* as a shorthand reference to describe these attributes and assessed men as well as women as "good" or "bad" *mesnagers*.

Middling families shared households that were complex rather than conjugal in their composition. A 1592 roll of city households listed twenty-six notarial households that included five or six people on average.[20] Of the twenty notarial households whose individual members were itemized, seventeen included one female servant and thirteen a variety of nieces, nephews, siblings, cousins, and clerks. Most other households also included a servant and some other kin beyond the conjugal family.

The membership of households frequently shifted in response to mortality and labor needs. The harsh demographic realities of early modern life caused the recurring breakup and reformation of families. Widowed mothers, siblings, or other young relatives taken in after the breakup of their families of origin were common additions to notarial households. Remarriages often involved a number of stepchildren on one or both sides.

Households also accommodated family members who needed a place to live or could offer services. Siblings or widowed mothers were most likely to fall into this category, although, especially for shorter-term stays, other kin might also be taken in. Pierre Mocet's family were compelled to leave their house when a neighbor's children were struck by a contagious illness in the summer of 1605. While his wife and children left for the countryside, Mocet stayed for six weeks in town with "a very distant relation" of his wife's "who called her cousin."[21]

Kin of wives seem to have been far more likely to enlarge the household in this way, perhaps as a consequence of the way property arrangements tended to accentuate this set of ties. Mathurine Pigeaud, Pierre Mocet's

20. "Dénombrement des hommes en estat de porter des armes et leurs armes et provisions," AMN EE30, 13 January 1592. I thank Alain Croix for providing me with his transcription.

21. ADLA, B5801, 15 March 1606.

widow, went to live with her daughter; Isabel Dubois's mother lived until her death with Dubois and Thomas Chauveau. Siblings were also common additions, usually after their parents died. Jacques Davy's sister-in-law continued to live with him until her marriage, even after his wife, Suzanne Rousseau, had died.[22]

Inheritance practices could also contribute to the presence of kin in households. Thomas Brisebois and his wife, Françoise Brossier, lived in one half of a house of which his wife had inherited one third. Her brother Philippe Brossier, who lived with them, also owned a third. (After Françoise Brossier died without children, both men were heirs to her estate. Enormous complications ensued concerning who owed whom what for the years preceding her death and for those after, for rent as well as for board and lodging, and for loans and money that Brisebois had paid on Philippe Brossier's behalf.)[23]

Households often needed additional assistance at some points, and older children—especially girls, who were the most likely to provide household help—regularly moved around to help meet the varying needs of kin, in a pattern that was probably common in early modern societies.[24] Françoise Leroy explained that her need for assistance had helped her decide to take in five grandchildren from the first two marriages of one of her daughters, "as much for the help and comfort she hopes [to have] from the older ones as for the enjoyable entertainment and company of the younger ones." Renée Jahanneau received 300 *livres* in the will of her paternal aunt's husband and was acquitted of her board and lodging for the time she had lived with them in compensation for the "great and special help" she gave them during their several long illnesses. Jeanne Chauveau, on at least one occasion, spent three months with her maternal grandfather "selling wine."[25]

Household members who were not kin were usually either female servants or male clerks. Almost all notarial households included one female servant, but very rarely more than one. Occasionally testamentary bequests

---

22. Other examples of this pattern include the mother and a younger sibling of Jacques Denan's wife; Michel Coupperie's widow, Clemence Collin, who lived with a daughter; the mother of Guillaume Garnier's wife; the aunt of Pierre Mariot's wife; and siblings of the wives of Thomas Robo, Hervé Trebillard, and Thomas Brisebois. I found no references to members of the husband's family, either parent, siblings, or other kin, living with him.

23. ADLA, 4E2/309, 18 August 1607.

24. A pattern of households supplementing their labor as needed by "importing" young female kin or servants has also been identified, for instance, in colonial America: see Laurel Thatcher Ulrich, *A Midwife's Tale: The Diary of Martha Ballard* (New York, 1991).

25. ADLA, 4E2/706, 12 July 1646; ADLA, 4E2/466, 28 December 1647; ADLA, B5810, 19 March 1639.

indicate long years of service, but most servants were young women who stayed with any one family for relatively short periods. Five servants in Thomas Chauveau's household each remained for just over three years, on average. Three servants of Vincent Bernard and Marguerite DelaVergne each stayed less than six months.[26] The young clerks who assisted in *études* were an equally transient group. Five of the twenty notarial households with specified household membership in the 1592 roll included clerks. Their position, as we have seen, resembled that of apprentices, and they stayed for one or two years, in a pattern that many artisanal households shared.

Other people—lodgers and, more rarely, tutors or wet nurses—also occasionally joined notarial households. Two young men each lived in Thomas Chauveau's household for a few months as tutors to the children. At other times, boarders were taken in, no doubt to increase household income. Jean Carte's household in 1592 included "a renter," while a court clerk's widow lived for fifteen months prior to her death with Gabriel Desprez and Jeanne Peloteau, during which time Peloteau "provided great cares and pains to help her in her infirmities."[27]

Household members who were subordinate to the husband or father had few resources to challenge his authority, and they faced cultural as well as legal obstacles in protecting themselves. Wives and female servants, for instance, who were both subject to the authority of the head of the household, were vulnerable to physical abuse of all kinds, against which they often had little protection or recourse. It was difficult for them to get help from kin or courts, while there was apparently little cost for men who engaged in such behavior.

Even after Vincent Bernard's frequent physical assaults on his wife, Marguerite DelaVergne, her sister's husband first responded to DelaVergne's requests for help in initiating a separation petition, with the exhortation that "she had to be patient since she had married him." Bernard, meanwhile, insisted that he had "just cause" for the beatings, which he made no effort to deny. The threats and violence to which Françoise Ouairy was sub-

---

26. ADLA, B5810, 19 March 1639; ADLA, B5806, 10 January 1626. The typicality of this pattern is difficult to assess for this period. Cissie Fairchilds has suggested that servants stayed an average of four years for the period 1600–1750, and about one and a half years thereafter, while Sarah Maza has suggested that in the eighteenth century, servants' stays averaged six to ten months. Cissie Fairchilds, *Domestic Enemies: Servants and their Masters in Old Regime France* (Baltimore, 1984), 69; Sarah Maza, *Servants and Masters in Eighteenth Century France: The Uses of Loyalty* (Princeton, 1983), 104.

27. ADLA, B5810, 19 February 1639; AM, EE30, 13 January 1592; ADLA, 4E2/1088, 24 November 1659.

jected led Robert Ouairy, her father, to remove her from the conjugal household. But the Nantes court ordered her to return and him to stop interfering.

Although proof of good character was necessary to be confirmed as a notary, domestic violence did not constitute a sufficient blemish. Nicolas Jourdanot, for example, experienced no prejudice from the fact that as a young clerk, a servant had accused him of using "great violence" to force her to have sex with him. The resulting pregnancy had led to the servant's dismissal, although she later made a successful petition for some financial support.[28]

Yet despite the difficulties that women faced, to perceive household relations only as simplistic patriarchal oppression is to ignore the greater complexity that day-to-day demands and negotiations created. In particular, the diversity of relationships in early modern households and the importance of *mesnagement* in conceptions of the "right ordering" of the world were key elements of early modern households for urban middling families, even though the general authority of the husband or father, as head of the household over all its members, remained. Lines of authority, alliances, and conflicts were created between servants, children, clerks, and wives, who were all subordinates.

The potential for conflict existed because the diverse people living in these households each had his or her own interests, demands, and needs. In some cases, at least, the arrangements were unsatisfactory for all concerned. Renée Cosson's remarriage was followed by a chorus of complaints from both the children of her first marriage (who included Robert, later also a notary) and their stepfather. The children charged that the stepfather's daily "bad treatment" of one of the girls had forced her to seek shelter "with one of her godfathers." Their stepfather claimed that they were ungrateful for the great efforts he had made on their behalf, for which he had sacrificed the interests of his own children. Françoise Leroy, Pierre Belon's mother-in-law, sheltered her grandchildren after they were "chased out and evicted by their mother [another of her daughters] and stepfather."[29]

The management of this internal hierarchy complicated lines of power

28. ADLA, B5806, 16 January 1626; ADLA, B6652, 10 [illegible] 1626; ADLA, B6131, 22 December 1633. ADLA, B5812, 26 March 1642; and ADLA, B6136, 31 March 1642. When the DelaVergne-Bernard petition later came before the court, several witnesses admitted that the brother-in-law had asked them "to tell the truth," which suggests that he had become more sympathetic to his sister-in-law's plight, a change that may have enabled her to bring the petition.

29. ADLA, B6375, 13 July 1640; ADLA, 4E2/706, 12 July 1646.

in the household, as issues surrounding the roles, responsibilities, and supervision of servants illustrated. Middling households observed an internal status distinction between family members and servants. A dispute between Jeanne Chauveau and her stepmother, Isabel Dubois, focused on the question of whether Chauveau had done servants' work, drawing out the fine lines between the two groups. Among the tasks considered to be the work of a servant were the purchase of food, tending the cooking pot and the spit in the hearth, doing the "base" tasks in the household, and generally doing "the low chores which servants do." Jeanne had been most involved with child care and looking after linen, and the parties disputed the status of these activities. The female servants did not define these as responsibilities of servants alone, and thus they insisted Jeanne had never done "any servant's work" nor any servant's "*mesnagement*." By their measure, "she was not in her father's house as a servant," and she lived there very decently, in line with her status.[30]

Sleeping and eating patterns were also opportunities for the drawing of lines of exclusion or inclusion within households. A witness supporting Jeanne Chauveau, included, among the instances offered of her being wrongly treated, that "Dubois made Chauveau sleep with her servants"; but a servant denied that Chauveau was treated like a servant by pointing out that she "drank and ate ordinarily at the table of her father and stepmother." When Vincent Bernard was charged with mistreating his wife, Marguerite DelaVergne, reasons given included the fact that he "did not want to put up with her sleeping in his bed" and made her sleep in the servant's bed.[31]

Although some studies have suggested that elite patriarchal rhetoric translated into masters' responsibility for the supervision of servants and other household members, in middling families, wives rather than husbands were responsible for the day-to-day management of the servants.[32] Marguerite Bouvier deducted the cost of items she had given to a servant from what she owed her when the servant left her employ. Marguerite DelaVergne refused to pay a needlewoman, on one occasion, because she

---

30. ADLA, B5810, 19 March 1639, and 18 April 1639.

31. ADLA, B5810, 19 March 1639; ADLA, B5810, 18 April 1639; ADLA, B5806, 16 January 1626.

32. Maza, *Servants and Masters*, esp. 9–13, 163; Fairchilds, *Domestic Enemies*, 137–50. The differences evident in the notarial households may be due to the use of sources that reflect actual practice in urban middling families, rather than the prescriptive, literary, or elite sources of the studies that have emphasized men's supervision of servants.

had no money. In another household, a servant noted that it was Isabel Dubois "who hired her and paid her."[33]

Servants rarely mentioned their masters, although the distance between the notaries and their female servants was social, not physical. In such close quarters, privacy was hardly possible. Servants in the Bernard household witnessed his beatings of his wife "with fist, feet and sticks," and heard his accusations that she was a whore. Even a servant sleeping in a different room saw DelaVergne pushed out of bed "all naked in her shirt."

Yet in other ways, masters' relations with servants seems to have been quite indirect. In Thomas Chauveau's household, for instance, servants discussing their work only referred to him in noting that his wife, and sometimes his daughter too, took care of most of his needs. A neighbor confirmed that Chauveau's daughter, rather than a servant, served dinner. Vincent Bernard was apparently equally disengaged from the daily routine of his servants, turning to them only when he wanted them to corroborate his suspicions about Marguerite DelaVergne's having an extramarital affair.[34]

The wives who hired, paid, and supervised servants had a very different relationship than did their husbands to those women, in terms of the quality as well as the quantity of their contacts. Servants' attitudes in the dispute between Vincent Bernard and Marguerite DelaVergne suggested how these differences could affect life in middling households. Whether or not Bernard's complaints that DelaVergne kept "bad company" with another man were more than a figment of his imagination, all the servants who had worked in the household over the years agreed that they did not know the reason for the spouses' quarrels and denied ever having seen the purported lover of DelaVergne. Their denials outraged Bernard, who accused them of complicity in the vices of his wife and her purported lover. He tried to persuade one servant to poison his wife, and he offered another a new skirt in exchange for testifying that she had seen DelaVergne with another man—all to no avail. Perhaps even if the liaison happened, the servants were anxious to protect DelaVergne, for, as one servant pointed out, Bernard was a "big villain."[35] Clearly their sympathies were with her.

33. ADLA, 4E2/246, 29 June 1649; deposition of Julienne Saupin, ADLA, B5805, 16 January 1626; deposition of Michelle Legal, ADLA, B5810, 18 April 1639.

34. Depositions of Michelle Legal, Michelle Tertoux, and Sebastien Gaudin, ADLA, B5810, 18 April 1639; depositions of Renée Guillou and Jeanne Villetard, ADLA, B5806, 16 January 1626.

35. Depositions of Renée Guillou, Jeanne Villetard, Jacquette Hode, Claude Villetard, Marie Dutay, Julliene Saupin, and Vincennes d'Autheiller, ADLA, B5806, 16 January 1626. Bernard's response, ADLA, B6652, 10 [illegible] 1626.

The sources of solidarity between wives and servants seem to have been based in their similar tasks and in flexible attitudes to job allocation and to the close nature of their relationship. Although a hierarchy of household chores existed, wives worked hard without standing on their dignity. Dubois and her servants shared a frustration with Jeanne Chauveau's reluctance to do household tasks. One servant, recalling the quarrels between Dubois and Chauveau over the latter's behavior, confirmed firmly that the daughter was very idle.

The servants' descriptions of their relationships with their mistresses give little hint of the distance or of the recognition of the inequality that characterized their relationships with the men who were heads of households. Marguerite DelaVergne showed her bruises to her servants and asked to borrow money to buy necessities. Women, as wives and servants, shared similar tasks and ways of life. In the Chauveau household sometimes Dubois went to supervise the rural holdings, leaving her servant to hold the fort, while on other occasions, the servant accompanied Jeanne Chauveau to the countryside, leaving Dubois to handle everything in the city.[36]

Other similarities in experiences and expectations also served to reduce the distance between mistress and servant in middling households and to provide common ground on which alliances could be built. Notaries' wives largely shared the life courses of the women they employed as servants. They too might well have lived for short periods in the households of kin during their adolescence, to provide assistance. Even if their position was not formally that of a servant, it was an analogous role in many ways. The servants themselves usually married after leaving residential service, and often they continued to work on a more informal basis as laundresses or pewter cleaners for their former employers. The former servants of the Bernard and Chauveau households mostly married local artisans and lived nearby in the adjoining streets. In all probability, they hired servants of their own and were busy with many of the same activities that consumed notaries' wives.

The solidarity of wives and female servants suggests some of the ways in which lines of authority operated within households and some of the possi-

---

36. I do not mean to portray the servants' position too sanguinely here. One of the Chauveau servants said if she went to sleep before them, she was woken up to see to their needs later. Vincent Bernard, as we saw above, admitted beating various servants. A servant of Louis Coudret and Marguerite Rousseau's left after accusing them both of ill treating her. Deposition of Michelle Legal, ADLA, B5810, 18 April 1639; ADLA, B6652, 10 [illegible] 1626; ADLA, B6127, 23 October 1624.

ble resources that women had in their day-to-day lives. Their alliances gave them some informal leverage against husbands, as Vincent Bernard discovered, but women could also hold each other responsible for keeping certain standards. As we have seen, Isabel Dubois and her servants solidly denied that her stepdaughter Jeanne Chauveau had done servants' work or been otherwise harshly treated.

A central theme of intra-household negotiations was the centrality of the *mesnagement* of the domestic economy, in which all household members had to play a part if the household was to be successful. For these families, capacity for *mesnagement,* which they understood in very specific terms, was valued above almost all other qualities. Head-of-household status entailed obligations for *mesnagement* as well as the right to authority, and the emphasis on a successful, well-managed household carried implications for wives and other household members as well as for husbands and fathers.

Men who headed households were expected to be *bons mesnagers,* meaning that they worked hard, kept good company, and showed astuteness in their financial affairs. Such expectations were often elucidated most clearly when the issue was in question. Evidence of aptitude for *mesnagement* was the key to independence for young men. Their *émancipation* from the supervision of a father or guardian in managing their property before they reached their majority (at the age of twenty-five) rested on kin satisfaction that they were *bons mesnagers.* This quality implied not only sound financial sense, but respectable behavior (usually referred to in contrast to debauchery) and diligent work; in other words, the attributes that befitted a good householder.

Julien Coquet's son, for instance, wanted to be emancipated in December 1618, but his kin (various uncles and cousins) turned his request down and required him to stay under the authority of his guardian until he showed "good *mesnagement* and behavior." Twenty-six months later, the son tried again, claiming that in the intervening period "he had always comported himself very well without engaging in any debauchery . . . and has worked and works assiduously" in the *étude* of a lawyer. He asked that his kin give evidence of his "good *mesnagement,*" and they declared him "to be a *bon mesnager* capable of administrating his property."[37]

Veneration of *mesnagement* among families of this rank was an important source of pride for middling men, in part because it reinforced their own social identity and differentiated them from the disorderliness that they

37. ADLA, B6125, 19 February 1621.

could perceive as characterizing the elite, as well as from poorer urban families below them. Claude Geneste chastised his married son for his "lazy life" and failure to pursue a career, in favor of living "in liberty and fancy, idling and passing his time with people as little concerned as he."[38] Geneste's critique of his son clearly implied a distinction between hardworking, upright people and slothful men of leisure living off unearned income. The virtues of financial astuteness, respectable comportment, and hard work that were embodied by the concept of *mesnagement* were also those demanded (rather than a university education, for instance) as proof of eligibility for office for notaries as well as for other minor legal officials. Notaries' active participation in public life, as we will see, similarly offered avenues to hold up these values and promised social differentiation.

The domestic economy of *bon mesnagement* had profound implications for other household residents, too. Everyone had to contribute either labor or goods. Servants, obviously, earned their keep. Clerks and boarders paid fixed sums as their shares. Relatives who joined the *ménage* were also expected to pay their way. In 1654, Jeanne Bouvier moved in with her sister Marguerite and brother-in-law Hervé Trebillard. The three agreed by contract that she would stay for eight years, during which time Jeanne would receive bed, food, and clothes and would contribute her help "well and decently according to her ability," in return for turning over the income (from *rentes* and other revenues) produced by the property that she had inherited from her parents. Other families made similar arrangements less formally. Jacques Denan's mother-in-law confirmed in her will in 1631 that she had given him "possession" of properties that she owned in the parish of St. Similien in exchange for the "board and lodging" of her and one of her daughters.[39]

In other cases, specific agreements were made beforehand to cover the financial ramifications, or retrospective accountings were made at later stages. Mathurine Pigeaud arranged to live with her daughter and bookseller son-in-law "for the time that it will please God to leave her to live." They were to take care of all her material needs, including medical assistance, in return for the income from her property.[40]

These considerations were liable to cause tension if they were not covered quite specifically. Jean Leroy went to live with his sister Françoise and Thomas Robo, and a dispute quickly ensued over expenses. Leroy insisted that after the death of his father, "Robo had asked him to go to live with

---

38. ADLA, B5817, 24 July 1658; ADLA, B7080, 5 December 1608.

39. ADLA, 4E2/173, 22 October 1654; ADLA, 4E2/1458, 9 July 1631.

40. ADLA, 4E2/141, 26 June 1643. Judging by the very small dowry of 150 *livres* that Pigeaud had given her daughter, these revenues would, however, have been small.

him, promising him not to ask for anything for his board." After "very little time," Robo began to treat him badly (including allegedly breaking his arm), so Leroy left. Robo repeatedly asked him to return again, but the same problems immediately reoccurred, and they ended up in court fighting over who owed whom what.[41]

The priorities of this version of *mesnagement* also affected children, whose costs and contributions were often carefully weighed. Marriage contracts often included discharge of the bride or groom's "board and lodging" until the wedding day as part of the parental gifts. Jeanne Chauveau and her stepmother, Isabel Dubois, ended up in court over whether Chauveau had to pay the costs of her board and lodging while she had lived in her father's household during his second marriage, or if, as one witness suggested, "it would not be reasonable to make her pay in view of the continual services she had rendered in the house."[42] The servants' sympathy with Dubois, on the other hand, which we have already seen, was largely tied to the ways in which they perceived that Chauveau was not a good householder.

For women, the consequences of a household authority structure that was premised in part on sound *mesnagement* were critical. By emphasizing *mesnagement*, these families gave women important roles, with some power and recognition within the household. A successful domestic economy on the terms espoused by middling families required cooperation and contributions from the wife as well as from her husband, not only in the smooth daily management of the servants, but in many aspects of life both in and out of the household.

Women's labor was essential in the maintenance of the *ménage* in all its senses.[43] While this necessity created rigorous burdens for them, it also pro-

---

41. ADLA, B6114, 23 October 1598. Leroy added that during the second stay, he had earned his living by helping Robo at the latter's behest in many activities, most of which "were not respectable nor worthy of brothers."

42. Deposition of Pierre Bizuel, ADLA, B5810, 19 March 1639.

43. Several historians have noted that the debate over purported changes in the emotional lives of elite families has largely neglected the labor and commodities that domestic life required. They stress the need to examine women's roles in the creation of the domestic environment. Case studies of the nineteenth century have demonstrated the potential for control over material culture to determine domestic relations between men and women, although they draw contradictory conclusions as to who benefited. Carole Shammas, "The Domestic Environment in Early Modern England and America," *Journal of Social History* 4 (Fall 1980), 4; Bonnie Smith, *Ladies of the Leisure Class: The Bourgeoises of Northern France in the Nineteenth Century* (Princeton, 1981); Delores Hayden, *The Grand Domestic Revolution* (Cambridge, 1981); Sybille Meyer, "The Tiresome Work of Conspicuous Leisure: On the Domestic Duties of the Wives of Civil Servants in the German Empire, 1871–1918," in Jean Quataert and Marilyn Boxer, eds., *Connecting Spheres: Women in the Western World, 1500–Present* (Oxford, 1987).

vided possibilities for their acquisition of power through their control over certain important aspects of the household. In daily practice, women's labor was an important element in property accumulation and allocation as well as in capital infusion through dowries.

Women in middling families contributed to the *mesnagement* of their households in myriad ways. Many notarial families owned small vineyards and other agricultural holdings, including cottages where they could stay, in the rural parishes surrounding Nantes. Wives and daughters went to rural holdings as necessary, not only to supervise the grape harvest and to sell the wine, but also to collect other produce.

Marguerite Bernard's journeys included going "to take the grain to the Mill to make flour for the Nourishment of her family and to have the rest of the grain that is in one of the top rooms removed to avoid losing it." They probably also gathered the vegetables that many sharecroppers were required to grow, and made their choice of the "cabbage, peppers . . . and other good plants used to make soup together with all kinds of other lesser plants good for making salad" that were typically reserved for the owners' households. Isabel Dubois and her stepdaughter Jeanne Chauveau took it in turns every year to go "to the fields" to supervise bringing in the grape harvest and selling wine "by the jug."[44] Women, who were more able to leave the city than their husbands by virtue of their different obligations, were probably often away to oversee these responsibilities.

Nor were women's activities limited to such quintessentially female work, as their tasks in support of the household interests were wide-ranging, and women often filled in when their husbands were otherwise occupied. At Nicolas Jourdanot's behest, for example, Jeanne Bellanger found someone to "hide" the 600 or 700 *livres* in the house just before his death, presumably to protect this sum, at least, from the demands of creditors. When Guillaume Chapelain died in 1657, Clemence Coupperie (herself the daughter and granddaughter of notaries) was away in Rennes attending a trial, in which their claim as heirs to certain property was at issue.[45] Wives' resourcefulness helped their households to protect their interests.

Wives' expertise did not always observe a division between familial or domestic matters and the public work of their notary-husbands. As in arti-

---

44. ADLA, B5810, 19 March 1639; ADLA, B6817, 15 May 1614; ADLA, 4E2/1564, 9 February 1615; ADLA, B5810, 19 March 1639.

45. ADLA, B5818, 10 December 1660; ADLA, B5695, 24 September 1657. Women's flexibility here is similar to that identified as "deputy husbands" in colonial New England. See Laurel Thatcher Ulrich, *Good Wives: Image and Reality in the Lives of Women in Northern New England, 1650–1750* (Oxford, 1980), 35–50.

sanal households, notaries' wives may have been significantly involved with production as well as housewifery, blurring at the edges the strictly gendered identity of the law. The law—in terms of its institutions and actors—was a masculine domain. Unlike the widows of artisans, who (albeit with increasing restrictions) could, on occasion, take on the management of their husbands' workshops, the widows of notaries (like those of judges and doctors) had no legally ensconced assumption of occupational competence.

Nevertheless, notarial wives could participate, in some ways, in their husbands' occupations. Notaries' *études* were staffed by teenage clerks learning the trade, much as apprentices did, and notaries' wives supervised them as well as their children and servants. Formal agreements as to the conditions of their stay emphasized the primacy of the notaries as masters to whom the clerks were beholden. Occasional clauses, though, overtly acknowledged that wives played a role. Complementary obligations in the form of money or gifts were to be paid specifically to the notary's wife. In October 1618, seventeen-year-old Antoine Hastier became the clerk of Jacques Denan for one year, and their agreement included not only 120 *livres* for his support, but also "six *livres* for the pins [*espingles*] of Denan's wife." Such tributes apparently did not occur in apprenticeship contracts for other occupations, and they seem to acknowledge more than the extra burden of another person for whom to cook and clean.[46]

Other evidence also points to the intertwining of the political and domestic economies of notarial households. Unlike lawyers, barristers, or other members of the elite, most notaries, like apothecaries and artisans, worked out of rooms that were adjacent to or even part of their own living spaces, rather than out of space in law courts or other public buildings. Clients often mentioned the presence of the notary's wife in the *étude*.

Almost all notaries' wives were literate, at least to the extent of being able to sign their names in an awkward hand. This skill was unusual in women of their social rank, and it may also have been related to expectations about their roles as well as to the emphasis on literacy in families whose husbands depended on writing for their livelihood. Very occasionally, a notary's wife might serve, instead of the clerk, as a substitute signer for an illiterate client on an act that her husband had made.[47] Wives of notaries in these ways

---

46. ADLA, 4E2/1452, 6 October 1618. Other cases include, for instance, the "*pistolle*" that a clerk gave to Vincent Bernard's wife "without diminution" of the fee of 150 *livres* arranged in the contract, and the "*écu d'or*" assigned to Simon Aubin's wife "in favor" of another contract. ADLA, 4E2/1728, 10 March 1629; and ADLA, 4E2/491, 13 December 1629.

47. For evidence of these kinds of hints see, for example, ADLA, B5660, 14 July 1628 (spinning wheel); B6664, 17 August 1647 (comment in passing on presence of notary's wife);

seemed to straddle the boundary between artisanal crafts in which women might have informal expertise and those skills and sets of knowledge such as law and medicine, which were defined as exclusively male.

Louise Lecoq's experiences, and the attitudes expressed toward her by a variety of clients and officials following René Guilloteau's hasty flight from the city in 1656 in face of accusations of malpractice, clearly illustrate the range of notarial wives' involvement in their husbands' work. Guilloteau left Louise Lecoq with a power of attorney allowing her "to act, manage and do for me in my name." He specifically included the ability to sell his office and any other property "at such a price as she will judge and see to be fitting," and to use the money as she saw fit, along with supervising all other activities such as leasing of properties, putting out money, and accepting the income of *rentes,* and generally all "necessary for [the] greater facility of my affairs."[48] Guilloteau entrusted her with this direction of their patrimony, although kinsmen were available: his brother-in-law, for example, was also a notary and lived on the same street. He was in no doubt that her competence was wide reaching.

Clients, as well as the judge and prosecutor overseeing the case, presumed that Lecoq had some familiarity with her husband's work. The judge and prosecutor repeatedly asked her if she knew where any other notarial acts made by her husband were, besides those sealed by the court, or if her husband "had revealed to her the state of his affairs." Although she denied knowing anything, her husband's entrusting her with the handling of their affairs—an act that the judge and prosecutor were not aware of—suggests that she was, in fact, very well informed, as they suspected. Clients asked Lecoq to locate their copies of contacts that they had asked Guilloteau to draw up. One aggrieved client named both Guilloteau and Lecoq in a court action over a notarial transaction, and asked her to recognize her husband's signature on a receipt, a task that notaries or lawyers were usually called on to perform.[49] Their attitudes point to the extent of notaries' wives' participation in the work of the *études,* exhibiting a flexibility that also characterized the work of artisans' wives in workshops.

Acknowledgements of the roles of notaries' wives in upholding sound *mesnagement* abounded. References to women's "assiduous work," "industry," and "*mesnagement*" suggest that their role in materially shaping the

---

4E2/1038 (torn), November 1653 (Louise Lecoq signing as substitute for an illiterate party to a contract that her husband, René Guilloteau, had been charged to draw up).

48. ADLA, 4E2/547, 17 November 1656.

49. See, for example, ADLA, B6127, 12 September 1624.

household was well known. Claude Geneste, for instance, credited the "diligence and thrift" of Marguerite Bernard with enhancing the value of her marital property community when her previous husband, René Dumolay, was largely confined to bed with gout.[50]

The issues surrounding the production of linen provide an example of some of the benefits and costs for women of *mesnagement*'s centrality in the domestic economies of middling families. Linens were important items in early modern households. They were more fully described in inventories than any category except furniture. Quantities and values were carefully enumerated, and fine distinctions were drawn, for example, between serviettes that were "new" or "almost new," and those that were "half used," and between first-quality linen and inferior grades.

The creation and care of linen shaped early modern household relations in multiple ways, both material and otherwise.[51] Linen and its accoutrements were valuable. Household linen formed quite a significant part of the overall wealth of middling families, representing, on average, almost 20 percent of the value of estates in notarial household inventories. Linen presses were among the two or three most valuable pieces of domestic equipment, along with, perhaps, a large water container and a big cooking pot. Stored in chests or laid out on buffets and dressers, linens served for these families, as for contemporary Dijon artisans and Massachusetts Puritans, as substantial and portable investments and demonstrations of personal wealth.[52]

A close correlation existed between wives and this important form of wealth, because women's dowries and labor supplied household linen. Women's trousseaux usually provided initial household linen supplies. In a typical case, Clemence Collin, the widow of Michel Coupperie, gave her daughter Magdelaine and Etienne Tesnier fourteen sheets, three dozen table napkins, six towels, fourteen tablecloths, six pillowcases, and a table runner. Trousseau linen was sometimes embroidered, which perpetuated

---

50. ADLA, B7080, 5 December 1608.

51. Anthropologists have pointed out the need to avoid a presentist attachment to preindustrial goods of the one-dimensional qualities (such as use or exchange value, prestige or essential item) that tend to characterize goods in industrial society. See, for example, Jane Schneider, "Trousseau As Treasure: Some Contradictions of Late Nineteenth-Century Change in Sicily," in Marion Kaplan, ed., *The Marriage Bargain: Women and Dowries in European History* (New York, 1985), 112.

52. The function of linen as an investment has been widely observed in the early modern context. See James Farr, *Hands of Honor: Artisans and Their World in Dijon, 1550–1650* (Cornell, 1988), 115–16; Shammas, "Domestic Environment," 10; John Demos, *A Little Commonwealth: Family Life in Plymouth Colony* (Oxford, 1970), 38.

the link between it and the women. When Catherine Guilloyais, for example, married Donnatien Ledoux, some of her trousseau linen was marked with a "C" and a "G."[53]

Like many other women, notaries' wives met the linen needs of their families, beyond those that their trousseaux satisfied, largely with their own spinning and sewing. Spinning wheels, winders, and large quantities of spun thread and flax were common in their households, although the absence of weaving equipment suggests that they took their work to a local weaver.[54] Isabel Dubois "had cloth made" that she then used to make "small linens." They did have long lengths of linen and other material, especially serge of various colors, indicating that all kinds of linens and clothes were made up at home.[55]

Spinning was a traditional resource for married women, as it could be done in odd moments free from other tasks, and, with the increasing restrictions on working opportunities that were available to early modern women, spinning may have become an even more important option.[56] Spinning allowed women to contribute to the material resources of the family in two ways. When women spun, they saved money that would otherwise have to be spent on buying linen. As well, they added the value of the linen they produced to the wealth of the household.

Wives' roles in the production of this resource and their control over it provided a material and specifically gendered measure of their contributions to the *ménage*. Widowers, for instance, often lacked the supplies of linen that characterized conjugal households. Thomas Robo did not own any linen when he died after having been a widower, in one instance of what seems to have been a broader pattern.[57] Women, rather than men,

53. ADLA, 4E2/292, 30 December 1653; ADLA, B5698, 22 December 1661. The rest of the linen was marked with a stitched cross, an "X" or an "EJ," the significance of which is unclear. The special connection that women felt to their trousseaux has been suggested by Agnès Fine in "A propos du trousseau: Une Culture feminine?" in Michelle Perrot, ed., *Une Histoire de femmes est-elle possible?* (Paris, 1984), 163.

54. See, for example, Alice Clark, *Working Life of Women in the Seventeenth Century* (London, 1919), 9, 95. The presence of spinning equipment in middling urban families has also been noted in other places. See Romain Baron, "La Bourgeoisie de Varzy au dix-septième siècle," *Annales de Bourgogne* 36 (July–September 1964), 190; and Lehoux, *Cadre de vie*, 516.

55. Deposition of Michelle Tertoux, ADLA, B5810, 18 April 1639; ADLA, B5686, 4 May 1648.

56. For the increasing limitations on work that women could do in the early modern period, see Martha Howell, *Women, Production, and Patriarchy in Late Medieval Cities* (Chicago, 1986); and Merry Wiesner, *Working Women in Renaissance Germany* (New Brunswick, N.J., 1986).

57. The absence of linen in the estates of widowers in inventories in the Paris basin is noted

tended to leave linens to specific individuals (often daughters) in their wills.[58] Jeanne Chauveau was very careful about preserving her dignity, as we have already seen in her dispute with her stepmother, but a servant noted that one of the few household tasks that she was willing to do was "to prepare linen on the press."[59] Women may have attached particular importance to linen as a source of property that was more distinctly theirs than property that was formally administered by their husbands.

Spinning may also have provided women in these families with a means of income that they would not otherwise have, as few of them had formal occupations or much opportunity for wage earning. Most of the households with spinning equipment also had a large quantity of flax, weighing between twenty and thirty pounds. This volume suggests that beyond production for domestic needs, these women were also selling or bartering spun thread. The income from this work would have been minimal, but it did give wives' access to a small amount of money not distributed by their husbands. Women might also have a couple of other sources of petty amounts of money. The sale of wine or of surplus from small holdings may have provided a small sum of cash.[60]

A separate financial resource could be important for women in a variety of ways. Husbands' authority, as we have seen, was conditional on their *mesnagement* of their households, an obligation that included the maintenance of subsistence. Any extra money that wives could earn might then give them access to items or services otherwise unavailable to them without asking their husbands. Moreover, by spinning, women emphasized their productive role, which was vital in the acquisition of status.[61]

Any money that women earned could also provide a safety net for themselves and their families: not all husbands lived up to their obligations, leaving women without any resources of their own, acutely vulnerable. And

---

in Michele Baulant, "La Famille en miettes: Sur un aspect de la démographie du dix-septième siècle," *Annales E.S.C.* 27 (July–October 1972), 961.

58. I thank Barbara Diefendorf for this observation.

59. Deposition of Danielle Legal, ADLA, B5810, 18 April 1639.

60. See, for example, ADLA, B5810, 19 March 1639, which notes Jeanne Chauveau and Isabel Dubois going to the countryside to sell wine by the jug.

61. Historians have correlated women's ability to earn money with enhanced status, and their loss of a productive role with declining status. Moreover, although potential earnings from part-time spinning are almost impossible to assess, even small amounts could make a crucial difference to family security and comfort. See Gay Gullickson, *Spinners and Weavers of Auffray: Rural Industry and the Sexual Division of Labor in a French Village, 1750–1850* (Cambridge, 1986), 71–74, 77–78, 84; and Clark, *Working Life,* 129–30.

men's and women's spending priorities often differed. Marguerite DelaVergne complained, for instance, that Vincent Bernard "did not give her a sou to live" and did not feed her adequately. Isabel Dubois, on the other hand, had a supply of money (although it is impossible to tell if this derived from Chauveau or her own efforts) that she used to pay for a variety of purchases and services.[62] When women mentioned paying out money, to buy either goods or services, their purchases concentrated on serving family needs. The revenue of women's productive work, whether from spinning or small holdings, may often have been "claimed" first by family necessities, whereas men felt freer to use their money to entertain themselves with drinks, food, and games in bars and other places.[63]

Spinning encapsulated an ambivalence that characterized much of women's household experiences. Linen was important in households for many different reasons, and, as women monopolized its production and care, it offered them an important resource. However, in the long term, the piecework basis of spinning and the low rates combined to minimize women's ability to earn much money. Moreover, the association of spinning and linen as household activities that occupied large shares of female time and labor reinforced longer-term trends toward a narrowing of opportunities for women. Spinning itself ultimately helped to keep women within the spatial confines of the household.[64]

62. Depositions of Perrine Levesque and Marie Dutay, ADLA, B5806, 16 January 1626; depositions of Marie Tertoux and Michelle Legal, ADLA, B5810, 19 March 1639 and 18 April 1639.

63. Work on early modern England and America has also pointed out the ways in which the use of women's income was restricted by the prior claims of family obligations, while men were much freer to spend their income as they wanted. It has also been observed that we should not assume that men's and women's interests necessarily coincided in the expenditure of time and money. See, for example, Margaret Hunt, *The Middling Sort: Commerce, Gender, and the Family in England, 1680–1780* (Berkeley and Los Angeles, 1996), chap. 5; Shammas, "Domestic Environment," 4.

64. Spinning came to be viewed very ambivalently. In folktales, spinning was portrayed as a source both of wealth for women and of their subjugation and imprisonment. Carole Shammas has observed that in the eighteenth century, the increasing complexity of household domesticity had a dual edge for women: initially empowering, in the long term it bred a series of conventions about the ideal domestic environment that trapped women. See Ruth Bottigheimer, "Tale Spinners: Submerged Voices in Grimms' Fairy Tales," *New German Critique* 27 (Fall 1982); and Shammas, "Domestic Environment," 19.

Domestic Sociability: Inter-Household Relations

Although each household was distinct in terms of its personnel and contents, in many physical and material ways, the boundaries of households
were quite permeable. The relative openness of individual households to
outsiders was the result of both necessity and choice, and it profoundly
shaped the patterns of sociability of urban middling families, such as those
of notaries. Interactions between households were an important part of the
cultural dialogues that defined and maintained authority within households and shaped patterns of authority between households.

The physical layout of early modern living spaces for nonelite families
necessitated shared staircases, courtyards, galleries, and latrines, and contributed in part to a porousness between households. The tiny, fragmented,
densely packed spaces in which notarial families and their peers lived compelled extensive contact with members of surrounding households, as the
spatial parameters of households literally blurred into each other.

The neighbors who lived alongside notarial families were a varied group.
Some were fellow members of the legal ranks, such as lawyers and court
clerks, but most were artisans. Louis Bretineau sublet three portions of the
building he rented during 1637 and 1638: he let one upper room to a merchant, another to a carpenter, and the ground floor to a baker.[65]

Kin frequently lived in the adjacent households, a practice that could
reflect personal preference and/or another aspect of the impact of inheritance or of agreements made in marriage contracts. In any case, presumably
the proximity of kin further facilitated interactions of all kinds between
households. Louis Coudret lived with his family in a building that also
housed his wife's sister's family and and his mother-in-law. The sisters Claude
and Adrienne le Gaigneux, who married Jean Carte and Guillaume Penifort,
also lived in the same building in property inherited from their parents.
They lived on alternate floors, with one household having the first and third
levels and the other the second floor, between them. René Guilloteau and his
two sisters Françoise and Catherine, who both married notaries, lived in adjacent houses. Again, statistical analysis of such arrangements is impossible,
but many similar examples suggest that they were quite common.[66]

65. ADLA, 4E2/1462, 19 June 1638; ADLA, 4E2/1462, 26 May 1638; ADLA, 4E2/129, 10
February 1637.
66. ADLA, 4E2/1038, 1 April 1653; ADLA, 4E2/577, 11 February 1649; ADLA, 4E2/1034,
23 February 1649. Tax rolls probably reflected a door-to-door listing of households, in which

Living in such close proximity, daily interaction was unavoidable, as innumerable references to conversations "at the door" attest. Neighbors were, as a result, intimately familiar with each other's lives. Disputes between husband and wife were common knowledge, and cries might attract attention and disapproval. The domestic violence of the Marguerite Dela-Vergne–Vincent Bernard household, for instance, was well known to people living in adjacent rooms or nearby buildings, who attested to the sounds of violence that had often drawn "several close neighbors" to the Bernard household. Moreover, several of them reported discussions with DelaVergne about her husband's abuse and said it was a matter of open discussion and "common rumor."[67]

Constant references to having "heard [it] said" and rumor suggest the role that gossip played in defining the boundaries of neighborhood and regulating accepted behavior. People talked about people they knew. Neighbors, encountered in casual meetings on the stairs, at the well, or in the street, oversaw many of the affairs of each individual household and helped to regulate community life.[68]

While residential patterns gave little choice but to open every household to neighbors' purview, cultural parameters recognized what physical boundaries could not, in these circumstances, demarcate. In this milieu, like in that of eighteenth-century Paris, neighbors often waited for kin to act rather than stepping into internal household affairs.[69] Community respect for the authority of household heads and kin compensated in part for the involuntary transparency of household life.

Neighbors in Nantes, as in other early modern communities, did supervise and even attempt to resolve disputes between members of different households. Male violence against women, which fell within the bounds of community acceptability when it was between husband and wife, apparently attracted intervention much more quickly when it occurred outside

---

case the tax list of 1593, for example, confirmed that kin often not only lived in the same locality, but were neighbors. The four households of Guillaume Leroy's widow, her son Ollivier, and two sons-in-law, Thomas Robo and Thomas Lemoyne (all notaries), were apparently adjacent in St. Saturnin (whether in the same or contiguous buildings is impossible to discern). The list contains many other examples of kin who occupied at least two adjacent households. AMN, CC86, April 1593.

67. ADLA, B5806, 16 January 1626.

68. This interpretation of neighborhoods in eighteenth-century Paris has been offered by David Garrioch, *Neighbourhood and Community in Paris, 1740–1790* (Cambridge, 1986), 16–55.

69. Garrioch, *Neighbourhood and Community,* 79–80.

of the bounds of the household. Both Anne Liborne and Marguerite Bouvier (the wives of Hervé Trebillard and Julien Belute, respectively) became embroiled in disputes with men whom they tried to stop from beating other men. When the objects of the men's wrath turned against the women, other bystanders were quick to jump in to prevent the women being hit, although insults might continue.[70] While early modern society conceded to heads of household large discretion to "discipline" their wives (or other dependents), it did not extend that right to all men over all women.

The regulatory role of neighbors became much more overtly interventionist in disputes between households, as an incident involving Hervé Trebillard illustrated. He lived in the parish of St. Croix on a sandbank in the Loire River. He recalled being "at the door" of the house in which a merchant lived when the merchant proclaimed to several bystanders that he had been robbed by a girl servant sent to him by some women orange sellers who lived nearby. Some of those present said that the merchant was justified in going to find the servant. With this community sanction, the merchant asked Trebillard and others (all artisans or "merchants") to accompany him to the servant's house. The incident ended violently, when the members of the servant's household (including her employer's brother-in-law, sister, and sundry other kin) and "several other men and women" of the neighborhood attacked the merchant, calling him an evil man for making accusations associating them with wrongdoing.[71]

Ideas about *mesnagement* were again key, here, in suggesting why neighbors who might gossip about the internal affairs of a household were nonetheless reluctant to intervene, whereas they would intercede far more quickly in disputes between members of different households. A man who beat his wife could do so within certain limits without attracting much response, but a man who beat someone else's wife overstepped the boundaries of authority that assigned husbands a monopoly of violence against their own spouses.[72]

The choices that members of middling families made, as well as structural necessities, determined the extensive household sociability that also contributed to a porousness between households. Early modern sociability

---

70. ADLA, B6664, 27 June 1647; ADLA, B6667, 27 April 1654.
71. ADLA, B6668, 27 November 1656.
72. This kind of community regulation could operate in other ways, too, with women regulating each other as well as men. See, for example, Georg'Ann Cattelona, "Control and Collaboration: The Role of Women in Regulating Female Sexual Behavior in Early Modern Marseille," *French Historical Studies* 18 (Spring 1993).

among this milieu was based in the household as well as in locations like bars, and it revolved around visitors as well as family members. A constant flow of visitors filled many middling households, and their presence helped to further the gender alliances that shaped them.

Middling people visited each other's households frequently, and such interactions could continue on a regular basis for many years. A woman described visiting François Chauveau's household "very often and as one of the family" for ten or twelve years. A master saddler, similarly, observed that he had visited for many years and during Chauveau's two marriages, adding that they "often each went to the other's."[73]

The great number of seats that middling families owned indicated the many visitors they expected and their desire to accommodate their guests. Almost all families possessed seats sufficient for far more people than lived in the household. The principal *chambre* of Chauveau's household, for example, contained nine chairs, six folding chairs, and two stools, while Louis Coudret's household had gathered five chairs, and eleven stools of various kinds.[74] The seats were overwhelmingly concentrated in the main *chambre*, where visitors would have been received. The abundance of folding chairs, easily movable stools, and other lightweight seats as well as trestle tables that we have seen not only allowed household members to compensate for the shortage of space, but facilitated its reorganization when company called.

The enormous quantities of table linen that most notarial households possessed suggest that mealtimes were a focus of household sociability. These middling households owned, on average, 115 table napkins and nineteen tablecloths.[75] Such stocks not only represented a valuable investment, but they enabled these families to conceive of entertaining guests on a regular basis. Laying the table with its cloth and table napkins was also part of the regular routine at mealtimes, as the details of the tasks of servants show.[76]

---

73. ADLA, B5810, 19 March 1639.

74. ADLA, B5693, 20 May 1655; ADLA, B5697, 15 July 1659. This superabundance of seats has been noted without comment in other contexts in this period, for example, Lehoux, *Cadre de vie,* 177; and Pardailhé-Galabrun, *Naissance de l'intime,* 256.

75. Twenty of the twenty-one inventories include linen, and the holdings seem to be related fairly clearly to wealth and length of marriage. Thomas Robo's was the only inventory that did not list any linen, which is explicable, since he was very poor and the only widower whose inventory survives.

76. Deposition of Marguerite Gerard, ADLA, B5810, 18 April 1639.

Mealtimes provided occasions for these families to assert their status as well as to entertain themselves and visitors, as their efforts to provide reasonably clean linen made clear. The sheer quantity of linen that the households accumulated in part served to meet this need, but frequent references to items sent to a laundress, and specific provisions in leases as to the permissibility of washing linen, also attest to the same motive. René Guilloteau's lease in 1620 specifically allowed that Marie Bouin, his wife, could "when she sees fit do or have done her washing in the yard."[77] Agreements made between the notaries and the peasants who sharecropped their rural small holdings also frequently included the provision that the latters' wives would help the notaries' wives "do the washing" whenever required.[78] The concern to maintain clean linen and the need for it indicate that this linen was regularly used, and was not merely displayed or stored in chests as an investment. At the same time, the desire for clean linen may also have been part of the ongoing efforts of notarial families to differentiate themselves from their social inferiors. Cleanliness of clothing and, above all, linen became an important indicator of civility in the early modern period, when few people had adequate washing facilities.[79]

At least in urban middling families, entertainment within the household was already important. They frequently welcomed visitors, and sociability was apparently oriented, even below the elites, mainly around mealtimes, with their opportunities for gossip, display of silver and linen, and hosting of non–household members.[80] The sixteenth- and seventeenth-century households of middling families such as those of notaries certainly lacked the accoutrements, like tea services and musical instruments, that provided the focus for domestic sociability with the rise of consumer society in the eighteenth century. However, household sociability before the eighteenth century did not have the associations with the private consumption of the conjugal family that it was to develop later.[81]

---

77. ADLA, 4E2/1571, 4 April 1620.

78. Among many examples, see ADLA, 4E2/1572, 1 December 1622; ADLA, 4E2/492, 19 April 1634; ADLA, 4E2/173, 18 October 1654.

79. Jacques Revel, "The Uses of Civility," in Roger Chartier, ed., *Passions of the Renaissance: A History of Private Life*, vol. 3 (Cambridge, Mass., 1989), 189–90.

80. See Neuschel, "Noble Households," 609–12, for the importance of mealtimes and the display of conspicuous consumption associated with these mealtimes for early modern aristocratic elites.

81. For the correlation of the rise of domestic sociability in the eighteenth-century household with the emergence of luxury commodities, like tea services and musical instruments,

Wives' responsibility for the creation of the context for household sociability, from erecting the table on its trestles to laying out the linen, dishes,
and food, created a potential source of conflict or pride in households, as
contemporary popular cultural forms recognized. During the sixteenth
and seventeenth centuries, most nonelite families used utilitarian pewter
dishes (so undistinguished that inventories categorized them by weight
rather than by item), and food was simple (being dominated by the varieties of stews that could be cooked in one pot over a fire). In most households, therefore, the real opportunities for display to guests came with
linen and the odd piece of silver, rather than with the dishes and food. The
author of the *Quinze joyes de mariage* noted, for example, that a great grievance of husbands was to be refused "white and well worked tablecloths."[82]
The provision or lack of ample, clean, starched linen could provide a locus
for power contests between men and women, while the display of the same
illuminated the success of the household, bringing credit that women
could share.

Visiting helped to create bonds between members of different households that everyone recognized. Vincent Bernard identified the court
usher Claude Pouponneau as a friend of Bernard's wife's brother-in-law, on
the basis that they often ate at each other's table. Sebastien Gaudin, another court usher, saw his frequent meals at Chauveau's house as one proof
of their having regarded each other "as good friends."[83]

Although the smallness of scale and the mixing of domestic and occupational work prevented the physical differentiation into male and female domains, household sociability among these middling families seems to have
been gender specific rather than focused on spouses.[84] Shared meals and
frequent unspecified visits focused around gatherings of either women or
men, but rarely seem to have included both. Pierre Mariot recalled going
to visit an acquaintance at about five or six in the evening and finding "several other people" there, of whom the five mentioned were all men.
Women, as well as men, made frequent visits to the household of Thomas

and locates earlier patterns of sociability outside the household, see Shammas, "Domestic Environment," 3–24.

82. Quoted in Havard, *Ameublement*, 1,054.

83. ADLA, B5815, 14 December 1646; ADLA, B5810, 19 March 1639 and 18 April 1639;
ADLA, B6652, 10 [illegible] 1626; ADLA, B5810, 12 May 1639.

84. The separation of male and female physical space has provided a powerful model for
understanding gender relations, especially in rural areas. See, for example, Martine Segalen,
Love and Power in the Peasant Family: Rural France in the Nineteenth Century (Chicago, 1983).

Chauveau and his family, but only the men specifically linked their visits, and the events and conversations that took place there, to Thomas Chauveau. Women often referred to going to or coming from church, for example, but never in the company of their husbands. Louise Bouteiller, Pierre Quenille's wife, described leaving church after the main mass, the previous Sunday, in the company of three other women. Similarly, Anne Liborne and Marguerite Bouvier, the wives of Julien Belute and Hervé Trebillard, talked about returning home alone from church services.[85]

Material structures and choices in the household provided one terrain on which gender and power relations were mapped, in the daily lives of urban middling families in early modern France. The process of the accumulation and management of household property created obligations and responsibilities, albeit unevenly, for husbands and wives. These responsibilities helped to define patterns of power and authority. Distinctive relationships between households also developed.

The emphasis on the *mesnagement* of the household introduced expectations for husbands and wives as well as for other residents. Wives were essential contributors to the successful management of the resources of households, and their roles were clearly acknowledged. Wives' labor, whether in taking care of clerks, overseeing small holdings, producing and maintaining linen, or myriad other tasks, was indispensable and, as such, offered a structure of daily life in the household domain that had the potential to empower them. Women's control of linen, for example, whether its accumulation through their trousseaux and spinning work, its transformation into usable items, its maintenance via cleaning, or its display, gave them important roles in producing and portraying their household's wealth and status.

In these ways women as well as men constructed the particular form of early modern households. Their work had wide-reaching implications. The positive focus on *mesnagement* in middling families not only gave women a niche in the domestic economy, it also gave wives grounds for seeking community regulation of husbands who failed to meet their obligations as *bons mesnagers*. Their role in the domestic economy and in accommodating extensive household sociability provided them with access to a certain kind of

85. ADLA, B5807, 11 August 1628; ADLA, B6664, 27 June 1647; ADLA, B6667, 27 April 1654.

power in daily life, albeit de facto power that was neither secure nor insti-
tutionalized. Gendered patterns of sociability may also have provided
women with networks to contest and combat the monopoly on authority
that their husbands enjoyed. Yet members of these middling families—men
and women—were required by their families and peers to meet the standards expressed through the idea of *mesnagement* or face disapproval, or
worse.

The valorization of *bon mesnagement* among middling families pointed to
a key issue in determining gender and power issues. In terms of accruing
authority, management of property was as important as legal access to it.
These families constructed a household political economy that emphasized
the responsibilities of *mesnagement* and the ties between households, including the right of kin to intervene, in certain circumstances. This pattern
had important consequences as it was replicated in many other aspects of
their lives, as we will see.

5

Having and Holding

Managing Household Property

Aside from the creation of authority and opportunity in everyday household life, household members and their kin had opportunities, at particular moments, to influence who would manage property. In 1629, for example, a merchant asked René Desmortiers, Jean Verger, and five other of their kinsmen to recommend to a judge that his son be forbidden to transact any business. Soon after Claude Geneste and Marguerite Bernard married, at the start of the century, two of their children from earlier marriages also married each other. But angry recriminations and legal action over gifts of property that Geneste and Bernard made to each other soon marred their integration into one big happy family. When Jeanne Duvau died in 1647, two years after her husband, Mathurin Carte, twenty-three of their kin argued fiercely over who among them should be appointed as guardian of the orphaned children. Guyonne Carte sought the guardianship of her children after her husband died, whereas Mathurine Pigeaud suggested that another person fulfil that role for her children. In both cases, their kin gave advice before the judges made decisions.

In these incidents (explored in detail later), members of middling families expressed their priorities and imperatives in a variety of ways: efforts to limit a person's right to manage his or her property; married couples' decisions to seek to make mutual gifts to each other, or to pursue marital separations; family choices of guardians for orphaned children; and surviving spouses' experiences of widowhood. Such occasions, again, entailed the constant negotiation of issues of authority and power on terms that refined the bases of both gender and kinship. The consequences of formulating authority and competence around ideas of *mesnagement* were clarified at these moments in a household's life. This created contexts for affirming gender roles, building alliances or creating conflict between spouses, and shaping the reorganization of relationships as well as property, both within the household and between households of kin.

The management of a household's property was a matter for the possible intervention of kin, and this type of kin oversight affected all the members of that household, albeit in different ways—the husband and father, the wife and mother, and their children. The large role of lineage property in the patrimony of individual households and the consequent persistence of ties to kin seemed key factors in shaping such actions, illustrating how common interests in property structured kin relations and encouraged kin to act together. Repeatedly, patrimonial practices gave kin important roles in overseeing and supervising the affairs of individual households, even when kin had no material share in the property in question.

The Power of Prohibition

Poor *mesnagement* might occasion the intervention of kin into personal affairs, through efforts to put limits on the rights of a person whose capacity for *mesnagement* was in doubt. Kin gave advice, for example, on petitions to secure prohibitions (*interdictions*), which could be requested in a variety of circumstances to suspend the legal rights of persons considered incapable of managing their own affairs.

The merchant Jean Amproux, for instance, asked the court to issue a prohibition forbidding his eldest son to enter into any contracts that involved property. The son allegedly had a sickness that not only rendered him incapable of any business, but might lead him to actions that "tarnished the honor of the family." The seven relatives who gathered to give their advice included two sons-in-law of Amproux, together with four male first cousins (including Jean Verger) and René Desmortiers, who was married to another cousin. They agreed that they believed the son's illness made the request appropriate.[1]

Kin could use *interdictions* to protect their interests in the property of a household that they felt to be inadequately managed. Julien Lucas combined with his sister, maternal grandmother, and maternal uncle to secure an order prohibiting his mother, Isabel Daguin, and her fourth husband from having management of the property of Daguin, "seeing what results from the dissipations and poor husbandry [*mesnagement*] of Daguin."[2] André Charier's voluntary concession of control also acknowledged the interests of his heirs. Recognizing "his corporal incapacity for which reason he could not manage his domestic affairs nor ameliorate and maximize the value of his goods and properties," he gave his son and two sons-in-law control over his estate, for them to manage "as they see fit."[3]

Kin collaboration in the consideration and protection of the interests of a particular family member persisted over time, even after death disrupted the initial kinship tie. Pierre Guerin remarried in 1630 after the death of Judic DelaGasne, his first wife. Yet in 1647, he was still among "the closest relatives" of a niece of DelaGasne, as "an uncle because of his wife," called to discuss the petition of the girl's father to sell her part of the lineage property of her maternal grandmother's succession.[4] Again in this example, kin moderated the head of household's right to manage the patrimony.

Separations and Donations

The capacity of spouses to pursue goals either together or separately, as well as some of the reasons behind such decisions, and the interests of kin that were at stake in such decisions were illustrated in the use of two contrasting strategies. Petitions for separation of either property or property and person (*séparations de biens* or *séparations de corps et de biens*) and spousal

---

1. ADLA, B6372, 7 February 1629.
2. ADLA, B6377, 8 March 1658.
3. ADLA, B5873, 20 June 1656.
4. ADLA, 4E2/466, 6 February 1647.

agreements to make gifts to each other of property (*donations*) provided two demonstrations of the degree of flexibility that was available in the management of household property.

Women's petitions for separations, in their choice of explanation and chances of success, highlighted the role of kin and the parameters of *mesnagement*, as well as its importance as the key to authority for men. Mathurine Bretet, for example, cited Mathurin Garnier's "poor husbandry . . . and debts." Likewise, Renée Bretineau illustrated Julien Jouneaux's failure to maintain her appropriately by pointing out that "if he took a servant he would be obliged to feed her."[5] Men also mobilized this way of judging their peers. Mathurin Guillou gave evidence in support of a female neighbor seeking a separation of property, saying that he had known the husband to mistreat his wife during their marriage and to be a man "very given to gambling, debaucheries and excesses who . . . dissipates his property and that of Rohee [his wife], often making mad deals."[6]

The pivoting of men's authority around *bon mesnagement* in this community created a potential justification for intervention in households if the domestic economy seemed to be breaking down. While neighbors, kin, and the legal system tolerated a certain level of physical abuse, poor husbanding of the household's resources—in terms of handling financial affairs, disorderly behavior, or application to work—elicited negative reactions from kin and neighbors, and their cooperative testimony was a critical element for women seeking to challenge husbands' legal authority to run household affairs.

Kin played very important roles in facilitating women's petitions for separation. Besides DelaVergne's plea to her brother-in-law for help, Françoise Ouairy's father was accused of removing her from the conjugal household to save her from abuse; Mathurine Bretet's parents made a petition on her behalf, because she was still a minor; and Renée Bretineau took refuge with her mother-in-law.[7] Women called on their neighbors to provide corroborating evidence of the wrongdoing that their petitions alleged, after the requests for separation had been made.[8]

---

5. ADLA, B6140, 30 January 1648; ADLA, 4E2/1480, 28 January 1652.

6. ADLA, B5817, 24 July 1658.

7. ADLA, B5806, 16 January 1626; ADLA, B6131, 22 December 1633; ADLA, B6140, 30 January 1648; ADLA, 4E2/1480, 28 January 1652.

8. A study of divorce in Rouen at the end of the eighteenth century found neighbors more willing to intervene than kin, not least because of greater proximity. Whether this difference was due to changing demographic patterns that made kin less likely to be also neighbors by the end of the eighteenth century, or whether challenges to patriarchy as the principle of social organization in the revolutionary decade had contributed to this change is hard to tell.

Moreover, women's petitions to the Nantais court for separations of property enjoyed a high rate of success, whereas the outcome of petitions for separations of property and person were far more unpredictable. In what was a typical pattern in women's experiences with petitions for separations, two wives of notaries secured separations of property, which they justified by emphasizing their husbands' poor financial management and failure to provide adequate support, whereas two other petitions for separations of property and persons, where the primary evidence presented was about battery and adultery, were unsuccessful.[9]

Judges' greater willingness to grant petitions for separate property emphasized "good husbandry" as the basis of men's household authority, with its obligations and privileges, in a way that offered women some protection. The state had an interest, after all, in encouraging households based on this kind of orderliness. It did not have this direct interest in regulating domestic violence or adultery.[10]

Several motives could lie behind the decisions of the members of middling urban families who sought separations or renunciations of the marital community property.[11] Husbands and wives could use this legal means to protect a threatened patrimony. Facing charges of embezzlement, René

Roderick Phillips, *Family Breakdown in Late Eighteenth-Century France: Divorces in Rouen, 1792–1803* (Oxford, 1980), 180–89.

9. One hundred and seven cases of petitions for separation survive between 1598 and 1660, in series B of the ADLA. Of these, 105 were made by women. One-third were requests for separation of property and person, and these were rejected in two out of three cases. The remainder were petitions for separations of property, and these were virtually always successful.

10. David Sabean points out that agents of early modern Germany evaluated people "by their ability to manage 'households.'" David Warren Sabean, *Power in the Blood: Popular Culture and Village Discourse in Early Modern Germany* (Cambridge, 1984), 149–51.

11. For an expanded analysis of the dynamics involved in separations cases, see my "Seeking Separations: Gender, Marriages and Household Economies in Seventeenth-Century France," *French Historical Studies* 21 (Winter 1998). For a survey that focuses mainly on requests for separation of property in the eighteenth century, see Alain Lottin, "Vie et mort du couple: Difficultés conjugales et divorces dans le nord de la France aux dix-septième et dix-huitième siecles," *Dix-septième siècle* 103, 104 (1974).

Historians of early modern Anglo-America have debated the possible meanings of the evolving practice of separate estates for married women that elite Anglo-American families utilized beginning in the late sixteenth century, and that a broader group began to use in the eighteenth century. Was separate property a sign of the increasingly egalitarian nature of spousal relationships, a family strategy to protect at least part of the household property from creditors, or a reaffirmation of patriarchy that sought to ensure that the victims of spousal abuse had property to support themselves and did not become disruptive public charges? See the respective arguments of: Lawrence Stone, *Family, Sex, and Marriage in England, 1500–1800* (abridged ed., London, 1979); Marylynn Salmon, *Women and the Law of Property in Early Amer-*

Guilloteau left his wife, Louise Lecoq, to face creditors and judicial officials, but he gave her power of attorney, allowing her full discretion in the management of all their property. One of her first actions was to renounce their marital property community. By this means she too became a creditor of their household and could claim, for instance, the proceeds of the subsequent sale of his notarial office and any other money liquidated, at least to the amount of her dowry.[12] One consequence of this series of actions was to shelter some of the household's property from the husband's creditors, by specifying it as the property of his wife.

Wives' petitions for separations also employed language that suggested that women's property and interests could be distinct from those of their husbands. Wives were acutely aware that "their" property was endangered and were determined to protect their interests, while at least some husbands clearly conceived control over property as significant power levers in the internal dynamics of the household. Renée Bretineau claimed that Julien Jouneaux had not supported her and their children adequately, which had forced her to seek a property separation; he had demanded that she, as "mistress of her property and revenues," contribute to their living expenses.[13]

Women could also seek to protect the lineage property that they had brought to the household. Yvonne Maillard wanted her husband, Jean Lemoyne, to compensate her for her dowry and for lineage properties that she had inherited from her deceased mother and father, which "Lemoyne and she had sold and alienated at the instigation and persuasion of Lemoyne." Lemoyne agreed to transfer to Maillard as her lineage property some land that he had inherited, to take the place of the property sold and in order to free himself of all obligations with regard to Maillard's *propres*.

Maillard subsequently took other steps to protect herself from the repercussions of Lemoyne's financial misdemeanors, in a strategy that highlighted the importance of lineage property, both for women and for kin involvement in the internal affairs of a household. Lemoyne had been the guardian of his widowed sister's daughter, and the niece's estate sued him

---

ica (Chapel Hill, N.C., 1986); and Susan Staves, *Married Women's Separate Property in England, 1660–1833* (Cambridge, Mass., 1990).

12. ADLA, B5694, 13–22 December 1656; *procure* attached to ADLA, 4E2/547, 28 June 1657.

13. ADLA, 4E2/1480, 28 January 1652. Bretineau apparently did return to live with Journeaux eventually, as they had more children later, but they maintained separate property. See, for example, ADLA, 4E2/1203, 1 December 1657; and ADLA, 4E2/181, 5 December 1660, both made by Bretineau as "*femme séparée de biens.*"

for the return of the money that he had managed for her. Maillard was apparently concerned (as perhaps were her kin) that she also might be held responsible, as she helped Lemoyne raise the money to settle the case in return for a promise that she herself would be free from further claims against him from the niece's estate. Lemoyne agreed to pay his niece's estate 3,000 *livres* to be acquitted of all claims. To raise the money, he sold his office of notary for 1,000 *livres* to his sister, a move made possible by Maillard renouncing any claim she had to the office as part of her lineage property (presumably it had been purchased with her dowry). The other 2,000 *livres* came from the sale of some of Maillard's lineage properties to her brother.[14]

The presence of inalienable lineage property in the capital that women brought to marriages emerges here as a key in creating the context in which women claimed interests that could be protected from their husbands. But their interests were familial in ownership and gendered in management. The frequent involvement of wives' kin in efforts to secure separations of property suggests that we should be cautious about interpreting such resorts as signs of the potential autonomy of women in these families. Such actions often point to the way in which property practices revolved around securing the management of property for male kin.[15]

Married couples could also seek to assert their financial independence as a couple from the interests of their children, siblings, or other kin. Breton customary law strictly limited spousal gifts, forbidding testamentary bequests between spouses, but it did give them options to protect the profits of their marital partnership, if they chose.[16] Couples could seek, for instance, to protect the marital patrimonial estate against claims on lineage or community property. As we have seen, marriage contracts for children sometimes protected the lineage property of a surviving parent for use in their lifetime.

Spouses could also choose to make mutual gifts (*donations*) that provided that the surviving spouse should receive as his or her property all the per-

14. Maillard raised the money by selling some rural property that she had inherited to her brother for 2,000 *livres* earlier the same day. ADLA, 4E2/1499, 18 May 1621; ADLA, 4E2/666, 10 July 1621; ADLA, 4E2/666, 10 July 1621.

15. In an early study, Jacques Lelièvre argued that a Parisian wife in the late eighteenth century, "in face of the juridical omnipotence of the husband [with regard to her property], was protected quite efficiently" by a balancing system of rights that included the ability to seek separate property and to renounce the marital community. Jacques Lelièvre, *La Pratique des contrats de mariage chez les notaires au Châtelet de Paris, de 1789 à 1804* (Paris 1959), 148–56.

16. *La Coustume de Bretagne avec les Commentaires et Observations . . . par Maître Michel Sauvageau* (Nantes, 1710), article 215.

sonal property (*biens meubles*) that they owned and, in addition, proprietorship of half of all the real property that they had acquired by personal effort during the marriage (*acquets*) and usufruct of the other half until death. In return, the surviving spouse paid the debts of the estate, acted as executor of the will, dealt with burial-associated matters, and supported any children. If a donation had not been made, community property was split in half on the death of a spouse, between the surviving spouse and other heirs, with each being responsible for half the debts as well as gaining half the assets.

Donations between notaries and their wives indicated a desire to affirm the distinct and mutual interests and affairs of the married couple. Such agreements typically included some version of a statement that described their motivation, as in the donation between Mathurin Goheau and Jeanne Tareil: "For the reciprocal love and affection they feel for each other and for the good and agreeable favors, assistance and treatment they give each other daily."[17] Beyond such general formulations of mutual admiration, donations seemed to acknowledge the role of a couple's own efforts (rather than kin contributions) in any success that they had enjoyed, and to convey the sense that they alone should enjoy subsequent rewards. Toussaint Charier and Jeanne Cercleux added that they had made the donation not only "in consideration of their reciprocal affection and the good treatment that they receive daily from each other," but also in consideration "of the effort and care they had [taken] to amass and conserve the said property."[18]

The language of the agreements recognized the contribution of each spouse and the accumulation of property through their own efforts, as opposed to any inherited lineage property that emphasized their ties to kin. (As a result, middling families only seem to have included donations as part of marriage contracts in exceptional circumstances. Robert Poullain and Anne Menart included a donation in their contract, but she, as it carefully noted, had earned the 1,000 *livres* that her dowry was worth in money and household goods, "from her own trade and the dealing in merchandise she does.")[19]

17. ADLA, 4E2/292, 11 April 1654.
18. ADLA, 4E2/1481, 9 April 1655.
19. ADLA, 4E2/1615, 4 October 1643. Poullain and Menart also formed a marital property community at once, instead of waiting the year and day designated by customary law (a rare decision, usually only taken when one of the parties was remarrying). In a similar vein, when Jeanne Lucas, a linen worker (the sister of Jean Eon's wife, Marguerite Lucas, and, like her, the granddaughter of Bertran Lucas), married, her mother declared that the dowry, which comprised the stock of Lucas's boutique, "belonged to her [daughter] and came from the profits she had made." ADLA, 4E2/469, 13 September 1657.

The oft-married Claude Geneste and Marguerite Bernard made a donation after their marriage to each other, and their attitudes to their current
and former households juxtaposed what they saw to be the positive and
negative possibilities of household viability. Geneste praised Bernard for
her contribution to the value of her community property with her first husband, saying the latter had "few means" and "if God by his blessing had favored their community, it was more from the diligence and thrift of
[Bernard] than her deceased husband."[20] Bernard, on the other hand, observed that the personal property (*biens meubles*) of the community of Geneste and Perrine Jonnet, his first wife, "were not of great value" and largely
taken up on her death by paying their debts, "the majority created by Jonnet at the merchants of this town for material and other goods."[21]

Although mutual gifts reflected recognition of the complementary efforts of spouses to be worthy *mesnagers,* an important attribute among middling families, children and other kin were often suspicious and hostile to
such donations. Donations were, to some degree, out of line with the usual
thrust of customary laws regarding the distribution of patrimony. By
strengthening the claims of husband and wife over household property, donations potentially prejudiced the patrimonial expectations of other kin,
expectations that were uppermost in most of the inheritance rules. The potential loss involved for other heirs seemed to come into focus most acutely
when either husband or wife had children from a previous marriage who
had a claim to part of their estate. In such cases, a marital donation benefited the surviving spouse at the cost of claims that children would otherwise have expected to make on the parental estate.

Both customary law and the contracts recording donations sought to ensure that the agreements were made in good faith, and not designed to
cheat heirs out of what they would, in the normal course, have pointed to
as their right. Breton customary law decreed that donations were invalid "if
they were made in hatred or fraud of the presumptive heirs," and Parisian
customary law forbade couples with children to make donations at all.[22] Donations always started by carefully stating that husband and wife were mak-

---

20. ADLA, B7080, 5 December 1608.
21. ADLA, 4E2/450, 24 March 1611.
22. *La Coustume de Bretagne,* article 199. In the Paris customary region, other postmarital
gifts of all kinds between spouses were also forbidden. Contemporaries feared that the affection of spouses might lead them to favor each other over their heirs and lineages. Breton custom permitted donations during a marriage with children, but nullified them if the surviving
spouse remarried. Barbara Diefendorf, *Paris City Councillors in the Sixteenth Century: The Politics
of Patrimony* (Princeton, 1983), 229–30; *La Coustume de Bretagne,* article 213.

ing their gifts "of their own free will without inducement, [the] persuasion nor constraint of anyone."[23]

Despite such precautions, clearly donations did sometimes involve attempts at deception. In her 1604 will, Marie Jahanneau, the wife of Alexander Chebuet, revoked a donation that she and Chebuet had made and urged her heirs to take what belonged to them. She claimed that Chebuet "had made her agree by force and violence . . . and to avoid the maltreatment he did to her day and night." For these reasons, she said, she had agreed to the donation, "although her intention had never been such since she knew very well that he was making it to defraud" her heirs.[24] In this case, far from representing mutual spousal recognition, a second husband who, presumably, saw the opportunity to advance his own interest coerced his wife into making the agreement. Jahanneau and Chebuet were so far from being the happy couple that a donation seemed to suggest that she asked to be buried with her father and first husband.

Even when no such coercion was involved, as in most donations, in all probability, children of earlier marriages had reason to feel aggrieved, as donations implied a narrow emphasis on spouses that contrasted with the general tendency of property arrangements to emphasize the interests of all heirs. Claude Geneste and Marguerite Bernard fought with the children and heirs that each had from earlier marriages over the legality of the donation they made, and the charges and responses of all parties illustrated clearly some of the tensions that such acts created or allowed to crystallize.

Bernard became Geneste's third wife after the death of her first husband, René Dumolay. Geneste's sons from his first marriage leveled the charges—one son had married Bernard's daughter from her first marriage, giving him cause to assert grievance from both sides. The long, drawn out, and bitter dispute had begun by 1607 and was still pending before the Parlement of Brittany in 1614, four years after Geneste died.

The children appealed to that court to overturn the donation, because "it was made out of the hatred and fraud Geneste and Bernard bear towards Geneste [the son] and his wife."[25] The younger Geneste had previously claimed that Bernard "and her thief of a husband . . . had stolen most of his property" and accused Bernard of thinking of "other children who

---

23. This particular form was adopted by Mathurin Bruneau and Mathurine Hervouet. ADLA, 4E2/676, 20 March 1634.

24. ADLA, 4E2/326, 12 March 1604.

25. ADLA, B6817, 14 May 1614.

she wants to enrich, forgetting those of her first husband."[26] The children felt that the donation was prejudicial to their inheritances.

Bernard countered that the donation that she and Geneste had made fairly gave her key pieces of his property. The offices of notary and lawyer that Geneste had held were central to the dispute. Bernard argued that Geneste had purchased the office prior to his marriage to their mother, and, as such, they "held the nature of personal property [*meubles*]." For her, the offices were part of her community with Geneste and became hers as a result of their donation, whereas Geneste's sons contended that the offices belonged to them. Bernard also denied her stepsons' claims to furniture, on the grounds that it was covered by the donation. She also alleged that Geneste's sons had made "atrocious and scandalous remarks" designed "to make the honorable life they [Geneste and Bernard] had lived seem odious."[27]

Geneste had fiercely denied the charges of wrongdoing that his sons leveled, saying that he had always acted in their best interest, as their other kin had agreed. He pointed out that other kin of the children had witnessed and approved both the marriage contract between his son and Bernard's daughter and the inventory of Bernard's community with her first husband (obvious potential occasions for subversion of justice).[28] As always, the presence of kin from outside the household was meant to ensure that the interests of all parties were fairly represented.

Children and other kin were hostile to donations because they ran counter to the collective emphasis of other property arrangements in at least two ways. They accentuated the separate interests of the marital couple, and other kin were not called on to give their advice as to whether the contract prejudiced the interests of any party. Donations also gave women control over patrimony that clashed with practices that generally minimized women's capacity to manage their own property, even when they owned it. Ironically, despite the equation of royal rhetoric with the absolute authority of each household head to make his own decisions, middling wives may have come closest to equality when their households were the most isolated, as in the case of donations, from the influence of kin.

Although neither separations nor donations were the rule in sixteenth- and seventeenth-century marriages, these options indicate that the importance of good *mesnagement* in middling families was nevertheless more of a

26. ADLA, B7080, 5 December 1608.
27. ADLA, 4E2/450, 24 March 1611.
28. ADLA, B7080, 5 December 1608.

two-edged sword for women than for men.[29] Wives' contributions to successful *mesnagement* gave them an important role in a domestic economy
built on complementary contributions from husbands and wives. Additionally, the priority attached to that concept gave them a cause to seek separation of their property, if not their persons, the threat of which may have
proved a useful lever. On the other hand, the emphasis on *mesnagement*
gave wives little protection against domestic violence, if it was inflicted by a
husband who otherwise safeguarded household resources satisfactorily.

Unlike donations and separations, guardianships and widowhood were
very common in early modern families. Years could pass, however, before
the ultimate partition of the entire estate among its heirs after the surviving
spouse's death completed a household's patrimonial cycle. During this
transition phase, the appointment of guardians for any surviving children,
and the experience of widowhood, provided critical decision-making moments for household members and kin, during which issues about gender
and authority were again negotiated.

Guardianship

The selection of guardians for minor children was a frequent task, given
early modern mortality rates, and it was another process through which the
parameters of authority in middling families were reaffirmed, and the differential authority of husbands and wives was spotlighted. Guardians were
appointed only when fathers died, as Breton customary law regarded the
father as "the natural guardian of his children and they must not have any
other." When mothers died, fathers remained charged with the responsibility for their children. In the case of a father's death, however, discussions
about and attitudes toward guardianships revealed some of the claims,
obligations, and interests involved in the recognition of kin ties and women's
capacities.

29. The frequency of donations is impossible to assess accurately, and the trend toward the
recognition of the material efforts of the household was apparently upward in the long term,
but they were probably not common in the seventeenth century. In contrast, by the end of the
eighteenth century, almost 90 percent of marriage contracts in Paris included a donation between spouses. The frequency of separations is also difficult to address, in view of the lack of
systematic study, but, so far, conclusions have emphasized that this resort was uncommon.
Lelièvre, *Pratique des Contrats de Mariage,* 165–66; Roderick Phillips, *Putting Asunder: A History of
Divorce in Western Society* (Cambridge, 1988), 159–62.

Customary law charged kin with choosing a guardian and provided guidelines that favored the choices of the late fathers or of paternal kin, and the selection of mothers. It required maternal and paternal kin of the children to select the "most effective, competent and advantageous" among them to have the guardianship and administration both of the persons and property of the minors. Customary law favored the mother as guardian "if she is adequate and wants to take the charge." It called on kin who were related by either blood or marriage to give their advice on the appointment, but observed that the opinions of paternal kin should be given the most weight and gave priority to the testamentary wishes of fathers regarding guardians for their children.[30]

In practice, kin pursued emphases that more closely observed other aspects of their management of patrimony, in involving kin from both sides and disregarding the observance of either the late father's wishes or the preference for mothers in favor of making their own choice. Michel Sauvageau, in a 1710 commentory, noted this divergence in advocating reforms to the Breton customary law on the basis of Breton practice. He claimed that kin discarded the customary obligation to respect the testamentary preference of the deceased father, and recommended that the provisions favoring the mother be dropped, leaving kin free to elect the guardian of their choice "following the usage of this province where this [preference] has never been observed." Sauvageau added that the customary law's preference for paternal kin should be dropped, because both sides inherited equally, "often there is more property to hope for in the maternal [stock] than in the paternal," and the principal consideration should be the adequacy of the guardian rather than the kin tie. Instead, customary law should be based on the prevailing practice, which was for "the nearest and best suited" kin to be called with equal numbers from the maternal and paternal sides.[31]

Kin were often reluctant to act as guardians, and many sought to be excused from a charge whose responsibilities could be time-consuming, weighty, and fraught with problems. Unlike in some countries, guardianships brought no hope of material rewards, and most middling families already had their hands full securing an adequate life for themselves and their immediate families. Contemporaries seemed to have regarded

---

30. The mother, if she was alive, or the nearest heir of the minor had to notify judicial authorities within two weeks after the death of the father, to initiate the appointment of guardian. *La Coustume de Bretagne*, articles 486, 500, 502, 506, and 507. This particular example is taken from ADLA, B6371, 29 November 1618.

31. *La Coustume de Bretagne*, articles 484, 500, 501, 504, 506, 507, and commentaries.

guardianships as burdens rather than privileges, despite the control it gave them over property. Guardians often asserted, in declaring their willingness to accept the duty, that they were motivated only by "the affection and goodwill" that they felt for the children.[32]

Even the first essential task of a guardian, the liquidation of the estate, entailed a good deal of time and effort. When François Rapion became the guardian of his second cousin, the son of an apothecary, he had to oversee the disposal of the apothecary's tools, stock, and shop as well as supervise the rest of the property. In apparent recognition of the energy and expertise required to safeguard the interests of the child and his property successfully, the kin who chose Rapion as guardian asked a paternal uncle of the child, another apothecary, to help him.[33]

Guardians often also pursued time-consuming legal actions to defend the rights of the children. The guardian of Etienne Poullain's children, for example, emphasized the great efforts he had made on their behalf for over fifteen years in pursuing lawsuits in the Nantes court and in the Breton Parlement in Rennes. He claimed that they had consumed "the best years of his life" and impeded his ability to amass resources for his own children, whose interests had subsequently been sacrificed to those of his wards.[34]

Guardians' responsibility for the children's welfare was a serious commitment, too, because it involved overseeing their marriages and establishment in careers. All manner of other problems inherent in the supervision of young people could crop up. In 1592, the guardian of Noel Bezic's sons was taken to court by a tenant who claimed that one son had "removed by force" two casks of wine from the residence. The tenant was asking that their value be deducted from the rent due.[35] We saw earlier the role of guardians in guiding the marriage prospects of their charges in consultation with other kin.

Besides such responsibilities, guardianships often ended contentiously when children questioned the final accounting, a pattern of which we have already seen many examples, and the high mortality rates that characterized the early modern period created the potential for massive complications in efforts to settle estates.[36] Sometimes both factors operated at once.

---

32. For example, ADLA, B6377, 10 April 1631; ADLA, B6373, 16 June 1630; ADLA, B6377, 13 October 1657.
33. ADLA, B6313, 3 December 1631; ADLA, B6130, 12 March 1632.
34. ADLA, B6135, 11 August 1640.
35. ADLA, B6113, 27 May 1592.
36. See, among many instances, ADLA, B6370 (Thomas Ouairy's ward demanded an ac-

In 1631, Pierre Levallet, the guardian of the children of Jean Brisebois, was taken to court by former wards of Brisebois, who disputed the latter's handling of their estate when their father had died, thirty-five years earlier, in 1596.[37]

The problems that encumbered guardianships partly explain why discussions among kin over the choice of a guardian were often contentious—because several kin were usually trying to avoid being selected. But debates also took place, because the issues involved in making the choice were open to interpretation. A guardian's primary responsibilities, to administer the property of the children and to see to their welfare until they attained their majority or were otherwise capable of earning their living (although guardians did not necessarily have physical custody of the minors), were not, necessarily, compatible. What was best for the preservation and growth of the patrimony was not always the best for the children. The qualities that would make one person "the most effective, competent and advantageous" candidate for guardianship were open to debate, not only subjectively, but also in terms of whether the advantage of the children or that of the property was prioritized. The "nearest and most adequate" guideline for which kin were to be consulted was also open to interpretation, depending on whether the emphasis was on the kin tie or the capacity, and on adequate for what purpose. Kin were potential heirs to the property that would be managed, a factor that meant some of their arguments were certainly self-interested.

The guardianship decisions of assembled kin could and did prevail over fathers' preferences, reflecting both the general weakness of testamentary powers in customary law and the powerful role of kin in overseeing the internal affairs of households. In 1587, for example, Noel Bezic requested in his will that the husband of a distant paternal cousin be appointed the guardian of his children. After his death, however, family members selected another kinsman as guardian.[38]

Kin in this urban middling milieu almost always chose the mother as guardian when she survived the father, although Breton practice left kin free to elect another guardian. Mothers were appointed in almost 90 percent of the cases where notaries were involved. Middling widows were seldom excluded from the guardianship of their own children, but such cases

---

count of his management of the ward's patrimony); and ADLA, 4E2/90, 14 March 1647 (an *accord* made by Jean Bonnet and his wards resolving "differences" arising from his management of their patrimony).

37. ADLA, B6373, 4 March 1631.

38. AMN, II131, 30 March 1587.

suggest some of the issues that widows faced. Renée Albert, for example, was still a minor (meaning she was under twenty-five) when Charles Demons died, and her father instead took the charge of their children until his death, fifteen years later, when she finally took over. Mathurine Pigeaud, Pierre Mocet's widow, suggested another relative as guardian for her children. Her kin agreed, and the children's paternal uncle took the charge. Pigeaud's reasons are unclear, although she may have been anticipating her own remarriage (which had occurred by the time of a court case eighteen months later) and so chose not to submit either herself or her future husband to the kin scrutiny involved in the selection of a guardian.

"The greatest part" of Françoise Bellanger's kin recommended her, on condition that she provide sufficient surety, but when she failed to do so, her brother was appointed instead.[39] The failure of Bellanger's kin to act as her guarantors, as kin usually did for the person they nominated as guardian, suggests that their support of her was not wholehearted. Perhaps they were not entirely convinced of her competency, but their ambivalence highlighted the reliance of widows on kin.

Although kin usually selected widows as guardians of their children, mothers' inability to assume that position automatically pointed to differing and gendered expectations about competence among these families. While the competence of widowed fathers to be the guardians of their children was unquestioned, mothers' capacity to carry out such duties was always subject to deliberation. Widows' frequent selection as the guardians of their own children signified kin acknowledgement of individual women's competence, but kin did not extend that recognition automatically, nor did they regard women as competent to be guardians for other people's children. Widows were made guardians only of their own children or grandchildren.[40] Moreover, perceptions of the burdensomeness of guardianship meant that its assignment to mothers may have had as much to do with kin avoidance as with anything else.

When both parents were dead, kin had no alternative to look among themselves for a guardian, and their decisions were far more erratic when someone other than the mother had to be chosen.[41] The issues involved re-

39. ADLA, B6373, 15 [illegible] 1630; ADLA, B6376, 12 June 1645; ADLA, B6371, 13 May 1609; ADLA, B6377, 8 June 1652. Mothers became guardians in twenty-two out of twenty-five extant cases involving notarial families.

40. *La Coustume de Bretagne,* article 506. In this regard, usage seems to have closely followed law.

41. In contrast, the naming of the nearest relative was almost a formality among the Parisian elite in the sixteenth century: Diefendorf, *Paris City Councillors,* 280–81.

flected the flux and complexity of early modern family life. In 1631, for example, twenty kinsmen met to choose guardians for the minor children of two deceased brothers who were cousins of Simon Ertaud's.[42] One brother had married twice and had also been the guardian of his deceased brother's children. His own death meant that guardians were needed for three sets of children. Eight different kin were put forward as candidates during the deliberations, with five others mentioned as possible substitutes in case the first choices all made convincing excuses.

Various kin claimed excuses why they should not be chosen, or offered particular services in exchange for not being appointed. The husband of a maternal aunt of one set of children claimed that his occupation exempted him. The husband of the children's paternal aunt asked to be excused because his work often took him out of town. A paternal second cousin argued that his old age should exempt him. The husband of a maternal great-aunt pleaded that he already had four guardianships. Three distant paternal cousins (one in the "third degree" and the other two in the fourth) claimed they were only "poor peasants" who could not be expected to fill the charge. Three other kin promised to raise one child each without making any charge to the children's patrimony. These offers were phrased in terms of "the affection" they felt for the children, but they were also bargains by which the kin would avoid the guardianship of all the children. Ultimately, the husband of a paternal aunt (who had offered to take one child) and the husband of a woman who was the children's paternal cousin "in the fourth degree" were each made guardians. Two other offers to take care, but not be guardians, of a single child were also accepted.[43]

This pattern of nominations, excuses, and counteroffers typified many kin debates about guardianship. Occasionally efforts to avoid the charge went to greater extremes. Perhaps anticipating his nomination as guardian of the minor son of Jacques Davy, one kinsman "contested" the very fact of his kinship with the child in 1633. His objection was overridden when another cousin produced acts going back to 1575 as proof of the relationship, and his own brother confirmed their kinship.[44] Pierre Mariot had to pursue through the courts two kinsmen appointed as guardians of his nephews when they refused to take the oaths accepting the duties. One claimed that he was out of town and another that he was too ill. Mariot decried both ex-

42. ADLA, B6373, 4 and 5 February 1631.

43. ADLA, B6373, 8 February 1631.

44. ADLA, B6373, 17 December 1633. The kinsman in question had what were presumably his worst fears fulfilled when he himself was appointed guardian.

cuses as inadequate, as he had seen the former in town only the previous evening, and the latter attended daily to his business. A judge ordered both men to take the necessary oath.[45]

The multiple tensions that guardianship embraced, between the "interests" of the minor children themselves, of their property, and of their kin, were mediated in the outcomes of kin negotiations over the charge. Kin offering to take care of one child tended to express their action in terms of the affection they had for the children and their deceased parents, language that recognized, and perhaps diffused, the potential dialectic between the best interests of the children and the preservation of their property. This compromise also served the interests of the kin, while acknowledging the obligations inherent in kin relations.

Siblings were often split up among several households as the result of such compromises, pointing again to the competing interests at stake and raising the question of how well these solutions served the children's interests. In terms of protecting patrimony, these solutions worked satisfactorily. Usually the child was supported at the care provider's cost, thereby preserving the inheritance intact.

How the children themselves fared is more questionable. Early modern demographic patterns meant that complex households were common, and stable, permanent domestic situations had not yet come to have the importance attached to them that they attained in the modern era. It is striking that kin did not choose to articulate their offers in terms of the childrens' own nonpatrimonial needs or preferences. The welfare of the children, as far as the guardian was concerned, seems to have been interpreted largely as a question of patrimonial management. Moreover, the frequent disputes between guardian and children when the latter reached adulthood invariably focused on the alleged mishandling of patrimony during the period of guardianship, rather than on other aspects of the children's welfare.

Nevertheless, contention over selection of the guardian could result from genuine differences of perception of how the best interests of the children could be met. Kin differences over the guardianship of the children of Mathurin Carte articulated explicitly some of the possible permutations in individual constructions of how and by whom the interests of the children might be best served. Carte died in 1645, and his widow, Jeanne Duvau, became the guardian of their children. Her own death, two years

45. ADLA, B6123, 21 May 1618.

later, necessitated the choice of a new guardian, about whom twenty-three kin were consulted.

The Carte-Duvau kin split into two main groups during the deliberations. One set of five kin (which included Carte's nearest surviving relative, François Oger, a paternal cousin) lived in Ancennis, a small town a few miles away from Nantes. They nominated Simon Meneust, a barrister and distant ("in the fourth degree") maternal cousin of the children, "finding him competent, effective and advantageous," and offered to act as guarantors for him. Menuest and another kinsman, Raoul Boucaud, who was also a barrister, protested, accusing the Ancennis kin of forming a "league" and "plot" to avoid the guardianship.[46]

The reasoning of both sides throws light on the differing ways that the best interests of the children could be interpreted. The Ancennis kin argued that the professions of Boucaud and Meneust, their financial well-being, and residence in Nantes best fitted them to be guardians of children who were, after all, the offspring of a Nantais notary.

Boucaud and Meneust claimed that the Ancennis kin, who were "first cousins and in a closer degree [of kinship]" than themselves, "had not considered the advantage of the minors" in making their nomination. The property of the children was in the Ancennis area, and Oger, as a notary and lawyer there, could look after their affairs "without expense" to their estate. Moreover, another distant paternal cousin ("in the fifth degree"), who was also a lawyer, had offered to take care of all the children's affairs in the Nantes courts "without salary and for the affection he has for the minors." Presumably this offer compensated for the advantage of a Nantes resident's having the guardianship. Meneust added that he was only a distant maternal cousin (fourth degree), that he was not married and not permanently resident in Nantes. His appointment as guardian, he warned, "would be the total ruin of the children." For him, a guardian who was on the spot to oversee the patrimony, whose household included a wife, and who was the nearest suitable kin would serve the best interests of the children.

Property was a central factor for all sides in this debate. When offering to provide the necessary surety of solvency for Meneust, the guardian of their choice, the Ancennis kin noted that they were "perfectly cognizant" of the fact that Carte and Duvau had died owing "a large sum of money" that the sale of their personal property (*biens meubles*) would not cover. Meneust ad-

---

46. ADLA, B6376, 23 April 1647 and 9 May 1647.

mitted that he had "important business" with the children, who owed him more than 2,000 *livres* in inherited debts. Boucaud and Meneust questioned the financial solvency of most of the Ancennis kin, who were, they felt, for that reason, dubious providers of surety for the guardian, presumably leaving the latter with the possibility of lone responsibility for the settlement of the debts in question.

Meneust finally suggested that the advice of the "distant kin," who had given their opinion with Oger in Ancennis and who "did not have any property," should be disregarded. In their place, six or seven of "the most solvent kin" should be asked to consider the issue. He apparently included himself among this group, as he went on to suggest that Oger or a maternal first cousin be appointed. Oger was appointed as guardian, and the seven kin who had nominated him were named as the guarantors.[47] Significantly, these included both Boucaud and Meneust and their respective brothers, suggesting that the opinion of the "most solvent" had been given weight.

Affective and economic interests were two sides of the same coin, as the rearrangements of kin relationships necessitated by the parents' death were worked out. Boucaud and Meneust felt that neither of them should be appointed guardian as long as other candidates, more appropriate in their eyes, were available. In their opposition, though, they continued to acknowledge the obligations that ties of kinship imposed, and to participate in overseeing the patrimonial affairs of the household by providing security for the eventual guardian.

Guardianship deliberations revealed again the extensiveness and obligations of kin ties in this milieu. Cousins of the fourth degree were commonly included, and it was not rare to include as well those of the fifth or sixth degree. Moreover, when nominating guardians and acting as guarantors for a person's solvency or offering other help, such as taking one child or providing professional expertise, kin accepted the obligations that their relationship imposed.

Negotiations over guardianships highlighted the lines of gender and authority in middling families. Fathers, as "natural" guardians, were not subject, as mothers were, to either initial approval or subsequent supervision of this kind. As at other key moments in the household's handling of patrimony, consultation with kin provided a social guarantee that the property in question was being appropriately managed. The reluctance of kin to ac-

---

47. ADLA, B6376, 13 May 1647. In addition, Boucaud undertook to support, at his own expense, the youngest child; and the offer of Claude Pellier, the *procureur* in the Nantes court, to take care of the children's actions there without expense was also taken up.

cept the guardianship of minors also points, as we shall see in greater detail later, to the existence of distinctions between the many kin who could be called upon for advice and the much smaller group who could be mobilized for material aid. All kin expected to give advice on the patrimonial management of individual households, but they also expected that only certain kin would be primarily responsible for the provision of aid.

Widowhood

The contingency of widows' appointments as guardians, in contrast to the automatic continuation of widowed fathers as their children's guardians, is one illustration of the differing attributes of gender in households. A spouse's death inevitably disrupted a household, affectively and logistically, but the consequences for the surviving spouse and for the ways that property was held were quite gender-specific. Although widows became heads of households, they did not simply replace their husbands, as their differential situation with regard to surviving children indicated. Widows' experiences of widowhood suggests how the gender patterns that were integral to the creation of authority in a household and between households affected men and women differently.

Widows did acquire, as heads of households, all sorts of rights that married women lacked. They could make contracts alone, manage their own property, and remarry without the permission of their families. Widows of notaries, like other widows, took advantage of their acquisition of a legal personality. They lent money in the form of *rentes,* and in myriad other ways took on many of the activities associated with head-of-household status.[48] They made leases as tenants and owners, sued landlords for repairs, bought and sold land, and dealt with unexpected crises, as in the case of Louise Lucas, who petitioned the city for help in ransoming a son seized by pirates in the Mediterranean and held captive in Algeria.[49]

For these reasons, widowhood has often been viewed as a time of expanded opportunity for early modern women. Freed from the constraints

48. For the financial dealings of rich urban widows in Nantes and elsewhere in the seventeenth century, see James Collins, "The Economic Role of Women in Seventeenth-Century France," *French Historical Studies* 16 (Fall 1989), esp. 456–57.

49. Notarial records provide many examples of widows as landlords, tenants, sellers, and purchasers of real property and *rentes.* See ADLA, 4E2/21, January 1639, and 4E2/1760, 14 September 1639, for petitions seeking city help to pay the ransom of a son.

of marriage, widows were legally able to participate in many aspects of public and personal life, running businesses, managing their own financial affairs, and enjoying other advantages of head-of-household status. The household organization of society, historians have argued, allowed widows to enjoy significantly more status and opportunity than did wives.[50]

Despite widows' capacities, they encountered pressures that widowers did not face. In a variety of ways, a husband's death caused greater disruption and opportunity for contention than did the death of a wife. In early modern society, legal access to property was not enough to empower women. In reality, most widows did not own sufficient property to guarantee independent existences. But even financial security could not always counteract prevailing patrimonial practices that were often unfavorable to widows, as they were to wives, in their emphasis on oversight and supervision by a broad group of male kin rather than household autonomy.[51]

When a notary's wife died, he (like any man in his position) remained as the head of his household, and, although an inventory had to be made to ensure that their community property would be divided equally, the demands on the estate were relatively few, so long as children survived who could inherit their mother's lineage property. The widowed husband continued to have legal control over the family patrimony and over his minor children, just as he had previously (although, as we have seen, maternal kin expected to be consulted about the management of any matrilineal property). As among other social groups in early modern Europe, most notary-widowers remarried quickly, thereby restoring their households, at least practically, as new wives' labor and dowries replaced those of their predecessors.[52]

50. See, for example, Barbara Diefendorf, "Widowhood and Remarriage in Sixteenth-Century Paris," *Journal of Family History* 7 (Winter 1982); Sherrin Marshall Wyntjes, "Survivors and Status: Widowhood and Family in the Early Modern Netherlands," *Journal of Family History* 7 (Winter 1982); R. Vann, "Towards a New Lifestyle: Women in Preindustrial Capitalism," in Renata Bridenthal and Claudia Koonz, eds., *Becoming Visible: Women in European History* (Boston, 1977).

51. Factors other than wealth were critical in determining widows' freedom at other times and places. See, for instance, the variety of issues suggested by: Christiane Klapisch-Zuber, "The 'Cruel' Mother: Maternity, Widowhood, and Dowry in Florence in the Fourteenth and Fifteenth Centuries," in her *Women, Family, and Ritual in Renaissance Florence* (Chicago, 1985); Alice C. Metcalf, "Women and Means: Widows and Family Production in Colonial Brazil," *Journal of Social History* 24 (Winter 1990); Lyndal Roper, *The Holy Household: Women and Morals in Reformation Augsburg* (Oxford, 1989), esp. 49–54; Adrienne Rogers, "Women and the Law," in Samia Spencer, ed., *French Women and the Age of the Enlightenment* (Bloomington, Ind., 1984).

52. As a general rule, men remarried within several months. Michèle Baulant, "La Famille en miettes: Sur un aspect de la démographie du dix-septième siècle," *Annales E.S.C.* 27 (July–October 1972), 959.

When husbands died, on the other hand, widows found themselves in some quite different circumstances. As a practical matter, middling women, like all widows in early modern France, were far more likely to live out their lives without remarrying than were their spouses in the same situation. Although women who were widowed in their twenties with small children remarried more often than did other widows, the more numerous women who became widows after their late thirties tended to live as widows for years or even decades.[53]

Many women in notarial families shared this experience. Renée Coquet, the daughter of the notary Julien, was not yet twenty-five when she became a widow for the first time. She remarried Jean Bachelier in 1617 and was widowed for a second time in her early thirties, in 1626. She brought up her two surviving children alone and lived, without remarrying, for at least another thirty years. Clemence Collin was already a widow in 1605 when she married the widowed notary Michel Coupperie. He died in 1619, leaving her with three young daughters, and she remained a widow until her death in 1656.

Some pressures that were common after the death of either spouse affected widows more severely. Women were not especially disadvantaged in terms of the costs that occurred whichever spouse died (unless other arrangements had been made like those described in the preceding chapter), like funeral expenses and the evaluation of family property as a prelude to its division. Marital community property was divided after the death of either spouse. In fact, in that women were legally able to renounce their stake in community property and men were not, they may have had a certain advantage. However, the transmission of property entailed the division of debts as well as assets, and the settling of accounts presumably left widows with far less to live on than when their households had enjoyed the revenues of husbands' occupations. In addition, while the expenses and claims associated with patrimonial division always provided scope for conflict with kin, widows' dower entitlements were gender-specific burdens on patrimonies.[54]

---

53. Of 107 notarial marriages ending before 1660 where the date of death of the first spouse is certain, the death of the husband ended 71 marriages and that of the wife, 36. Of 52 cases where marital status was certain at death, 46 women died as widows, compared with only 6 men who were widowers when they died. About 50 percent of widowers remarried in early modern France, as opposed to only 20 percent of widows. André Burgière, "Réticences théoriques et intégration practique du remariage dans la France d'Ancien Régime, dix-sep-tième–dix-huitième siècle," and Guy Cabourdin, "Le Remariage en France sous l'Ancien Régime, seizième–dix-huitième siècles," both in J. Dupaquier, ed., *Marriage and Remarriage in Populations of the Past* (New York, 1981), 42, 274–78.

54. The death of the husband as an especially potent disruption for these reasons has been noted elsewhere. See, for example, Jonathan Dewald, *The Formation of a Provincial Nobility: The*

Moreover, widows in notarial families, like other widows who were below the elite, confronted economic obstacles that widowers did not. Notaries' wives shared with many of their counterparts the lack of a patrimony sufficient to guarantee a comfortable subsistence, and husbands' deaths removed a major source of income.[55] Most nonelite widows were left with few legitimate sources of income and many expenses. Widows of notaries, as well as those of artisans in crafts like goldsmithing, where wives could not carry on their husbands' occupations, had even fewer options than the widows of men whose work and income women might be able to continue, in some form. Widows' prominence as lenders was, in part, due to the fact that they had few other ways to employ their property profitably. Nevertheless, because many borrowers did not pay the interest due on time, even widows with some money to lend could not rely on a regular income.

Widows were also excluded from certain key family privileges and responsibilities that were normally associated with head-of-household status. Most notably, given the dynamic of family life in urban middling communities, while widows were not legally barred from the kin assemblies that played such important roles in the management of wide-ranging patrimonial matters, they almost never participated in these consultations.[56] In such matters, therefore, widows had no voice, or had to rely on adult sons or other male kin to represent the views and interests of their households, as husbands had done previously.

The rearrangement of property that deaths of husbands triggered provided a central focus for familial efforts to contain the parameters of wid-

---

Magistrates of the Parlement of Rouen, 1499–1610 (Princeton, 1980), 294–97. Judith Bennett has argued that changes in household status had far greater implications for women than for men in her *Women in the Medieval English Countryside: Gender and Household in Brigstock Before the Plague* (Oxford, 1987).

55. It seems noteworthy then that most conclusions about the autonomy of widows have been based on the experiences of elite women, a focus that hides the difficulties that the majority faced (see, for instance, the work cited in note 51, above). When historians have looked at a broader socioeconomic sector, they have emphasized the importance of economic factors in determining widows' autonomy. Vivian Brodsky, "Widows in Late Elizabethan London: Remarriage, Economic Opportunity, and Family Orientations," in Lloyd Bonfield, ed., *The World We Have Gained: Histories of Population and Social Structure* (London, 1986); and Olwyn Hufton, "Women Without Men: Widows and Spinsters in Britain and France in the Eighteenth Century," *Journal of Family History* 9 (Winter 1984).

56. Extant records of kin gatherings involving notarial families to give advice on many different issues include only two exceptions to this practice. In each case, a guardian was to be appointed, and a grandmother offered to act as guardian in one case and to take care of one of the children in the other. Their offers were accepted and may explain their insertion into a forum in which widows were generally absent. ADLA, B6376, 2 March 1644 and 30 September 1645.

ows' independence, through the patterns of guardianship and other actions. As well, it provided a setting in which widows could negotiate the various pressures they faced. Kin who chose a widow as the guardian of her
children, for example, not only endorsed her competence, but partially re-
solved the contradictions that a female household head raised, because kin
could continue to supervise a guardian's performance. The kin gatherings
that chose guardians settled other matters at the same time, such as the
terms on which successions should be accepted. Martine Coquet's kin, for
instance, gave her the guardianship of her six remaining minor children,
but made other decisions at the same time, including that she should rent
or sell her husband's apothecary shop on the best possible terms, to produce profit for the children.

In some cases, male kin exercised a more general supervisory role over a
widow's patrimonial management, extending far beyond the immediate
decision making at the time they appointed her as guardian. Martin Minquet's widow, Guyonne Carte, secured the guardianship of her children after her mother, Claude Legaigneux (Jean Carte's widow), guaranteed her
solvency. However, a provision that the children's paternal uncle or two of
Carte's male cousins had to be present when any loan was repaid—that is,
when any significant sum of liquid capital came into her hands—significantly restricted her patrimonial administration.[57]

Widows lost their guardianships if they remarried, and they had to either
submit themselves again to the judgment of their kin, if they wanted their
new husbands to take over the duty, or give up the management of their
children's property and persons. Kin, once more, deliberated on the appointment of a new guardian, and, although stepfathers were often chosen,
kin could express their disapproval by appointing someone else.[58] Isabel
Daguin, for example, "lost the charge for having remarried in haste for the
third time," whereas Daguin's second husband had been the guardian of
the children of her previous marriage. Her children became the wards of
their maternal uncle.[59] Through kin power to remove guardianship and the

57. ADLA, B6372, 3 July 1627; ADLA, B6374, 22 February 1635.
58. Examples of stepfathers' taking over guardianships include Raoul Boucaud, who became the guardian of Julien Mesnard's daughter on his marriage to Mesnard's widow, Olive
Berthelot; and Robert Poullain and his siblings, who were under the tutelage of their stepfather. A similar tendency to appoint stepfathers as guardians existed in the families of the Parisian municipal elite. Diefendorf, *Paris City Councillors*, 281.
59. See ADLA, B6376, 30 September 1645, for the appointment of the guardian following
Daguin's third marriage; and ADLA, B6373, 21 January 1633, for the appointment of her second husband as the guardian of her children from her first marriage.

rights it entailed, kin were able to discourage, if not prevent, widows' marriages of which they disapproved. Conversely, kin willingness to appoint stepfathers as the new guardians served to encourage the reconstruction of conjugal families that reaffirmed the structures of patriarchal households.

Widows could hope to defuse potential criticism by formally consulting male kin at an early stage, in order to validate their actions. Just as the presence and advice of kin validated the judiciousness of the decisions taken during the construction of patrimony of individual households, so widows could also use this resource to avert criticism and family dispute. When Clemence Coupperie, the widow of Guillaume Chapelain, accepted the guardianship of her children, she articulated what seems to have been a prevalent, but usually implicit, understanding with male kin. She "asked them to give advice to avoid expenses" (presumably connected to the settling of the estate), and to advise her "how she should behave in accepting the succession of her deceased husband and selling his office of notary."[60] Similar gestures characterized other such moments.

Such consultation, however, increased the influence of male relatives and circumscribed widows' ability to make their own patrimonial decisions, pointing to the ways in which widows were quite differently situated from widowers. Although all appointed guardians were subject to kin oversight of their stewardship, these kinds of limits went far beyond the role that kin usually had in assessing a husband or father's management of his household, a real supervision, but one that was predicated on the expectation of success. When the guardian was a male household head, kin would intervene only when given proof of failure or inadequacy, rather than assuming the need for a close eye on many day-to-day transactions from the start.

Widows had to negotiate the line between meeting cultural representations of model widowhood and the practical exigencies of managing daily life and handling the available patrimony, or face opprobrium. They seem to have been well aware of the issues involved. Renée Albert (Charles Demons's widow) petitioned in 1645 to be granted the guardianship of her son after the death of his previous guardian, appointed while she was herself a minor. She framed her request in a way designed to meet patriarchal assumptions about virtuous widowhood. During the fifteen years of her

---

60. ADLA, B6377, 13 October 1657. All successions could be accepted as they were ("purely and simply"), or "*sous bénéfice d'inventaire*," which protected the creditors. Widows also had the choice (which their husbands did not) of renouncing their marital property communities and simply taking back their dowries, an option that was to a widow's advantage if the community was heavily indebted, as many seem to have been.

widowhood, Albert claimed, she had "applied herself to her widowhood . . . with honor." The judge asked "four or five" of her son's relatives to give their opinion, and presumably they confirmed Albert's assertion, because she was granted the guardianship some weeks later.[61]

Widows with minor children who were facing financial difficulty could petition the city court to order kin to help support the children, a legal resource that epitomized the complexities of widowhood. Louise Lucas, left with three small children after the death of Charles Germont in 1623, requested a kin *contribution* one year later on the grounds that she had no means to provide for the children, the oldest of whom was only five. The court eventually ordered fourteen of the children's kin to share the payment of 60 *livres* a year to support the children, until they were old enough to earn their living.[62] Petitions like this one apparently usually succeeded, despite the occasional protests of kin as to the actual sufficiency of resources.[63] Widows who sought *contributions* took advantage of community expectations about kin support, but were also forced into dependency on those kin.

One dispute between a young widow and her kin illustrates some of the ways in which cultural expectations constrained widows' behavior, despite their legal abilities. In 1646, Jeanne Deniau, the widow of a pewterer, requested a court order to force her kin to contribute to the maintenance of her two children, as well to that of a third she was expecting, "since she had no means to feed them." The kin protested on the grounds that she had the stock of her husband's shop and was "able bodied." Moreover, they added, she had taken to going daily to bars, where she gambled; her clothes were "sumptuous and excessive in comparison to her status"; she had hired a servant at the highest wages; and she made all kinds of other "prodigal and superfluous acts." They pointed out that she would have an "abundance" of resources if she retrenched. Tellingly, Deniau's kin con-

---

61. ADLA, B6376, 17 May 1645 and 12 June 1645.

62. ADLA, B6370, 11 March 1625.

63. The kin of Alexander Houet and his five minor siblings complained, for example, that the patrimony of the children was more than sufficient for their mother to support them and demanded a copy of the inventory of the parents' community property. ADLA, B6376, 13 April 1649.

The order itself was, of course, no guarantee of payment. Nine petitions for *contributions* involving notarial families were all granted, but in one of these cases, for example, the mother, Gratienne Tantin, had to get a court order to force Hervé Trebillard to pay the six months of arrears that he owed to support her minor children. There is no way of telling how often such arrears arose. ADLA, B6138, 23 August 1641; and ADLA, B6134, 30 January 1638.

trasted her household management with that of her deceased husband, who, they asserted, had refused even to have a servant, "because he wanted to make the best [of his resources] to leave something to his children."[64]

On one level, the focus of Deniau's kin on her lack of *mesnagement* (in contrast to that of her husband) mobilized an important core principle of urban middling families. Kin, as we have seen, also criticized men for poor household management, on grounds of poor judgment and failure to be *bons mesnagers*, whether through spendthriftiness or idleness. This pattern is evident in their depositions in support of women's petitions for separations of property.

Deniau's kin also, however, constructed a more gender-specific critique in the particular complaints that they made of her behavior. They clearly perceived her as a disorderly woman, whose weaknesses had been given free rein by the removal of her husband's constraining hand. The natural proclivity of women for disorderliness was a powerful tenet in French culture. Women's subjection to their husbands was one means to counteract this tendency, as was the elevation of marriage as the only acceptable female secular state.[65] More than that, by charging Deniau with visiting bars, an important site of male sociability, dressing beyond her status, and committing other excesses, they emphasized the transgressions of sexual propriety that were often associated with prostitutes.[66] They not only complained that she was a poor manager of her household, but implied sexual license. In this sense, these kin critiques went beyond those that were likely to be leveled at male household heads.

Some widows, including the financially better off, chose to defuse the tension surrounding their status by transferring the public responsibilities associated with head-of-household status to male kin.[67] By choosing to cede

64. ADLA, B6139, 17 December 1646. Deniau, of course, denied their allegations as "against the truth." She claimed to have borrowed money that had to be repaid to restock her husband's shop, to have only one black dress and no servant. The court eventually ignored her kin and ordered them to contribute 62 *livres* a year to the support of the children. ADLA, B6376, 28 January 1647.

65. The power of the image of the disorderly woman is discussed in Natalie Zemon Davis, "Women on Top," in her *Society and Culture in Early Modern France* (Stanford, 1975), esp. 124–26. For the association between marital status and female honor, see James R. Farr, "The Pure and Disciplined Body: Hierarchy, Mortality, and Symbolism in France During the Catholic Reformation," *Journal of Interdisciplinary History* 21 (Winter 1991), 408–14.

66. For popular characterizations of behavior associated with prostitution, including luxurious dressing and their location in male cultural domains, see Lyndal Roper, "Discipline and Respectability: Prostitution and the Reformation in Augsburg," *History Workshop* 19 (Spring 1985).

67. The pattern of widows' preferring to leave the management of their public affairs to others has also been observed in eighteenth-century Montauban. Margaret A. Darrow, *Revolu-*

the public roles associated with the status of a head of household to others, widows may have been responding to the disjuncture between their legal capacity and pervasive cultural ambivalence about independent women.

When Clemence Collin's husband, Michel Coupperie, died in 1619, she dealt with a broad range of responsibilities. She rode out to rural small holdings with her stepson to oversee the making of an inventory, settled the division of the patrimony with the children of her husband's first marriage, and took care of her daughters. Yet, as her daughters married in subsequent years, she transferred the public management of her assets to a son-in-law and lived with a married daughter. In 1654, Collin declared that she "had not needed money for more than fifteen years," as one son-in-law "did all her business." She added that "when she needed money Tesnier her son-in-law gave it to her."[68] In public matters, it was almost as if she had remarried.

Like Collin, other widows took up residence in their adult children's households. The child in question was usually a daughter whose husband then managed the widow's affairs.[69] Mathurine Pigeaud, Pierre Mocet's widow, went to live with her daughter and bookseller son-in-law. They agreed "to give her the care and assistance required by a person of her age which is about 65," and in return she turned over her income to them.[70] Other widows made less formal agreements, reckoning costs in periodic accountings.[71]

Growing infirmity may explain some of these cases, but old age was not the only factor behind such arrangements. Françoise Rousseau, Jacques Denan's mother-in-law, and a child of hers who was still a minor lived with her daughter's family. The age of her young child implies that Rousseau was not elderly. Clemence Collin, Coupperie's widow, lived with her daughter Magdelaine, the wife of Etienne Tesnier, for about twenty years. Renée Rousselet lived with her daughter and son-in-law starting on the day of their marriage. The longevity of these arrangements and others suggests that more than frailty lay behind them.

Even widows who did not live with their children made similar arrangements to withdraw from the public management of their affairs, belying the

---

tion in the House: Family, Class, and Inheritance in Southern France, 1775–1825 (Princeton, 1989), 117.

68. ADLA, B5816, 28 July 1654.

69. For more on the way a wife's kin, including her mother, were more likely to reside in the same household, see Chapter 3.

70. ADLA, 4E2/141, 26 June 1643.

71. See, as a typical instance among many examples, ADLA, 4E2/463, 15 May 1638.

possibility that shared households alone accounted for the practice. Hester Mellet, for example, arranged with her son Julien Mainguy that he would enjoy all her revenues from her share of her community with his deceased father, as well as her dower, in return for acquitting her of all payments that she might owe and paying her 36 *livres* a year. Guillaume Garnier's accounting with his mother-in-law revealed that he had undertaken many activities on her behalf, including collecting rents and her share of inheritances, paying money that she owed for loans and *rentes,* settling with artisans who had repaired a roof, and undertaking legal actions.[72]

On the other hand, men in this milieu, whether married or widowers, rarely withdrew from management of their affairs or gave up the maintenance of separate households. Most notaries worked until they died, judging by the dates of the sales of their offices, and notarial records of all kinds of formal transactions indicate that they also continued to take care of their family's affairs.[73] While the difficulties that widows faced in maintaining head-of-household status may have encouraged them to look for ways to minimize the challenges that their position offered to the patriarchal order, men found it equally important to retain that status, to emphasize their social and political authority.

The pressures that female head-of-household status entailed motivated widows to turn the public handling of many of their affairs over to the next generation. When women took care of these responsibilities, they practically and symbolically exceeded the boundaries of guarded speech and behavior that were regarded as the pillars of female honor. Widows who conceded their public roles compromised the independence that the status of widowhood formally bestowed, but they protected their own status as honorable women. Although widows may certainly have continued to have a powerful say in family affairs, as wives seem to have done, their concession of the public actions of head of household combined with the cultural bias against independent women to compromise the authority that widowhood legally offered.

Women's understanding of the state of widowhood and the availability of other options may also have shaped their handling or concession of their

---

72. ADLA, 4E2/835, 2 July 1652; ADLA, 4E2/1700, 18 March 1643.

73. I have found only one exception to this practice. In 1656, André Charier handed over management of his affairs to his son and two sons-in-law, as a result of an illness that he felt did not allow him to manage his domestic affairs or his property. Even this solution was markedly different from the kinds of choices that widows made: they chose one child alone to have control, whereas Charier split the responsibility between all his heirs. ADLA, B5873, 20 July 1656.

public head-of-household responsibilities. Their willingness to hand over the role of patrimonial manager and public representative of the household may be explained by their perceiving widowhood as a transitional phase, during which they were responsible for preserving the patrimony as it passed between generations, rather than as a definitive and self-contained status. Renée Albert's own characterization of her fifteen years of widowhood as a time in which she applied herself to that status may reflect this role.

Generational timing partly explains why some widows were active managers of their affairs, while others allowed a son or son-in-law to handle the public business associated with head-of-household status. Many widows acted as heads of household only as long as their children were still minors, when they did not have even the option of transferring management.

Cultural ambivalence about widows combined with inheritance practices to create contexts for contention about the division of community property between widows and heirs. Which property was included in the marital property community, to be divided in half between the wife and the heirs of her husband, became a matter of prime concern, and the insecurity of widows' authority perhaps encouraged children to challenge the process. Marguerite Bernard and the sons of her second husband, Claude Geneste, quarreled endlessly about the division of community property, with Geneste's offices as fundamental points of contention. She maintained that the offices were marital community property, as acquisitions resulting from their own efforts, and not lineage property, as the sons maintained. Bernard and Geneste's sons were also locked in conflict over the personal property left at his death, as were the sons of Jean Quenille and their stepmother, Estmaguette Demasalne. In both cases, the stepchildren claimed property that they felt was theirs as heirs of their mothers, arguing that it should not be considered as part of the community of their fathers and stepmothers.[74]

Widows' tendency to use children or sons-in-law to act on their behalf could also highlight differences in the interests of widows and those of other heirs, including their own children or stepchildren. Jeanne Duchesne, for example, eventually reached an out-of-court settlement after a prolonged dispute with her eldest son, Pierre, over the "payment and reimbursement" of various monies after the death of his father, Jean Charier.[75]

---

74. ADLA, 4E2/450, 24 March 1611; ADLA, B6215, 15 June 1620.
75. ADLA, 4E2/1572, 19 March 1622.

Duchesne pointed out that she was not responsible for paying the funeral expenses of her husband and was liable for only half of the debts of their community property. In addition, their children, as his heirs, had to pay her dower and compensate her for the portion of her lineage property that her husband had alienated. For these reasons, Duchesne wanted her son to account for the money in the house at the time of his father's death, as well as for revenues from community property received since then. She was not appeased by her son's assertion that she knew that such income "had for the greatest part been consumed" by the upkeep of the family's two households (one in Nantes and a rural property), the other children, and household expenses. No doubt Duchesne resisted this reasoning on the grounds that their community ceased with the inventory made after her husband's death. Thus she was not liable to bear such expenses alone.

In this case, like others, tensions were fueled not only by the widow's assertion of her own distinct rights, but also by her designation of one child to act in the public sphere in matters for which the head of household was ordinarily responsible. Duchesne admitted that her son had "handled and managed" the business of the family after his father's death. Clearly it was the division of responsibility that had created the space for conflict to arise.

Perhaps more commonly, a widow's chosen public representative did not himself fall out with her, but the intermingling of their affairs aroused the suspicion of other siblings. The possibility that such arrangements subverted the strict egalitarian tenets of the Breton inheritance system was a trigger for sibling rivalry. During Françoise Rousseau's widowhood, for example, her son-in-law Guillaume Garnier, rather than her son Charles Demons, handled many of her affairs. After her death, Garnier attempted to get his sister-in-law Renée Albert, who was Demons's widow and Rousseau's daughter-in-law, to pay half of what he claimed Rousseau owed him. Albert asserted that his claims had been "extorted" from Rousseau with the intention of frustrating the claims of her own son, who was his grandmother's legitimate heir. Albert also claimed that Garnier and his wife had been favored with gifts of wood, grain, money, and furniture that had not been accounted for. One son-in-law's handling of Clemence Collin's affairs also divided her three daughters' husbands, leading the other two to charge Collin with intending to deprive their wives of their inheritances.[76] In a slightly different slant on a similar theme, the children of

76. ADLA, B6138, 31 August 1645; ADLA, B5816, 28 July 1654. The animosity between Collin's sons-in-law was presumably shared by their wives, but in the public world of the law, this element manifested itself only between the men, as heads of households.

Guyonne Carte (Martin Minquet's widow) also ended up in a legal battle. The son-in-law appointed as Carte's guardian (after she had been declared incapable of handling her own affairs) was accused of using the charge to his own profit and to the detriment of Carte, and, by implication, that of the family patrimony in which they all had a stake.[77]

Widows and their contemporaries tried to resolve the incongruity of female heads of household by constructing close ties between widows and their kin. Widows could not escape the constraints of a gender hierarchy, with all its implications for the ordering of power relations, maintained by male kin between households as well as by husbands and fathers within households. As wives, women faced multiple legal restrictions, but many opportunities for practical action and influence as well. As widows, they enjoyed unprecedented legal rights, but faced pervasive cultural and economic constraints closely tied to their access to property.

Practices surrounding donations, separations, widowhood, and guardianship appointment illustrated the extent to which patrimony linked individual households to other households of kin. The pattern of kin supervision of the affairs of any given household replicated, in the patrimonial domain, the structures of supervision, reinforcement, and upholding of obligation that were evident in other aspects of daily household life.

While royal rhetoric and marriage laws emphasized individual households as the locus of gender relations and strengthened the hand of fathers over marriage, kin supervision of affairs of individual households tempered the power of husbands and fathers as heads of household.

Kin oversight appears at first glance as an important counterbalance to the gender hierarchy at the heart of early modern social and political organization, but gender hierarchies were just as powerful in the context of overall patrimonial practices of middling families. The implications for women were most clear when widows were left as heads of households. Legal access to property did not in itself secure female power or status, because it was only one part of a larger system of property management that male kin dominated. Gender disabled widows even at this most opportune moment for female independence, just as at other times in women's lives. The access to property that women legally enjoyed in this community less enhanced their position vis-à-vis their husbands in their own households than reinforced the links between households that served to consolidate power and gender hierarchies in middling urban communities. The coop-

---

77. ADLA, B6374, 2 May 1639; and ADLA, B6377, 12 May 1656.

eration of male kin—as well as that of husbands and fathers—whose households were linked by shared patrimonial concerns was an important source of authority on a day-to-day basis. Men dominated kin gatherings, which had both the legal right and the cultural authority to oversee the affairs of individual households and to intervene when the *bon mesnagement* of any one household appeared to be breaking down.

The role of kin as a critical element in patrimonial practice underlay the maintenance of gender hierarchies, which continued to be at the heart of power axes and daily relations among these families. While husbands did not totally control their wives' interests, women's ability to counteract the power of their husbands lay largely in the continued and active collaboration of their own kin, rather than in a capacity of independent action. Customary law and the preferences of some family members structured patrimony in ways that made kin ties extremely important. The role of kin in playing important supervisory roles in managing patrimony became clear at what were culturally defined as key moments in the transmission of property.

The patrimonial practices of middling families illustrate, again, the ways in which daily practices could provide a means of framing larger political debates. The pervasiveness of familial analogies in the critiques of the king's ministers and advisers that were rampant in much of the seventeenth century, for example, were perhaps the macro-equivalent of the contention over guardianships and patrimony that divided kin in the microcosmic contexts of managing households. The power of familial politics in early modern France lay in the way it could epitomize the goals of many different groups. The brick-by-brick process of maintaining and naturalizing cultural hierarchies also involved the labor and energy of ordinary people in relationships beyond the familial, a process that subsequent chapters explore.

6

Dividing Patrimony

When Jean Bonnamy made his will in 1630, he asked that after his death, six priests from his local parish church of St. Saturnin carry his body to the church and bury him there, and he left the details about other prayers to his mother, Renée Rousselet, widow of François Bonnamy. The following year she made her own will, in which she, too, wanted to be buried in the parish church of St. Nicolas, but she asked more specifically to be buried "in front of the altar of St. Anne near her deceased husband." Like Bonnamy and Rousselet, most notaries and their wives were buried in their local parish churches, usually asking in their wills to be laid to rest there with services and memorial masses that varied according to their means and tastes. Sometimes they wanted to be buried near deceased spouses or parents, sometimes near a specific altar, and sometimes they left the decisions about the exact place of burial to their kin or the church's priests and vestry members.[1]

A spouse's death paved the way for the ultimate division of a household's

---

1. ADLA, 4E2/94, 9 September 1630; ADLA, 4E2/461, 17 May 1631. Too few wills for notaries and their wives survive to allow more specific patterns to be discerned.

patrimony, a moment of critical decision making for children and other heirs. In the process of dividing a household's patrimony, as in its construction, laws, together with individual and familial decisions, again shaped and reflected personal relationships in determining patterns of property holding and management. Lines of friction and cooperation crystallized as the claims, obligations, and expectations of different parties were satisfied or frustrated. Steps in this last process included the reporting of gifts that heirs had received, the making of shares to be distributed, and subsequent efforts to sort out inheritances in ways that met individual goals.

Partitioning Patrimony

A household finally dissolved with the final division of its patrimony among the heirs, a two-stage process that involved a preliminary reporting by each heir of what he or she had already received from the estate, followed by the making of shares and the selection by each heir of a share. The final decisions in property transmissions, like all the earlier decisions, depended on both legal guidelines and family strategies. The tendencies of patrimonial management and the intra-familial tensions that had evolved throughout the construction and gradual breakup of a household all came into play again during the household's final dispersion.

Breton customary law, like that of the rest of northern France, set very egalitarian standards for inheritance. Daughters as well as sons had equal claims on non-noble estates, and the principle of forced return to the succession required that gifts received previously be declared, so that the final portions that each claimant received would reflect long-term equality. Parents' testamentary powers were severely restricted, so they had few means, at this stage, to evade the legal requirement of partibility. The legal code once again invoked the idea of consultation with other kin, to guarantee the acceptability of decisions affecting household patrimony. If the heirs were unable to agree over the settlement, it suggested, they should put the matter "before their relations to agree amiably" and without resorting to legal action, if possible.[2]

As a first step in the process of dividing an estate, all heirs met to report any monies or property in kind that each had previously received. These

---

2. *La Coustume de Bretagne avec les Commentaires et Observations . . . par Maître Michel Sauvageau* (Nantes, 1710), articles 455, 587, 596, and 566.

declarations might include large sums for dowries or offices, as well as many smaller amounts. Sometimes these statements were quite straightforward, as when the two surviving children of Jean Bachelier reported what their parents had given to each of them. (Their exceptionally large inheritance also attested to a successful social mobility that many notarial families may have hoped for but few achieved.) The children reported having received a total of 30,400 *livres*. Twenty-four thousand *livres* had been used to purchase a legal position for the son, and 8,000 *livres* had gone to the daughter's dowry, but she returned 1,600 *livres* to her mother as loans, in the form of *rentes*. The son also reported 100 *livres* that he had already given his sister, and 60 *livres* that he had given his mother.[3]

The accounting was more complicated in other cases, and heirs could disagree over what was to be included and what was exempt. In 1601, for example, the deaths of Guillaume Leroy and Jeanne Callo left their five children and the widower of a sixth to report what each had already taken out of their parents' property. Olivier had received more than 1,400 *livres*, including 1,180 *livres* to buy his office of notary and a 258-*livres* loan from his mother. Jeanne and her husband, Michel Coupperie, had been given a dowry of 540 *livres* and a cow worth 6 *livres*. Pierre had already been given more than 2,500 *livres*, including 2,010 to purchase his office as a court usher and loans from his mother totaling more than 500 *livres*. Two siblings claimed that Pierre should also report almost 3,000 *livres* that he had "extorted" from their mother for living expenses and debts. Thomas Robo, the widower of Françoise, said they had received just over 2,350 *livres*, including a 750-*livres* dowry, 300 *livres* to pay their rent, and a 150-*livres* loan from her mother.

The exactness with which each heir's share was calculated meant that the worth of every small property transmission had to be determined. Robo and Olivier deducted from what they had to report the payments they made for Callo's funeral. Robo also deducted money he had paid for food for the marriage of Jeanne to Michel Coupperie, and for the planting of trees and other "improvements and additions" made to some rural properties at Callo's request.[4] Yet Robo's siblings-in-law thought he should report 10 *livres* that their mother had given him for grain, 16 *sous* (less than 1 *livre*) that she had paid him for "a quarter of a milk calf," and the value of two years of support that she had allegedly provided for her grandson.

The emphasis on absolute clarification of who had received what at this

3. ADLA, 4E2/1036, 16 January 1651.
4. ADLA, B6115, 19 February 1601.

stage also manifested itself in other ways, notably the minute attention paid to the costs of board and lodging, where co-heirs were keen to see that no advantage was gained. Two sons of Gilles Thomin, for example, François (who was also a notary) and Yves (a lawyer), came to court over François's demands that Yves pay him for board and lodging during three years when the latter had allegedly lived with François as a young clerk. Yves said that while he had resided in the same building, he had lived with another brother above François's residence, in a room that his now-retired father kept to use during visits to town, and that his father had supported him. Yves went on to claim that François's "fraudulent and slanderous" demand was motivated by the latter's desire to reduce the amount that he had to report to his siblings before the division of their inheritance.[5]

With the initial reporting done, heirs moved on to determine the shares that each would receive and divide the estate (*partage*). As in other regions, Breton customary law included safeguards to ensure that its commitment to equality among heirs was observed. Heirs selected lots according to their sex—with all sons (or their heirs) choosing first—and age, with the eldest having first pick, an ordering that might seem to give the eldest son a considerable advantage over the youngest daughter. Yet the last in line was charged with making up the lots from which the other heirs chose, and because the lot maker would receive the share that was left over, he or she had a clear incentive to make the lots as fair as possible.[6] Although this legal arrangement recognized a hierarchy in giving the first choices to sons, it was also meant to provide equal shares to each heir, regardless of sex or age.

In practice, the heirs of middling families closely observed equality of lots, and the emphasis on equality extended to all aspects of inheritances. Etienne Poullain and his siblings, for example, divided their parents' estate in 1620 into three lots estimated to be worth 387 *livres*, 5 *sous*; 375 *livres*, 6 *sous*, 6 *deniers*; and 385 *livres*, 8 *sous*, 11 *deniers* respectively. Even these small discrepancies had to be compensated for: they agreed that the first lot should pay 3 *deniers*, 18 *sous* a year owed on a *rente*, and that the second lot be given an extra piece of meadow to make the shares more equal. Only after making these adjustments did the siblings move on to the choice of lots. Jacquette Monnier, Pierre Granjon's wife, split the estate of her sister with

---

5. ADLA, B6126, 17 January 1626.

6. *La Coustume de Bretagne*, article 587. The customary laws of Anjou and Maine, to the east of Brittany, similarly ensured equality of lots, but by a reverse procedure where the eldest made the lots and the youngest chose first. Xavier Martin, *Le Principe d'égalité dans les successions roturières en Anjou et dans le Maine* (Paris, 1972), 161–63.

her three surviving siblings in 1630. They first agreed to divide "among them equally" all the "personal property [*biens meubles*] both in money and household goods" of their sister, as well as the costs of the "funeral rites and burial and testamentary gifts and legacies." Two months later they each chose from the lots of real property that Jacquette, as the youngest, had made up.[7]

The shares that each heir received when the final division of property occurred were similar in content as well as value, an important factor in making sure that the equality was real. The lots of daughters as well as sons included real property as well as cash, *rentes,* and debts. The practice of "preferential partibility"—that is, the favoring of sons and the preservation of real property by assigning it to one or two sons while giving cash or movables to daughters and younger sons—has been noted among peasant communities in nineteenth-century Brittany and in other partible-inheritance regions. In the sixteenth and seventeenth centuries, this practice was not at all evident.[8]

Like parents, heirs to the patrimony of middling urban families made little effort, in making shares, to evade the egalitarian impetus of the customary law. At the same time, neither particular siblings nor other heirs seem to have expected that any one of them should sacrifice their own interests to advance those of another. On the contrary, they apparently accepted that all heirs, male and female, should inherit equally.

The emphasis on absolute equality of shares in a partible inheritance system raised the prospect of multiple heirs to one estate, thereby encouraging the recognition of even quite distant kin ties. Many heirs could exist, and at quite distant relationships to the deceased, if an immediate heir had died and was "represented" by his or her own descendants. Mathurin

---

7. ADLA, 4E2/1571, 22 February 1620; ADLA, 4E2/460, 12 April 1630 and 15 June 1630. The total value of the estates or the equity of division are impossible to assess with absolute certainty. *Partages,* for example, frequently omitted any mention of personal property (although other evidence suggests that this was also divided equally). Moreover, the total value of each share was not always given. Nevertheless, a consideration of all documents dealing with the division of the estate, including accountings and other agreements as well as *partages,* allows some conclusions about the nature of the division.

On the difficulty of establishing the size of estates, see Barbara Diefendorf, *Paris City Councillors in the Sixteenth Century: The Politics of Patrimony* (Princeton, 1983), 262; and Daniel Dessert, *Argent, pouvoir, et société au Grand Siècle* (Paris, 1984), 113–16.

8. For examples drawn from nineteenth-century rural Brittany, see Martine Segalen, "'Avoir sa part': Sibling Relations in Partible Inheritance Brittany," in Hans Medick and David Warren Sabean, eds., *Interest and Emotion: Essays on the Study of Family and Kinship* (Cambridge, 1984), 135–38. For "preferential partibility," see Toby Ditz, *Property and Kinship: Inheritance in Early Connecticut, 1750–1820* (Princeton, 1986), 69.

Verger and Jacques Bernard were cousins and heirs to the estate of their childless aunt Perrine Verger, the widow of René Desmortiers. Their claim was to one half of her estate, but that half alone had to be divided into six lots, "in each of which were several kin." When Julien Rousseau died without children in 1627, the heirs to his estate included paternal kin, whose claim was based on their being cousins of Rousseau's father.[9]

These multiple claims could make the partition of estates difficult, when each share had to be equal. Verger and Bernard pointed out in frustration that it was "impossible to make any division" of their aunt's estate, when the property to be divided into six lots, each with multiple claimants, comprised one half of a house, half of a rural small holding, and payments of 160 *livres* a year for religious bequests. The logistical nightmare of the partition led them to predict "the waste of property and perpetual strife."[10]

Sometimes the form of the property made it simply impossible to divide. Offices were a primary case in point, and, although they were usually sold to avoid the problem of indivisibility, in some cases they were included in the partition. The office of Pierre Guihaud was split between his three children in the division of his estate in 1623, and it was not until 1628 that one sibling realized the asset in a useful form, by buying the other two out.[11]

Other pieces of patrimony, like the right to nominate appointees to chaplaincies, were similarly inheritable but impossible to divide. One solution was to create shares in a property that was not then actually divided or liquidated. This approach had its own problems: Marguerite Bernard argued with her stepsons after their father's death, for instance, about the patience she felt she had shown in allowing one of them to visit whenever he wished a rural property that had been in the estate of his father, "although he had only a small share" in it—one twelfth.[12] But he doubtlessly considered that his right to visit was the legitimate outcome of his own share.

Familial Alliances and Tensions

The emphasis on equality and the complexity of partibility created a potent context for potential antagonism between heirs, but nevertheless, specific

9. ADLA, 4E2/177, 26 October 1655; ADLA, B6129, 29 May 1629.
10. ADLA, 4E2/177, 26 October 1655.
11. ADLA, 4E2/1726, 23 March 1628.
12. ADLA, B6817, 14 May 1614.

patterns of conflict and cooperation among kin emerged around the efforts to pursue equitable patrimonial division. Family members valued warm relations with each other and were keenly aware of the potential costs of even the appearance of lack of equality between heirs. Stepparents and half-siblings were frequent targets for the expression of resentments. Siblings made wide-reaching efforts to accommodate the consequences of the fragmentation that ensued in each of their individual interests.

All heirs faced recurring problems in trying to make equal shares from diverse assets and debts that were always possible sources of tension. Julien Mainguy and his siblings came to an agreement that acknowledged the "differences, difficulties and disturbances" that the division of their parents' community property had created. The attempt to divide real as well as personal property into equal shares inevitably created potential difficulties for the future. Raoul Boucaud divided the estate of his first wife's parents with her four siblings. In this partition, the house of the rural small holding fell into two of the five lots; one sibling inherited the "big new main room and the two rooms above," and another the "*logia* at the end of the room and the small cellar below it."[13]

Despite such complications, even the appearance of one heir having been favored caused tension with others. Contention on these grounds was often associated with the idea that one child had somehow gained undue influence over parents or their affairs, and, as a result, had been able to "extort," to use a common phrase, some advantage. As we saw earlier, widows seem to have been especially vulnerable to this sort of suspicion.[14]

Parents sometimes tried to avoid this development. When André Charier gave up the management of his affairs due to his illness in 1656, he carefully allocated the responsibility for supervision of the patrimony to his son and two sons-in-law.[15] The assignment of joint responsibility, ensuring that none felt excluded or potentially disadvantaged, was especially prudent in this case, as Charier *père* admitted that the inheritance was heavily indebted.

Members of middling families frequently expressed the commitment to equal treatment of heirs in terms of the ties between equity and close rela-

13. ADLA, 4E2/834, 24 June 1650; ADLA, 4E2/1588, 5 December 1607.
14. See, for example, the accusations of the siblings of Pierre Leroy that he had extorted more than 2,000 *livres* from their mother; the similar accusations aimed at Guillaume Garnier by his sister-in-law after his mother-in-law's death; and the charges of favoritism leveled at Clemence Collin by two of her three sons-in-law, who felt that the third had gained some advantage by handling her affairs. ADLA, B6115, 19 February 1601; ADLA, B6138, 31 August 1645; ADLA, B5816, 28 July 1654.
15. ADLA, B5873, 20 June 1656.

tionships. Many acts involving property referred to a desire to "nourish peace and goodwill" in the family. Françoise Leroy, whose heirs included Julien Lucas and Pierre Belon, expressly articulated this sentiment in making a gift to Lucas on behalf of all his siblings. She specifically noted that they were to have equal parts of the 300 *livres* in question, "as much to acquit and discharge her conscience, not wishing to give more to one than to the other" of the children "as to prevent the lawsuits, disagreements and hostilities that could rise between them." The siblings of Guillaume Jahanneau and other heirs to his father's estate agreed to resolve a dispute "in order to nourish peace and goodwill between them as previously seeing the closeness of their kinship."[16]

The constant interplay between the qualities of family relations, which the pioneering work of Hans Medick and David Sabean has termed "interest and emotion," was at the heart of the interactions that members of these middling families had with each other. Clemence Collin, for example, was at the center of the notarial milieu. She was the daughter-in-law, wife, and stepmother of notaries, and two of her three daughters married notaries as well. In 1654, two sons-in-law charged her in a civil suit with making property arrangements that advantaged the third. In defending herself against these accusations of favoritism, Collin not only denied the formal charges but added that "she loved all her sons-in-law equally."[17] Similarly, by listing the material advantages that one of his sons had received—including education, office, and a "rich" wife—Claude Geneste refuted that son's accusations that his half-siblings were favored and that Geneste *père* had defrauded him.[18]

Tension over the handling and division of the patrimony seems to have been funneled into relationships that were viewed as less valuable in these communities, while diverting pressure from the most important relationships. The frequency of remarriage among notarial families and their contemporaries created a potent context for conflict within the family. Both half-siblings and stepparents were lightning rods for the manifestation of resentment and suspicions of wrongdoing.

The combination of a partible inheritance system that could create a

16. ADLA, 4E2/179, 8 April 1656; ADLA, 4E2/466, 19 December 1647.

17. ADLA, B5816, 28 July 1654. Collin, the daughter of a Nantes merchant, was the daughter-in-law and wife of Sebastien and Michel Coupperie, respectively, and the stepmother of Jean Coupperie. Two daughters married Guillaume Chapelain and Etienne Tesnier, and the third married Julien Martin, a *procureur.*

18. ADLA, B7080, 5 December 1608.

plethora of heirs and the complex household structures that resulted from the demographic realities of early modern life nourished the potential of remarriages to create intra-familial tensions. Pierre Lebreton and Perrine Benoist, his wife, became enmeshed in a dispute over her claims to her mother's property, made vastly complicated by the permutations that her parental household had experienced. Benoist's mother had remarried after the death of her father, and then her second husband had remarried after the mother's death. The stepfather's death left Lebreton and Benoist to take up their claim for their share of her mother's community property with the second wife of her stepfather.[19]

The negative consequences for family relations could be profound. Robert Poullain and his siblings, the children of Renée Cosson's first marriage to Etienne Poullain, came under the guardianship of the court usher Jacques Germont when their mother remarried. As the children reached adulthood, a bitter quarrel broke out when they complained of ill-treatment and the mismanagement of their patrimony. Germont complained of their ingratitude, after the effort and personal expense he had devoted to the advancement of their education, welfare, and property. The rupture was lasting and spilled over into other aspects of all their lives. Germont and Cosson sought to annul one daughter's marriage to a man they claimed had "the smell of a peasant," on the grounds that it had been clandestine. When Robert Poullain married, three years later, neither his mother nor his stepfather signed the marriage contract, a very unusual absence.[20]

The evolution of Thomas Chauveau's household revealed the process behind the growth of such hostilities. His first wife, Catherine Daniel, died, leaving three surviving children. The two older boys were old enough to start work as legal clerks, but the daughter, Jeanne, remained with her father when he remarried. Isabel Dubois, his second wife, ran a household that included Jeanne Chauveau as well as her own mother, a female servant, and an increasing number of her own offspring. After Thomas Chauveau's death, Dubois and Jeanne Chauveau fought over Dubois's effort to

---

19. ADLA, 4E2/294, 21 September 1658.

20. ADLA, B6135, 11 August 1640; ADLA, 4E2/615, 4 October 1643. Similar examples of tension between stepfathers as guardians and their stepchildren occurred over the management of their inheritance. See, for instance, ADLA, 4E2/1746, 4 August 1634 (Mathurin Carte's wife and siblings contesting with their stepfather over the account he had given of his management of their property); and ADLA, B7080, 5 December 1608 (accusations of wrongdoing by Claude Geneste in the management of his stepdaughter's affairs).

deduct 120 *livres* for each year of Jeanne's stay in their reformed household from what she had to pay to Chauveau's heirs as their part of his estate.[21]

The possibility of differential (and hence unfair) treatment of birth children and stepchildren was widely acknowledged. A stepson-in-law of Marguerite Bernard, who had been twice married to notaries, expressed the fears that lay behind such tensions in charging that by "fraud and deceit," she was advantaging the younger children of her second marriage while "forgetting those of her first husband." Bernard's second husband, Claude Geneste, defended her (his third wife) against these "infamous and scandalous" accusations of his children from earlier marriages. Geneste insisted that they were misplaced, as Bernard had "shown them so much affection and goodwill that she did not seem like a stepmother, but a true natural mother."[22]

Besides the potential grounds for hostility that were always latent in the stepparent's assumption of the parent's role in the household, the stepparent also posed a material threat to the children's future. By establishing a second household in which the new spouse could claim half of the property, and by producing more children among whom the patrimony would have to be divided, a stepparent threatened to erode the material expectations of the children of an earlier marriage.

Stepfathers who were guardians of children's patrimony (as often happened, because widows lost the legal guardianship of their children by remarrying) were often criticized by their wards on that front. Julien Belute and his siblings, for example, accused their stepfather of bringing about the "demolition and ruin" of their mother's property after her death, and thereby reducing their own expectations.[23] As we have already seen, families sometimes anticipated and maneuvered around possible disputes by including clauses in marriage contracts stipulating that the terms of the contract cleared all patrimonial obligations of guardianship.

Tensions over the partition of patrimony created splits within sibling groups and between the children of different marriages, as well as dividing children and stepparents. Guillaume Jahanneau and his siblings from his father's first marriage combined forces against a son of his second marriage who claimed that his half-siblings had taken all the documents pertaining to their father's estate as a means to maximize their share, while they "had prevented him from asking a single thing." Alexander Chebuet

21. ADLA, B6135, 3 August 1639; ADLA, B5810, 19 March and 10 May 1639.
22. ADLA, B7080, 5 December 1608.
23. ADLA, 4E2/614, 27 March 1639.

and his half-siblings ended up in court over his claim that their common mother had allegedly given the others 500 *livres* to use as a dowry, and that this gift should be reported prior to the division of their inheritance from her.[24]

The dispute between the children of the first and second marriages of Thomas Chauveau illustrated the fertile ground for conflict along the fault line that the structures of inheritance and property holding created. Differences arose regarding the successions "both of the deceased [Jeanne] Daniel [Chauveau's first wife] and of the common succession of Thomas Chauveau and the division of it between" the children of both marriages. The numerous points of dispute included the value of half of Chauveau's community with his first wife, to which their children were entitled; the 1,200 *livres* designated in the marriage contract of Chauveau and Daniel as her lineage property, to which only her children were heirs; and 200 *livres* that Daniel's father had borrowed from Chauveau more than twenty years before, for which Isabel Dubois, Chauveau's second wife, claimed that Daniel's children were liable. Dubois also claimed that the children of the first marriage should reimburse her for the costs of their mother's funeral, for the 900 *livres* that were designated as her lineage property in her marriage contract with Chauveau, and for their share of Chauveau's debts that she had paid since his death.[25]

Post-Division Strategies

Whatever tensions partibility, in law and practice, created in middling families seems to have been largely displaced onto stepparents, half-siblings, and other kin, facilitating the maintenance of good relations between siblings and their spouses. While heirs always had the choice of compromise or conflict in response to the practical difficulties that partible inheritance posed, siblings usually preferred cooperative strategies to overcome the minefield of problems that partible inheritance could create. Generally the experience of notarial families suggests that egalitarian inheritance practice fostered mutual help, rather than competitiveness and hostility, between siblings. By acting together, siblings and their spouses helped to

24. ADLA, 4E2/466, 19 December 1647; ADLA, B6113, 3 October 1594.
25. ADLA, 4E2/891, 31 October 1642.

combat some of the negative effects that partible inheritance potentially posed to their family patrimony and individual interests by fissuring the patrimony of their parents, and they furthered all their interests by combined action in defense of the patrimony as a whole.

Siblings frequently combined to resolve problems raised by the division of property, and to avoid the unnecessary losses that individual actions might entail. Jacques Denan pursued legal actions pending over the estate of his parents-in-law "at the prayer and request" of his wife's three siblings and their spouses. The latter gave Denan the power to make the settlement as he saw fit on their behalf, and agreed to split all the costs equally. Pierre Belon and his siblings chose to purchase jointly a *rente* to raise the money to pay their mother's debts rather than meeting the obligation individually. Pierre Boullery and his siblings joined together to try to make their uncle pay board and lodging for the three years and eight months when he had lived in their father's household, twenty years earlier.[26]

By exchange and purchase between and from each other after the division of patrimony into equal shares, siblings could counteract the effects of partibility. They accomplished this by consolidating the fragmented shares that partibility had created to their mutual benefit, thus minimizing the problems that resulted from the division of real property, such as houses. Numerous examples of such cooperation survive. Pierre Boullery and his siblings admitted the "great inconvenience . . . the plurality" of parties created in dividing their parents' estate. One sister, who after her marriage had moved to Poitou, articulated her desire to avoid "too much expense, trouble and inconvenience," as well as to encourage "peace and goodwill" among the siblings. She and another sister sold their shares to some of their brothers.[27]

In these efforts, siblings displayed a practical concern to enhance everyone's prospects by reorganizing the lots that they had inherited after the partition. These ends were achieved in ways as diverse as the properties in question. Pierre Liger sold the land in his own lot that adjoined that of one of his brothers to that sibling, a very common pattern. Jacques Gloriet and Marguerite Scarin, his wife, exchanged with her brother the house that he had inherited, next door to the one she had been allotted, for the rural property included in her lot. Julien Mainguy and his sister agreed that he

26. ADLA, 4E2/1464, 12 February 1642; ADLA, 4E2/1758, 15 February 1639; ADLA, 4E2/1688, 12 June 1634.

27. ADLA, 4E2/1461, 26 September 1635.

would give her the rural property that his lot had included from their mother's estate, adjacent to the property that she had inherited, and he would receive *rentes* in exchange. Thomas Bruneau purchased from his sisters the wine-making equipment that had been initially divided among them equally. François Cosson and his siblings agreed to exchange property among themselves to "avoid the expenses of valuation and division" that the partition of their deceased sister's estate would otherwise have involved. Thomas Ouairy's daughters carefully rearranged their shares to liquidate enough money to provide a dowry of 800 *livres* for one of them.[28]

Distant kin often chose another type of cooperative strategy to overcome the extreme fragmentation that equal lots often involved and to facilitate an outcome that was mutually satisfactory. Faced with dividing real property many ways into small pieces, for, after all, these were only middling families, they frequently chose to sell out their individual shares after the partition of the estate. Julien Bachelier and Renée Coquet, as the widow of his brother Jean, each claimed a one-ninth share of the estate of the Bacheliers' mother's cousin. They both chose to sell their shares, no doubt preferring cash to scattered parcels of rural small holdings.[29]

These varying responses reveal that inheritance strategies were in the hands of heirs—siblings or otherwise—as well as parents, where partible inheritance practice prevailed.[30] The inheriting generation actively made de-

---

28. ADLA, 4E2/616, 3 December 1645; ADLA, 4E2/326, 9 June 1598; ADLA, 4E2/1368, 23 February 1656; ADLA, 4E2/95, 30 November 1632; ADLA, 4E2/100, 19 February 1642; ADLA, 4E2/90, 6 February 1643.

29. ADLA, 4E2/1463, 11 May 1641; and ADLA, 4E2/1705, 25 March 1645. Among many such cases, see the following for arrangements made by one group of extended kin: ADLA, 4E2/454, 27 November 1623 (Guillaume Jahanneau sold to another heir one-quarter of one-quarter of one-half that was his share in an estate); ADLA, 4E2/326, 5 June 1600 (Guillaume Penifort purchased half of a *rente foncière* owed on a house of which his wife had inherited a part; he purchased it from the kin in whose lot the *rente* had fallen); ADLA, 4E2/488, [torn] February 1615 (Guillaume Jahanneau and Guillaume Penifort and his brother, Jean, who had sold their share in a part of an estate to another kinsman, repaid two-eighths of what they had received to two others, who shared the same portion of the estate).

30. Historians have, generally, focused only on the perspective of parents as the decisive decision makers in this process. Giesey, for example, emphasizes the active role of parents in manipulating the inheritance system to protect the integrity of the family patrimony. Diefendorf and Wheaton, drawing on practice rather than legal stricture, have suggested that parental preference for partibility led parents to fail purposefully to make such provisions during their lifetime. Ralph Giesey, "Rules of Inheritance and Strategies of Mobility in Prerevolutionary France," *American Historical Review* 82 (April 1977), 274–76; Diefendorf, *Paris City Councillors,* 264–70; Robert Wheaton, "Affinity and Descent in Seventeenth-Century Bordeaux," in Robert Wheaton and Tamara Hareven, eds., *Family and Sexuality in French History* (Philadelphia, 1980), 121–23.

cisions about the future of the patrimony. Occasionally, glimpses emerge of how far this dynamic could allow heirs to go in taking the initiative in shaping the fate of the family patrimony and their individual shares. Gilles Thomin, for instance, was a widower by 1625. His children, who presumably wished to have immediate access to the property they would inherit, apparently persuaded him to divide the family patrimony in advance of his death. The children met and decided to divide the estate "as if their father had died," except for the personal property that he was to retain for his own use. The sibling whose lot included the house where their father would live until his death was to be compensated, and the others also agreed to pay 80 *livres* a year each to support their father. To guarantee this payment, none of the inherited property could be sold while their father lived. They were also to share equally his debts and any legal costs incurred. In an indication of where the decision-making power lay, they noted that if their father should object in the future, they would use the consent that he had given to get legal confirmation of their decisions.[31]

In choosing to uphold rather than evade equality among themselves, heirs in middling families participated in patrimonial practices that had important ramifications for family and gender relationships among siblings and kin. Egalitarian legal codes in France have sometimes been interpreted as the source of competitiveness, suspicion, and distrust between siblings, and as favoring the extended lineage over the household.[32] The experience of the Nantais notarial families suggests a more complex dynamic: the prospect of an egalitarian patrimonial division fostered strategies among kin that emphasized cooperation as well as raising the possibility of conflicts. While cooperation served the interests of all heirs, and in that sense enhanced their ties to the lineage and its patrimony, it was pursued to further the interests of each heir's household, rather than secure the integrity of the patrimony and the future of the lineage.

---

31. ADLA, 4E2/490, 18 July 1625.

32. See, for example, Segalen, "Sibling Relations," 141–43; Emmanuel Leroy Ladurie, "A System of Customary Law: Family Structures and Inheritance Customs in Sixteenth-Century France," in Robert Forster and Orest Ranum, eds., *Family and Society: Selections from the Annales Economies, Sociétés, Civilisations* (Baltimore, 1976), 90–91; Jean Yver, *Egalité entre héritiers et exclusion des enfants dotés: Essai de géographie coutumière* (Paris, 1966).

Yver equated the western system with egalitarianism and lack of marital property community (echoing the earlier observation of Alexis de Tocqueville on the consequences of partible inheritance in the United States). Le Roy Ladurie extended Yver's formulation, to point out that community property emphasized the household as a distinct unit, while partibility could also enhance lineage awareness.

Indeed, the cooperation that characterized sibling attitudes to the patrimony in which they all shared strengthened ties between households of collateral kin, rather than between households linked by lineage bonds. The equal interest that women claimed in their family patrimony gave them a pivotal position in the formation of kin ties and helped to maintain their household ties to their family of origin. Strong relationships between brothers-in-law in particular and same-generation collateral kin in general, affinal as much as consanguinal, resulted. To take only one example, the frequency with which kin lived in adjoining households, a pattern that we have already noticed, was the result of property divisions as well as choice.

The sisters Claude and Adrienne Legaigneux, for instance, married Jean Carte and Guillaume Penifort. They both lived as married couples in a house on a corner of the Place du Pillori, inherited from their father in a partition that gave the first and third floors to Adrienne and the second to Claude, a spatial organization that their household arrangements observed.[33] Their husbands, who worked out of *études* on the ground floor, perhaps in the same *étude*, constantly co-signed for each other in their notarial capacities and were frequent companions in a multitude of other activities. Same-generation male kin, especially brothers-in-law, typically undertook many public activities together, and the bonds between them, material and affective, made them primary members of each other's social networks, as the next chapter will examine.

The division of property among heirs formally closed the patrimonial cycle of each household, initiated with the decision to marry. Between these two moments, the priorities of various family members were worked out in practices that dealt with household patrimony. The transmission of, access to, and management of patrimony illuminated the particular dynamics of the middling urban community. The interests not only of spouses—together and as individuals—but of their parents, siblings, and other kin shaped the patrimonial life course of every household.

The ethos of equality in regard to who should share in a household's patrimony was deeply imbued, reflecting both the pressure of the customary law and the challenges and demands of subsistence for ordinary people in an early modern city. Parents in a middling urban milieu of notarial families preferred to establish each child through marriage or career, rather

33. ADLA, 4E2/577, 11 February 1649.

than enhancing the long-term interests of their lineage or favoring one child. Heirs, similarly, seemed committed to equal shares for all.

The impact of this form of egalitarianism on familial relations was complicated, however, in the larger context of patrimonial management in these families. Expectations and obligations to patrimony under the partible inheritance system that was observed by these families served to link the households of some kin, while creating pressure points that raised barriers between others. The collateral orientation of kin relations and the importance of affinal kin were the outcome of a customary law and widely upheld practice that not only insisted on equality between heirs but narrowly limited the ability of parents to maneuver and select their own heirs. Inheritance strategies were in the hands of heirs too, and the tensions and alliances between different kin groups that resulted were critical elements of daily life. In particular, the cooperative response of same-generation kin and siblings to this situation contributed to the collateral orientation of kin ties.

Property relations were at the heart of a construction of authority among middling families that revolved around concepts of good husbandry—*mesnagement*—with its attendant rights and obligations both for spouses and for their kin, whose interests in a household's patrimony were, by virtue of how property was held, both material and emotional. Each household was embedded in a network of ties to other households, ties that encouraged and justified the oversight by kin of every household. This way of managing their lives was exemplified by the common claims and the role of kin in overseeing the many occasions when major decisions were reached about a household's patrimony.

7

Kin and Friends

Networks of Daily Life

When twelve kinsmen gathered to discuss the proposed marriage of Mathurin Verger and Françoise Merceron, when Antoine Charier and Jeanne Garnier asked his father, André, and her sister Catherine to be the godparents for their child and invited the six other witnesses who also attended the baptism, when Etienne Tesnier's two sisters and two brothers-in-law guaranteed the loan that he needed to buy his position as a royal notary, and when Louise Lecoq, the wife of René Guilloteau, lent 20 *livres* to the wife of a lawyer who lived in her parish, they were all mobilizing personal ties and contacts of diverse kinds and in diverse ways.

Like them, early modern people called on numerous of their peers as they sought to prioritize their resources and to meet the challenges of daily urban life. Notaries and their families identified particular people—among the kin, friends, neighbors, clients, and strangers they encountered every day—on whom they relied for diverse purposes. Circumstances (for example, the existence of surviving kin) as well as individual choices shaped these complex networks. The number, variety, and quality of interactions that every individual maintained helped to shape the social topography of the seventeenth-century urban landscape.[1]

These interactions made up networks that provided the foundations for larger social and cultural structures. People had overlapping networks, each with potentially distinctive purposes. Key family decisions might draw on one set of ties, financial help on another, daily sociability on a third. Recovering some specific urban solidarities provides a basis for exploring links between personal experiences and their public political counterparts.[2]

Kinship and gender patterns in early modern life were fostered in the making of networks. Gender roles for men as well as for women were continuously negotiated and shaped in daily interactions, and the networks that emerged out of those contacts shaped relations of power among men and between men and women. Like gender, kinship is culturally rather than biologically defined, and the structures of gender and kinship are closely related.[3] Yet the role of kin remains one of the great unknowns of early modern European historiography. Hans Medick and David Sabean, more than a decade ago, echoed a frequent lament about historians' ignorance of the "nature of specific structures and networks of kin mobilized

1. For discussions of the theory and practice of network analysis see, for example, J. Clyde Mitchell, "The Concept and Use of Social Networks," in Mitchell, ed., *Social Networks in Urban Situations* (Manchester, 1969), 1–50; Hans Medick and David Sabean, "Interest and Emotion in Family and Kinship Studies: A Critique of Social History and Anthropology," in their *Interest and Emotion: Essays on the Study of the Family and Kinship* (Cambridge, 1984), 13–18; Keith Wrightson and David Levine, *Poverty and Piety in an English Village: Terling, 1525–1700* (New York, 1979); Judith M. Bennett, "The Tie That Binds: Peasant Marriages and Families in Late Medieval England," *Journal of Interdisciplinary History* 15 (Summer 1984); Christiane Klapisch-Zuber, "Kin, Friends, and Neighbors," in her *Women, Family, and Ritual in Renaissance Italy* (Chicago, 1985), 68–93.

2. For recent discussions of the need to look beyond the conjugal family and examine the links between personal and public life, see, for instance, Claire Dolan, "The Artisans of Aix-en-Provence in the Sixteenth Century: A Micro-Analysis of Social Relations," in Philip Benedict, ed., *Cities and Social Change in Early Modern France* (London, 1989), 174–77; and Katherine A. Lynch, "The Family and the History of Public Life," *Journal of Interdisciplinary History* 24 (Spring 1994), 665–84.

3. Recent anthropological analyses of kinship and networks have emphasized the intersections of gender and kinship and stressed the importance of not assuming any particular form of social organization. See, for instance, Jane Fishburne Collier and Sylvia Junko Yanagisako, introduction to Collier and Yanagisako, eds., *Gender and Kinship: Essays Towards a Unified Analysis* (Stanford, 1987), who note that in regard to gender and kinship, "neither can be treated as analytically prior to the other, because they are realized together in particular cultural, economic and political systems." They point out that "instead of asking how rights and obligations are mapped onto kinship bonds, thus assuming a genealogical grid, we need to ask how specific societies recognize claims and allocate responsibilities."

for these purposes, and into the foundations of those expectations, obligations and rights on which this mobilization of resources from kin rested."[4]

Distinctions between different kinds of kinship relations are useful in analyzing the dynamics of kinship and gender in networks. Although ties of blood and marriage provided the basis for all familial kinship, Pierre Bourdieu has usefully conceptualized as "official" kin those people who were liable to be called on to fulfill legal roles, but otherwise were of limited importance in daily life. People mobilized their "practical" kin, in contrast, for a variety of formal and informal purposes and perpetuated ties with them by constant use.[5] Moreover, at occasions like infant baptisms, for example, individuals could use their choice of godparents to reinforce existing ties or to incorporate people to whom they were not connected by blood or marriage into their kinship network as "spiritual" kin.

4. Medick and Sabean, "Interest and Emotion in Family and Kinship Studies," 21. Historians have recently been exploring the role of kinship in various communities. They have argued for the importance of kin ties in structuring power relations in Renaissance Italy, whereas analyses of nonelite groups in England have tended to minimize the consequence of kinship. French historians have accepted the importance of kin ties, but studies of noble families have dominated, with the exceptions of Robert Wheaton's early study of urban kinship in seventeenth-century Bordeaux and David Garrioch's recent examination of the Parisian bourgeoisie. Historians of the nineteenth century, meanwhile, have clearly framed the role of gender in family, class, and kinship.

For Renaissance Italy, see Diane Owen Hughes, "Representing the Family: Portraits and Purposes in Early Modern Italy," *Journal of Interdisciplinary History* 17 (Summer 1986); Klapisch-Zuber, *Women, Family, and Ritual*; Sharon Strocchia, *Death and Ritual in Renaissance Florence* (Baltimore, 1992). For early modern England, see Alan Macfarlane, *The Family Life of Ralph Josselin* (Cambridge, 1970); Lawrence Stone, *Family, Sex, and Marriage in England, 1500–1800* (London, 1979); Wrightson and Levine, *Poverty and Piety in an English Village*. For dissents from the view that kinship was relatively unimportant outside elites in England, see Miranda Chaytor, "Household and Kinship: Ryton in the Late Sixteenth and Early Seventeenth Centuries," *History Workshop* 10 (Fall 1980); and David Cressy, "Kinship and Kin Interaction in Early Modern England," *Past and Present* 113 (November 1986). For France, see Jean-Louis Flandrin, *Families in Former Times: Kinship, Household, and Sexuality* (Cambridge, 1977), 23–49; David Garrioch, *The Formation of the Parisian Bourgeoisie, 1690–1830* (Cambridge, Mass, 1996); Sharon Kettering, "Patronage and Kinship in Early Modern France," *French Historical Studies* 16 (Fall 1989); Robert Wheaton, "Affinity and Descent in Seventeenth-Century Bordeaux," in Robert Wheaton and Tamara Hareven, eds., *Family and Sexuality in French History* (Philadelphia, 1980). For the nineteenth century, see Leonore Davidoff and Catherine Hall, *Family Fortunes: Men and Women of the English Middle Class, 1780–1850* (Chicago, 1987); Tamara Hareven, *Family Time, Industrial Time: The Relationship Between Family and Work in a New England Industrial Community* (Cambridge, 1982); Mary Ryan, *Cradle of the Middle Class: The Family in Oneida County, New York, 1790–1865* (Cambridge, 1981).

5. This formulation is borrowed from Pierre Bourdieu, who argues that practical kin relationships are "something people make and with which they do something," while official kin relationships may merely reproduce "the official representation of the social structures." Pierre Bourdieu, *Outline of a Theory of Practice* (Cambridge, 1977), esp. 33–43.

The networks examined here—of people who participated in the management of household patrimony, or attended baptisms, or were engaged in the circulation of credit—were the outcomes of voluntary associations that entailed varying elements of choice and commitment.[6] The people who participated in key decisions about a household's patrimony, for example, were sometimes present at the behest of customary law and sometimes by invitation. Families were free to choose whom they pleased to attend baptisms, and people who were invited could choose whether or not to attend. Making loans met the mutual needs of borrowers and lenders.

Defining Kinship

While the interests of kin in a household's lineage property and in the management of individual household patrimony were clear, which particular kin were involved in what ways in the life of a household is more difficult to illuminate. Analyzing which kin were included at two different kinds of decision-making moments in terms of a household's patrimony points to the particular patterns of kinship that these middling families observed. The first were the myriad occasions when customary law mandated that kin advice be given about a household's patrimonial management. The second were the making of marriage contracts, a matter in which kin often participated, although the only legal requirement was for parental consent.

Breton customary law was generally vague about which "kin" it required to give advice, and so the extended and bilateral (that is, including those of both spouses) kin who were usually consulted reflected cultural rather than legal expectations as to what kinds of relations constituted official kinship in middling families.[7] The people who gave their opinions on these occasions had widely varied relationships to the parties whose interests were at

6. Methodologically, network analysis offers complex challenges. Record linkage from many different sources is necessary to establish the identities, occupations, residence, and especially the kinship ties of particular individuals. By looking at the participants in a series of different kinds of contacts, a variety of the networks in which each person became enmeshed can be reconstructed.

7. Occasionally, customary law appeared to favor a patrilineal slant, but, as in other instances, practice may not have followed this guideline. As we have seen in regard to the choice of guardian, for example, customary law maintained that paternal kin should be favored over maternal, but commentators noted that in practice, both maternal and paternal kin were consulted. *La Coustume de Bretagne avec les Commentaires et Observations . . . par Maître Michel Sauvageau* (Nantes, 1710), article 504 and article 501.

issue and were drawn from both the husbands' and the wives' sides.[8] Uncles and first or second cousins were common, but kin of all sorts appeared. Some people described themselves vaguely as cousins of the fourth or fifth "degree." For example, one cousin "in the fourth degree" and two more "in the fifth or sixth degree in the paternal branch" discussed the appointment of a guardian for the children of Mathurin Carte and Jeanne Duvau. Simon Ertauld described himself as "kin in the third degree" in a guardianship conference with kin who included two similarly placed, four who were cousins in the fourth degree, one in the third or fourth, and another in the fourth or fifth.[9]

Paternal kin were often in the majority, but maternal kin were usually well represented. The kinsmen who gave permission for Mathurin Verger and Françoise Merceron to marry included, for Verger, four paternal, two maternal, and one whose lineage was unclear; and for Merceron, three paternal, two maternal, and two uncertain. After Guillaume Chapelain's death, seven paternal and five maternal kin met to discuss the choice of a guardian for his minor children. The odd exception to this pattern did occur, as when five paternal kin of Mathurin Verger's met six years before his marriage to consult with Verger's father, Jean, about his son's request for emancipation.[10] The prominence of wives' families in other areas of household life, as we have seen, meant that these affinal kin were unlikely to allow such decision-making occasions to pass by without their having any influence.

How far these understandings about the extensiveness and bilaterality of official kinship translated into daily relationships that can be characterized as practical kinship is another question. Among middling families, kinship of any kind meant more than a biological or marital relationship. This differentiation emerged in legal proceedings, for example when trying to establish the veracity of kin ties in order to verify claims to an estate. Witnesses defined kinship or lack thereof in terms of how the parties addressed each other and whether they visited each other frequently, rather by detailed genealogical information.[11]

---

8. Other legal practices also upheld the ideal of extended kinship as an important bond. Witnesses in court proceedings, for example, had to declare that they were not related to the litigants in any way. For evidence that this manifestation of the kinship ideal was not peculiar to Brittany, see James R. Farr, *Hands of Honor: Artisans and their World in Dijon, 1550–1650* (Ithaca, N.Y., 1988), 147.

9. ADLA, B6376, 4 and 5 February 1631; and ADLA, B6376, 23 April 1647.

10. ADLA, B5690, 7 January 1651 (same date on documents for both Verger and Merceron); ADLA, B6377, 13 October 1657; ADLA, B6376, 7 January 1645.

11. See, for example, ADLA, B5801, 15 March 1606; B5805, 10 March 1621; B6129, [torn] September 1627.

While an extensive range of kin were considered equal in the giving of advice, popular understandings of the obligations of kinship intimated that responsibility for material help was more narrowly limited. This suggested that contemporaries clearly distinguished between official kin and practical kin. Raoul Boucaud apparently happily offered his opinion on the appointment of a guardian but fiercely resisted his own nomination, on the grounds that first cousins in a closer degree of kinship to the children than he were available, so their selection of him was against the "order and disposition of our custom."[12] This reasoning surfaced in other matters where material aid was at issue. Hervé Trebillard and his kin argued (unsuccessfully) against kin being required to help a widow to support her children, partly on the grounds that her father was alive and had not been called on for support, implying that his responsibility preceded theirs.[13]

But kin who participated in making marriage contracts—for which kin consultation was not legally required—expressed their "opinion and consent" on these occasions by invitation. Their presence at the gatherings witnessing marriage contracts pointed to how distinctions were drawn in middling families between official and practical kin, as well as to the extent of the involvement of other people in familial and patrimonial matters.[14] As a rule, a sizable gathering witnessed marriage contracts. About ten people, apart from the bride and groom, usually signed the document.[15] Besides this group, and in addition to the two notaries who would formalize the contract, a priest was often present to affiance the couple.

Making a marriage contract was primarily a familial affair in this milieu, as befitted the status of the event as the most important moment in the

12. ADLA, B6376, 9 May 1647. *La Coustume de Bretagne,* article 507, declares the preference for the closest available kin in the appointment of a guardian.

13. ADLA, B6139, 17 December 1646.

14. This element of choice meant that, on rare occasions, the bride and groom might enter into the contract almost alone. Such arrangements were, however, rare and usually linked to particular circumstances. Pierre Babin and Jeanne Denys were both orphans when they married and had only one witness, who was, apparently, a friend but not kinsman of the groom, Robert Poullain, who had fallen out with his mother after her remarriage, and Anne Menant, who, as a *femme marchande,* supplied her own dowry and was unusually independent, had no witnesses to their marriage contract. Contracts for second marriages were often smaller affairs. When Pierre Belon married his second wife, Jeanne Daniels, their contract was witnessed only by five of her kin. ADLA, 4E2/100, 28 June 1642; ADLA, 4E15/153, 16 April 1660; and ADLA, 4E2/615, 4 October 1643.

15. Based on 164 contracts in which notaries or their wives were involved in some capacity, with 1,749 signatures. The signatures of the priest who was sometimes present were excluded from this total, but substitutes for illiterate parties to the contract were included in their own right, too.

transmission of the family patrimony. In June 1619, for example, in a room on the second floor of a house on the corner of the Place du Pillori in the parish of St. Croix, twenty-two people signed the marriage contract between André Charier and Marguerite Penifort. They met in the residence of Guillaume Penifort, the bride's father.

The seventeen witnesses—who were present along with the bride, groom, priest, and notaries—included ten people related by blood or marriage to the spouses. The bride's father and mother, together with the groom's widowed mother and two of his brothers, represented the spouses' immediate families. Five other notaries, as kin of the bride, also signed. Two of these, Martin Minquet and Yves Boucaud, were the husbands of Perrine and Guyonne Carte, the bride's maternal cousins, while François Bonnamy and his brother-in-law Jean Pineau were her distant maternal kin, and Guillaume Jahanneau was a paternal cousin of the bride's father. Even the co-signing notary was a kinsman, Mathurin Carte, a nephew of the bride's deceased uncle, Jean Carte.

Three spiritual kin—that is, linked to the families by godparentage— were also among the signatories. The lawyer Guillaume Lemarie was a kinsman (probably uncle) of the bride's father and was married to the bride's godmother; Claude Delomeau, a nobleman and barrister, was the husband of the groom's godmother. The lawyer Guillaume Landaz was the godfather of Marguerite Penifort's younger brother.

Only four of the signatories were not kin of either family. Julien Templier was a nobleman and doctor of medicine, who, with Delomeau, was a member of the urban elite, clearly well above the stratum occupied by notarial families. He remained a resource for the Penifort-Charier households; for instance, he and his wife were later godparents to children of the Penifort-Charier marriage. The three other men (an apothecary, a merchant, and a court usher) had a history of contacts with the fathers of either the bride or groom and were presumably family friends.[16]

16. ADLA, 4E2/489, 10 June 1619. The occupations of witnesses and their connections with the families were identified by analysis of the parish registers held in series GG, AM Nantes, and from other documents made by the families and recorded by notaries in the ADLA, series 4E2.

Similar patterns were evident among the witnesses to other marriage contracts. The six witnesses who signed the marriage contract of Simon Aubin and Renée Gallet in 1609 included Gallet's mother (her father and both his parents were dead), a female cousin of the bride and her husband, the bride's paternal aunt's husband, another of her cousins, and a maternal cousin of Aubin's. Eleven of the fifteen people who witnessed the contract of Robert Rouille's daughter in 1655 were identified as kin. The groom's kin included his two brothers-in-law and

The collateral (same-generation) as well as bilateral orientation of practical kinship became clear in marriage contracts that notaries and their wives were invited to sign. Notaries and their wives were related by blood or marriage to the spouses in more than 85 percent of the contracts they signed.[17] The collateral orientation of kinship, evident in the handling of patrimony, was again paramount. Over a third (38 percent) of these occasions were the marriages of siblings, in-laws of the same generation or first cousins, with each of these groups being almost equally important. The same portion was for their own children or for nieces and nephews, and only about 10 percent was for more distant relatives.[18] Women relatives often signed as witnesses, and maternal kin were well represented.

The spouses Pierre Belon and Marguerite Daguin signed nine extant marriage contracts, in a pattern that indicates how, in daily life, kinship among these middling urban families clearly emphasized kin ties from the families of both spouses, rather than favoring patrilineal kin. Only one did not apparently involve relatives, and in that case the families of the bride and groom resided in Belon's own parish. Three were for Daguin's siblings, one for Belon's brother, and three involved nieces and nephews. In the other contract, Belon's future father-in-law acted on behalf of the groom's parents, who lived in a rural parish. At the time, Belon was a young clerk working for the notary who registered the contract, whose *étude* was opposite the home of Belon's future in-laws, and Belon may have signed for an illiterate witness or in anticipation of his future kinship.

This bilaterality of kinship did not, however, nullify gendered hierarchies of power, as the latter were replicated constantly through the expressions of kinship. The patterns of signatures or marriage contracts represented differential positions for men and women in family relationships. Although

---

his cousin, while the bride's included two brothers, a paternal aunt, a paternal first cousin, and three husbands of paternal first cousins, plus her guardian, who was also her first cousin. Four unidentified female witnesses may have been two relatives of the groom and two of the bride.

17. Based on 157 extant marriage contracts with 189 signatures of notaries or their wives or widows. Only 28 signatures (14.97 percent) were not, apparently, for kin. Given the difficulty of identifying kin, some of these occasions probably also, in fact, involved kin.

18. Seventy-one of 189 signatures were for this group, with 25 signatures each for siblings and same-generation in-laws, and 21 for first cousins. There were 41 signatures for children, and 30 for nephews or nieces. Of the total, 19 signatures were for more distant kin. These included quite extended relationships, like Guillaume Chapelain's signature on the marriage contract of the daughter of his wife's paternal second cousin. In 12 cases, the exact relationship between the signatory and the marrying parties was not clear, but the fact of kinship was inferred from their designation as such, and, in these cases, I have assumed more distant kinship.

women's equal claim on patrimony probably at least contributed to their being invited to witness the contracts, female kin (apart from the bride and the mothers of the couple) usually signed in a group, below the names of all the male kin, who, therefore, presumably signed first.

Practical kin ties among these families were strongest between same-generation households who would also have been linked by their mutual expectations or interests in the inheritance system. Their preeminence at the making of a marriage contract, a primary occasion of patrimonial organization within a single household, again reflected the degree to which the way property was held shaped emotional as well as material relations between kin. Moreover, this pattern of practical kin ties persisted when patrimonial interests were not at stake.

Sacraments and Sociability

Baptisms were opportunities for expressions of membership in a secular community as well as sacramental occasions.[19] The rituals of baptisms were regular features of early modern life, providing much more of a locus for community interaction than they do now: men (although not women, an important distinction) in this milieu attended many baptisms—five or six a year, on average. Eleven or twelve people usually attended, many of whom were not kin of the baby. Unlike the making of marriage contracts, baptisms were social as much as familial events. The father, godparents, and guests gathered at the font as the church bells rang, not only celebrating the christening of the child, but confirming their relations with each other.

The baptismal interactions of ten notaries, representing different generations of four families (as parents, godparents, or guests), suggest that the relationships forged at baptisms embodied key social and spatial patterns. These ten notaries had more than 10,000 contacts with almost 5,000 individuals at almost 1,000 baptisms (see Table 7.1).[20] The traditional focus of historians on the parent-godparent dyad ignores the multiple relationships

19. This point is also made by Philip Hoffman, *Church and Community in the Diocese of Lyon, 1500–1789* (New Haven, 1984), 129–30. For an eloquent discussion of the meanings and values revealed by rituals surrounding death rather than birth, see Sharon Strocchia, *Death and Ritual,* esp. introduction and pt. 1.

20. These figures are based on the baptismal registers of Nantais city parishes between 1560 and 1660, held in the series GG at the AMN. Witnesses who attended baptisms signed these

Table 7.1.   Baptism contacts

	Penifort Père, 1599–1628	Penifort Fils, 1623–46	Jean Charier, 1580–1615	André Charier, 1619–56	Antoine Charier, 1653–60	Toussaint Charier, 1646–60
Baptism	166	86	34	107	34	32
Contacts	1,588	1,066	308	1,140	341	305
[Women]	[166]	[86]	[40]	[110]	[39]	[42]
Individuals	663	563	196	529	203	244
[Women]	[130]	[71]	[38]	[91]	[35]	[39]
Kin contacts	334	229	12	284	94	32
[Women]	[44]	[35]	[6]	[39]	[12]	[7]
Individual kin	68	58	9	70	29	13
[Women]	[22]	[21]	[5]	[23]	[8]	[5]

	Jean Carte, 1582–1616	Mathurin Carte, 1618–45	Pierre Belon, 1630–60	Julien Belon, 1639–60	Total
Baptisms	200	85	174	35	953
Contacts	2,016	912	2,067	493	10,236
[Women]	[219]	[90]	[183]	[42]	[1,017]
Individuals	815	493	860	252	4,818
[Women]	[159]	[70]	[119]	[34]	[786]
Kin contacts	287	177	539	117	2,105
[Women]	[34]	[28]	[67]	[12]	[284]
Individual kin	47	46	77	29	446
[Women]	[17]	[16]	[20]	[9]	[146]

that were indicated at baptisms, considers only a limited period of the parents' life course—their child-bearing years—and excludes childless couples.
Baptism attendance reflected important choices, both by parents about
whom to invite as guests and godparents, and by those invited about
whether to accept the invitations. Men who went to many baptisms together
over a period of years were more than acquaintances; they shared a pattern
of sociability.

registers, as did the father and godparents. The ten notaries attended 953 baptisms with
10,236 other people, an average of 10.7 guests per baptism. In this table, the number of witnesses out of the total in each category who were women is listed in brackets. Illegible signatures were excluded, and they numbered, for baptisms attended by each of the notaries, as follows: Penifort *père,* 25; Penifort *fils,* 18; Jean Charier, 4; André Charier, 13; Antoine Charier, 3;
Toussaint Charier, 8; Jean Carte, 37; Mathurin Carte, 12; Pierre Belon, 45; Julien Belon, 6. The
total number of illegible signatures was 171.
    This reconstruction was complemented by a sampling of all the interactions of city notaries
at baptisms for twenty-year intervals between 1580 and 1660.

Parents assigned "spiritual" kinship to the people they chose as godparents, drawing them into a formalized relationship with the parents and the child. Notarial families could use the opportunity to indicate which relationships they would most like to strengthen. In choosing godparents, parents could seek to extend their ties by inviting more socially or politically prominent men and women, reinforce already existing friendships, or emphasize existing kin ties.

The baptisms that notaries attended could be occasions to consolidate vertical bonds of solidarity, by inviting social superiors to sponsor the child. Well over a third of these children were given godfathers or godmothers who were of higher social status than their parents, and, in about a quarter of the cases, both godparents were of higher rank than the parents.[21]

Affirming relations with social superiors offered potential advantages, of which the most important in this milieu seems to have been the cementing of occupational ties. For children of the apothecaries and surgeons who shared middling rank with notaries, more senior medical professionals were popular choices. André Charier attended nine baptisms for the children of Jeanne Vaugour and the apothecary François Legrantel. Four of these nine children had doctors as godfathers.

Notarial families who chose godparents of higher social rank favored doctors and members of the highest court based in the city, the royal financial court (the Chambre des Comptes). Notaries, along with apothecaries, surgeons, and other men of middling rank, were, in turn, invited to be godparents for lower-status Nantes residents.

Yet notaries and their wives were much more likely to choose kin or people who shared their own social standing as godparents for their own children than to seek sponsors of higher social status. Less than a quarter of the godparents of their own children were of higher social status than notarial families, and both godparents were of higher social status in fewer than one in ten baptisms. The vast majority of the godfathers they chose were almost equally likely to be either kin or men of their own status, and godmothers were even more likely to be kin.[22]

---

21. In 958 baptisms, 380 godfathers (39.7 percent) were of higher social status than the parents, as were 335 godmothers (35.0 percent). In 241 cases, both godparents were of higher social rank (25.2 percent). Kin were not included among those of superior rank. The assessments of rank were made using the criteria observed in Table 7.2 for urban elite, bourgeois middle ranks, and artisans.

22. The networks of the ten notaries included 148 baptisms for their children or children of other notaries. Thirty-four of 148 godfathers (23.0 percent) and 35 of 148 godmothers (23.6 percent) were of higher social status than the notarial parents. Of 148 godfathers, 57

Nantais middling families seem, in practice, to have used godparent-hood as a flexible tool. The prospect of securing a patron through the extension of vertical ties was only one of the parents' concerns, rather than being a guiding principle. On the whole, baptisms more often saw the consolidation of existing kin ties and the confirmation of already existing relations within a social milieu.[23]

Grandparents were usually asked to be the godparents of firstborn children, suggesting the priority that middling families placed on reinforcing kinship ties. Although personal preferences and the demographic uncertainties that bedeviled early modern families led to individual variations, if grandparents were still alive, one maternal and one paternal grandparent frequently sponsored firstborn children, and the remaining grandparents took the second child.[24]

If, as often happened, some grandparents were dead, other kin commonly substituted as godparents. Guillaume Jahanneau and Perrine Clement chose godparents for their six children partly as a result of kin "availability." Jahanneau's own parents were dead when their first child was born in 1614, so Clement's father, a goldsmith, and the widow of a paternal uncle were enlisted. Clement's mother and a paternal uncle, a surgeon married to Jahanneau's sister, sponsored the second child. The godparents of five later children included four kin, three people of higher social status, and three people of similar status to the parents.

When middling families did not adopt this pattern of godparenthood,

---

(38.5 percent) were kin, with the same number being of similar social status to that of the notaries. Of 148 godmothers, 67 (45.3 percent) were kin, while 56 (37.8 percent) were from the same social milieu as the parents. The difficulty of fully identifying kin ties makes it likely that even these figures continue to underestimate kinship.

23. This flexibility combines the possibilities identified in earlier studies about the relations between parents and godparents. These, variously, have suggested that godparenthood was "a relation of formal amity" that extended kin relations by including non-kin; that spiritual kinship reinforced family ties; or that baptisms of infants were used to forge patron-client relations and cement vertical ties. See the respective arguments of John Bossy, "Godparenthood: The Fortunes of a Social Institution in Early Modern Christianity," in Kaspar von Greyerz, ed., *Religion and Society in Early Modern Europe, 1500–1800* (London, 1984), 197; and John Bossy, "Blood and Baptism: Kinship, Community, and Christianity in Western Europe, from the Fourteenth to the Seventeenth Centuries," in Derek Baker, ed., *Sanctity and Secularity: The Church and the World* (Oxford, 1973), 133; Flandrin, *Families in Former Times*, 30; Farr, *Hands of Honor*, 126–28; and Robert Schneider, *Public Life in Toulouse, 1463–1789* (Ithaca, N.Y., 1989), 240–52.

24. Bossy has suggested that beginning in the sixteenth century, "it has been widely held that grandparents had a special claim to the godparenthood of first-born children." Bossy, "Godparenthood: The Fortunes of a Social Institution," 198.

they sometimes failed to do so, in part, at least, because they had few available close relations. Guillaume Penifort and Adrienne Legaigneux had few family options when their first child was born in 1599, as their parents were dead, she had only one sister, they both had significantly younger brothers who were not married at the time, and patrimonial claims reveal the paucity of cousins. They secured members of two important households, the lieutenant of Nantes and the wife of the seneschal, to act as baptismal sponsors for their firstborn child. The godparents they chose for their six subsequent children included people of higher social status, kin, and peers. Two were of higher social status, and one of them, the doctor Pierre Bedeau, may also have been a kinsman. At least his ties to the Penifort family were very close: thirty years later, he and his wife were godparents to Penifort and Legaigneux's grandchildren. Four godparents were kin, including Legaigneux's sister's husband, Jean Carte, two other of her relatives, and Penifort's uncle's widow. The remaining godparents were the widow of Hardouin Bedeau (perhaps Pierre's mother), a priest, and the lawyer Guillaume Landaz and his wife, Anne Cottineau.

The choices of Landaz and Cottineau in 1604 and 1606 seem to have been ways to integrate neighborhood friends into the kinship group, because the families had many contacts over the years. Penifort and Landaz met at twenty-eight baptisms between 1603 and 1621, all but one in the parish where they lived. Landaz later signed the marriage contract of one of Penifort's children, a sign of real familiarity, as we have seen.

When notaries accepted invitations to baptisms, they revealed their own priorities and preferences in fostering particular relations in their communities. Notaries were guests, rather than parents or godparents, at more than three-quarters of the baptisms they attended.[25] Although at any single christening, the relationships between witnesses might be only the result of common ties to parents, the patterns of acquaintances revealed by a multitude of such gatherings illustrate the social world that the notaries fashioned. These patterns point to which particular kin, which other people middling men included among their inner circle, and to some of the boundaries of different kinds of relationships.

---

25. Of the 953 baptisms, 55 were for their own children and 216 for godchildren. Pierre Belon's experience slightly distorted these figures: he and Marguerite Daguin were childless, but as one of only two notaries during the century who became *échevins*, he was exceptionally active as a patron-godparent, acting in this capacity at 81 of the 174 baptisms that he attended. The other notaries and their wives only acted as godparents at 15 baptisms, on average, had about six children, and attended 594 of 779 baptisms (76.3 percent) only as witnesses.

This social world was dominated by men, by kin, and by narrow social boundaries. Early modern baptisms took place within days after birth, when mothers were absent, still resting. Women, as a rule, attended baptisms only as godmothers. Thus on average, a woman during her lifetime went to only one baptism with any one notary, and even a woman who was kin of a notary only attended two baptisms with him.[26] Over the course of a notary's own life, he could expect to encounter any one man at two baptisms, except for his kinsmen, with each of whom he could expect to attend six baptisms. Individual kin accounted for less than 10 percent of the people gathered at baptisms, yet they claimed more than 20 percent of the contacts made.

These averages, however, elide the importance of a few far more frequent contacts. Guillaume Penifort *père* met 530 other men at the baptisms he went to over thirty years, encountering people of every social rank, from the lowest segments of Nantais society to the most elite. The great majority of such contacts, as one would expect, represented casual meetings at baptisms of the children of mutual acquaintances. He was at only one or two baptisms with more than three-quarters of these people.

Yet Penifort attended more than five baptisms with fewer than 10 percent of these men, and the kin ties and narrowly circumscribed social status of the men he was frequently in the company of belied any impression of broadly based sociability. His brother-in-law Jean Carte was by far his most important frequent companion. Together they attended 85 of the 142 baptisms that Penifort went to before Carte's death. This sociability was only one expression of the interweaving of their lives. Their wives were sisters, giving them a mutual patrimonial concern; they maintained households on different floors of the same house; and they frequently co-signed for each other as notaries.

Penifort's most constant companions besides his brother-in-law were lower-level legal functionaries or their medical peers, who were often linked to either Penifort or each other by kinship. Penifort's cousin Guillaume Jahanneau and the husband of a cousin, Jean Pineau, both notaries, were the kin he saw most frequently after Carte. Three other men were equally

---

26. At 953 baptisms, 1,017 women were present. As baptisms prior to 1600 often had three godparents, with two being godmothers if the child was female, it was very rare for women to sign just as witnesses. Other women very rarely signed the baptismal registers as witnesses, although many were literate and did sign other documents to indicate their presence at other events, as, for example, in the case of marriage contracts. Their absence from the written record in this case seems to reflect their real absence from the occasion.

prominent in his social circle: the lawyer Guillaume Landaz, the apothecary Emmet Bourget, and the surgeon Issac Letourneux. Two notaries, Jean Brisebois and Pierre Guihaud, and the apothecary Urban Vaugour, as well as Penifort's cousin (the apothecary Robert Bonnamy), Carte's son-in-law (the notary and later lawyer Martin Minquet), and, later, Penifort's own son-in-law André Charier completed a core group of frequent contacts. Family groups dominated Penifort's network. Besides his own kin, Letourneux's father-in-law and brother-in-law, a surgeon and a court clerk, were also frequent associates, as was Bourget's surgeon brother-in-law.

Only three members of Penifort's inner circle came from even slightly broader social backgrounds. The tailor François Lebigot was the sole artisan, but his brother René was a notary who also had repeated interactions with Penifort. Two men of elite status were also frequent companions. The doctor Pierre Bedeau may, in fact, have been kin, and at any rate had numerous contacts with Penifort and his successors over a forty-year span. The lawyer Jean Bernard had a daughter, Marguerite, who married two notaries, and, as a militia captain, he was a local notable.[27]

Distinctive spatial and marital parameters accompanied the preeminence of kinship and shared socioeconomic status in the social world of baptisms. André Charier went to 107 baptisms between 1619 and his death, almost forty years later. He married Marguerite Penifort in the midsummer of 1619 and first witnessed a baptism the following September, for a child of a tailor, in the parish of St. Denis, where the newlyweds had established their household. In this instance, Penifort was godmother, and her maternal cousin's husband, Martin Minquet, was godfather. A couple of months later, Charier attended a baptism for Minquet's child. He or his wife were godparents at only twenty-one baptisms, twelve others were for their own children, and he attended seventy-five simply as a witness. Almost six out of ten of the baptisms that Charier attended took place in his own parish church. Twenty-nine of the forty-eight christenings he went to outside his parish involved only a trip to the neighboring parish of St. Croix. Kinship or acting as godparent accounted for almost three-quarters of the baptisms that drew him out of his own parish.[28]

27. Penifort saw the men mentioned at least at ten baptisms. One other person—with the surname Daniel—was also among this group, but his identity remains a mystery, as he never signed his first name nor acted as parent or godparent to provide further details.

28. Charier attended 108 baptisms: 60 were in St. Denis where he resided, and 29 in the neighboring parish of St. Croix. Of the 48 baptisms out of St. Croix, 23 were for kin, and in another 12, he or Penifort were godparents, so he only left St. Croix for 13 baptisms without

Generally, men became part of the social world represented by baptisms on a regular basis only after their marriage. Age did not seem a significant factor in this transition: most notaries married in their late twenties, but if they happened to wed more quickly, marriage signified the same turning point. Very occasionally, an adolescent acted as godparent, usually when the godparent bond established ties with a socially superior family, or where the baby was the youngest of many, and an older sibling acted as sponsor. Newly married men, whether as godfathers or guests, were integrated at baptisms into the social milieu of their in-laws and into the social world of their peers. As newly elevated heads of independent households, they began to participate fully in their communities.

The horizons of early modern sociability for middling men were parochial and localized. The parish was a distinct urban space with meaningful boundaries that functioned as a unit of real significance, however arbitrary and erratic its boundaries. The churches of St. Croix and St. Saturnin, for example, literally faced each other, as a 1636 traveler noted: "These two parishes and churches have door against door, [with] only the road between them."[29] Nonetheless, more than 60 percent of the baptisms that middling men attended were in their home parish, and more than 80 percent were held in either their own or an adjoining parish, a pattern that persisted between 1580 and 1660, regardless of parish size.[30]

André Charier, Jean Carte, and Pierre Belon, as residents of the respective parishes of St. Denis (with its population of 1,300 in 1600), St. Croix (about 2,600), and St. Saturnin (about 3,600), each attended about 6 out of 10 baptisms in their home parish. Mathurin Fegneux, who lived in the tiny parish of St. Laurent in the 1580s and 1590s, with its population of only about 350, followed a similar pattern, attending 88 baptisms, all but 10 of which were in St. Laurent. Gervais Denan, who lived in St. Nicolas, the city's largest parish, with about 6,000 people, attended 148 baptisms between 1581 and 1616, all but 8 in his home parish.[31]

---

these clear incentives. In addition, 4 of the latter 13 baptisms were for children of the extended Vaugour family, who were among Charier's closest friends (he had more than one hundred contacts with twelve male kin of this family). By ties of godparenthood, they were, in fact, his spiritual kin.

29. While St. Nicolas was physically separated from the rest of the city by a river, the nine other city parishes were folded into one another. Dubuisson-Aubenay, *Itinéraire de Bretagne en 1636* (Nantes, 1902), 62.

30. Of 958 baptisms attended, 575 (60.2 percent) were in the home parish. Of the total, 810 (84.6 percent) were in either home or adjacent parishes.

31. All the population estimates in this paragraph are taken from Alain Croix, *Nantes et le pays Nantais au seizième siècle: Etude démographique* (Paris, 1974), 206.

Middling men usually only went to another parish for baptism for specific reasons, such as ties of kinship or requests to stand as godparents. Gervais Denan restricted almost 95 percent of his attendances at baptisms to St. Nicolas, where he lived, whereas his son Jacques, who also lived in St. Nicolas, visited other parishes for more than a quarter of the baptisms he went to. However, two out of three of these "outside" baptisms only involved a quick trip over an Erdre bridge into the parish of St. Saturnin, on the opposite bank. Denan's wife's family lived there, and her kin accounted for almost all the baptisms he went to there.[32]

Practical kinship and other ties were maintained through repeated association between guests and godparents as well as between guests and parents. Guillaume Penifort worked as a notary from the 1590s to his death in 1629. He lived in St. Croix on a corner of the Place du Pillori, on the boundary with St. Denis residents. Ninety-six of the 167 baptisms he attended were in St. Croix and 50 others in St. Denis. Of the 21 baptisms he went to in more distant parishes, he was a kinsman in 12 and a godparent twice. Bonds of kinship accounted for 9 of the 10 christenings that took him out of the central city parishes altogether, to St. Nicolas, St. Similien, and St. Clement. Two generations later, Penifort's grandson, Antoine Charier, lived in St. Denis. He attended 34 baptisms in the 1650s, only 2 of which predated his marriage in 1655. Fifteen were held in St. Denis. Of the others, 8 were for kin and he attended 1 as a godparent. He apparently attended 8 of the remaining 10 baptisms because of the involvement as guests or godparents of his kin. His wife's brother and brother-in-law, Jean Garnier and Jacques Novel, were present on 7 of these occasions, and his sister and brother were godparents at another.

Kin of the same generation formed a primary cohort in these kinds of networks, as they did on other occasions. Two-thirds of the kin Penifort had contacts with were men of his own generation. Their dominance of practical kinship manifested itself both in the absolute number of kin, as they represented more than 70 percent of all interactions with kin, and in their relative importance in the total number of kin contacts, where six out of ten kin were members of the same generation.[33]

---

32. Gervais Denan attended 148 baptisms between 1581 and 1616: 140 in St. Nicolas (94.6 percent), 3 in the neighboring parish of St. Saturnin, and 5 in other city parishes. Jacques Denan attended 80 baptisms between 1609 and 1645: 59 in St. Nicolas (73.8 percent), 14 in St. Saturnin, and 7 in other city parishes. St. Nicolas and St. Saturnin together thus accounted for more than 91 percent of the baptisms he went to.

33. Interactions with kin numbered 136 of 232 male kin of eight notaries, where the generation of the kin in question could be clearly established, making 1,167 of 1,616 total contacts.

Same-generation ties between brothers-in-law and cousins from both spouses' families were quickly established after marriages and persisted over the long term, well past the stage where the baptisms of their own children might seem to explain this particular emphasis. Jean Carte, for example, had relatively few kin among the large number of people he saw at baptisms, probably because he had very few of his close family living. His only brother-in-law, Guillaume Penifort, was by far his most common companion, from the time of Penifort's marriage to Carte's sister-in-law to Carte's death. Various cousins, almost all related to Carte's wife, also maintained ties with him over twenty or thirty years. Similar collateral kinship configurations persisted over three generations in the networks of Penifort *père,* Penifort *fils,* and Penifort's grandson, Antoine Charier.

Wives' kin were at least as important as those of the husbands' families in these social networks, both within and across generations. The importance of women as generators of kin alliances was reflected in every situation. Kin from the families of wives or mothers accounted for about half of all kin contacts among the ten notaries whose complete networks have been reconstructed.[34] Just as a wife's family members managed to retain an interest in the shaping of patrimonial accumulation and in the management of her household through a variety of legal and cultural practices, they also filled important roles in social interactions.

Brothers-in-law and cousins or husbands of cousins usually formed a core distinguished from the general mass of kindred by the frequency of their contacts with each other. But nearness of relationship was not the only determining factor in practical kin ties, as individual compatibility also came into play. Penifort's most active kin ties included the second husband of his brother's widow and this husband's brother, as well as the brothers of his cousin's husband. André Charier met at least seventeen same-generation kin at baptisms, among whom kin of his wife were again prominent. Four men were far more frequent companions than the others: Charier's brother Pierre, brother-in-law Guillaume Penifort *fils* (also a notary), Penifort's brother-in-law's brother-in-law (a court clerk), and Mathurin Carte, who was Charier's wife's cousin's cousin. The relationships of these four

---

The kin of Jean Charier and his grandson Toussaint were excluded, as they had only four and six male kin, respectively, and the generational alignment even of these few is not clear in all cases.

34. Of male kin contacts among eight notaries, 53.6 percent (112 of 209) were with kin linked by wives or mothers.

men to Charier varied widely, while some immediate relations, like his wife's two cousins, were less important members of the network, and Carte's brother Jean, a lawyer, were very peripheral.

The practical kin of Pierre Belon, who was most frequently in the company of his innumerable brothers-in-law and cousins, exemplified personal preferences that operated within the collateral and bilateral nature of practical kinship. His two brothers, the husbands of his two sisters, and the brothers of brothers-in-law and sisters-in-law were among his effective kin, but he had even more contacts with his wife's brother, five brothers-in-law, and cousins or husbands of cousins. Marguerite Daguin's father-in-law and two uncles were also among Belon's most frequent companions, and kin from her side of the family predominated among the younger kin with whom he had frequent contacts. Belon took her nephew into his own notarial practice, and he also had repeated interactions with her niece's husband and with the husband of her nephew's wife's sister.

Propinquity and personal affinities may have shaped Belon's preference for his wife's kin. They almost all lived in same parish of St. Saturnin as Belon and his wife, whereas he grew up in St. Similien, and, although two of his brothers also came to live in St. Saturnin, his sisters lived in St. Croix. Although Belon must have chosen to live and work there initially, St. Croix was literally across the street. The sense of the parish as a distinctly defined social space apparently came into play again here. Additionally, Belon's relations with his sisters in particular, and by implication with those brothers-in-law, were sometimes uneasy. They questioned his management of their property while he was their guardian, and later he threatened to seize the furniture of one sister for nonpayment of debts. Belon's ties with his wife's family persisted after her death in 1657, despite a dispute over the value of her estate, of which her family inherited half, as she died without children.

Practical kin constantly mobilized their ties in early modern urban daily life for myriad purposes, as a few examples illustrate. Louis Coudret's brother-in-law Jean Nude twice helped him beat up a clergyman who claimed that Coudret owed him money; the brothers-in-law abused the priest, threatening to cut his throat and calling him thief and apostate. Gabriel Desprez and a brother-in-law provided the money to release another brother-in-law from prison for debt, and Mathurin Goheau's kin did the same for him. René Guilloteau and Marie Bouin, his wife, secured a loan to send money to her brother, who was studying to be a doctor in Montpelier. A young clerk who worked for Simon Ertault allegedly removed from the *étude* of Etienne Poullain an act that was prejudicial to the interests of the mother of the clerk's brother-in-law.[35]

A handful of other men, as well as kin, emerged as primary members of these networks, and they shared the occupational, familial, and residential characteristics of practical kin. Their preeminence suggests whom men in the middling milieu of notaries drew on for day-to-day sociability besides kin, whom they might regard as friends. Their characteristics and the kinds of other contacts between these men suggest some of the parameters of friendship in early modern urban society.

Such friends were drawn from a narrow social and often familial group, and they closely resembled the notaries themselves in terms of occupational and socioeconomic status. Various members of the family of the apothecary Urban Vaugour, for example, dominated André Charier's social network. Vaugour, who died before Charier's marriage, had been one of the most frequent companions of Charier's father-in-law. Vaugour's sons and sons-in-law (who included a surgeon, two apothecaries, an assistant court clerk, a bookseller, and another notary, Louis Lepetit) were among Charier's most frequent companions. All these Vaugour kin lived either in St. Denis, like Charier, or in the neighboring parish of St. Croix.

The precise spatial aspects of this largely intra-parish sociability were not necessarily bounded by very localized neighborhoods. Pierre Belon's most frequent baptismal companions were thirteen men who all lived within the same parish of St. Saturnin, but not in direct proximity to each other.[36] Eight were kinsmen: Belon's brother, his father-in-law, his wife's uncle, a cousin of hers, the husband of another of her cousins, and three of his brothers-in-law. Six of the eight lived in St. Saturnin clustered around the parish's main square, and the other two in adjacent parishes.

The five men who completed the inner locus of Belon's social network lived along the streets that radiated from St. Saturnin's central square. Guy Jumeau, the host of a bar called the Pelican, lived close to Belon on a street off the northern side of the square. Bonnaventure Papin, an apothecary, lived on the same side of the square as Belon's wife's family. Jacques Bernard, the notary, lived and worked on an opposite corner of the square. Pierre Chastelier, a merchant, lived in the fifth building on a street leading south from the square. The court usher Giles Dergonne lived at the end of

---

35. ADLA, B6650, 30 October 1621; ADLA, 4E2/1919, 20 June 1654; ADLA, 4E2/291, 27 April 1650; ADLA, 4E2/1749, 14 January 1636; ADLA, B6122, 16 June 1617.

36. The residences of Belon's most common contacts were located with the help of a house-by-house parish roll. "Rolle et déclaration des maisons," 14 July 1633, ADLA, G507.

the third street leading from the square. Although Belon had fewer but still repeated contacts with a few other men who lived on his own street, notably with the baker Jean Rousseau, his most frequent companions lived across the parish.

Frequent companionship at baptisms over the course of many years built and reflected other bonds of sociability between these men. Multiple ties linked men whose friendship was expressed by multiple attendances at the same baptisms. Jacques Bernard and Belon had been clerks in the same *étude* on a corner of the square in the building where Bernard later worked. They went to baptisms together, both in St. Saturnin, where they lived, and in the *faubourg* of St. Similien, where they had grown up and now owned property. Belon's younger brother Julien began his own career as a notary in partnership (*société*) with Bernard. The friendship between the couples was solidified into spiritual kinship when Daguin became the godmother of one Bernard-Jouneaux child.

While friends had similar profiles to practical kin, bonds of friendship had different meanings from ties of kinship in daily life: friendship among men seems primarily focused on gender-specific sociability. Friendship was sometimes confirmed by godparenthood, binding companions more closely together in spiritual kinship. Either friendship or spiritual kinship, however, occupied distinctive domains from kinship per se. Friends like these did not sign marriage contracts for each other, indicating that clear boundaries existed between friend and kin in matters concerning property. André Charier, for example, had close ties to the extended Vaugour family, as we have seen, but he did not sign any of their marriage contracts. Friends attended innumerable baptisms together, for each other's children and for those of people outside their inner circle, but they rarely consolidated their bonds into kinship through marriage of their children. Nor did friendship, on the whole, entail the provision of financial aid: they rarely provided loans or co-signed for each other. The web of material, patrimonial, and affective links that bound the households of practical kin was absent from friendship between men; it served instead as a simpler and distinct complement to—or possibly relief from—the complex world of kinship.[37]

Thomas Chauveau's choices epitomized the possibilities and limitations of male friendship. Sebastien Gaudin, a court usher, and Pierre Bizeul, a saddler, knew Chauveau well for more than two decades and through his

---

37. The friendship of middling urban men, in this sense, shares some of the characteristics of aristocratic friendship identified in Jonathan Dewald, *Aristocratic Experience and the Origins of Modern Culture: France, 1570–1715* (Berkeley and Los Angeles, 1993), 104–45.

two marriages. They had frequently spent time with Chauveau, in each others' houses and elsewhere. As Gaudin explained, they had "shared a table like good friends."[38] Neither were invited to be the godfathers of his children, however, nor did they invite Chauveau to act in that capacity.

The primarily social and female rituals surrounding early modern maternity (in contrast to the medical and male environment that evolved later) provided a parallel experience to baptisms for women, yet their meanings remain elusive. Historians have debated whether this time of lying-in, as new mothers recovered from their confinement, was a time of isolation and impurity or whether the mother-centered female gatherings that followed childbirth created an unusual, if temporary, empowering space for women in early modern society that marked a site of resistance to patriarchy.[39]

Although wives' patterns of sociability are very difficult to reconstruct in similar detail, they also seem to have been overwhelmingly gender specific, but oriented around help and support as well as companionship. Women were involved in patterns of sociability that seem to parallel men's, not only having their own celebrations to welcome newborns, but, for instance, walking home together after church services. Women also though seem to have used friends as sources of material help as well as of companionship. Jeanne Bellanger asked other women for help in hiding household items before an inventory was made, and she later told the women about her anxiety over recovering safely the large amount of money she had temporarily "lost" for the same purpose. Women also lent each other money, and in these and other ways may have formed different kinds of friendships than men did.[40]

While women had their own rituals for newborns that for them may have been as significant as baptisms and surely maintained their own networks, men's claiming of the public celebration of a child's birth reflected and reinforced the associations between gender and authority that pervaded early modern urban society.[41] The predominantly male character of baptisms as social occasions and the gendering of the public expression of

---

38. Depositions of Pierre Bizeul and Sebastien Gaudin, ADLA, B5810, 19 March and 12 May 1639.

39. For the debate over the meanings of lying-in, see Adrian Wilson, "The Ceremony of Childbirth and Its Interpretation," in Valerie Fildes, ed., *Women As Mothers in Pre-Industrial England* (New York, 1990); also David Cressy, "Thanksgiving and the Churching of Women in Post-Reformation England," *Past and Present* 141 (November 1993).

40. ADLA, B5818, 10 December 1660.

41. For the need for caution in assuming that women felt excluded because men defined them as such, see Caroline Bynum, *Fragmentation and Redemption: Essays on Gender and the Human Body in Medieval Religion* (New York, 1991). For the importance of women's exclusion

community that they entailed offered middling men the opportunity to affirm solidarities. At such events, they represented their households, cemented kinship, and built ties with other men, especially residents of the same parishes.

Raising Credit

The provision of credit drew borrowers and lenders into different kinds of commitments from the giving of advice or attending of familial and social occasions. The success of middling families in meeting the financial demands of their daily lives rested, in large part, on their ability to mobilize a variety of resources. Notarial families, like their middling peers and much of the rest of early modern society, developed credit networks that would enable them to borrow money either through formal loans, in the form of *rentes* that provided large sums of money, or through informal ones that covered many of the expenses of everyday life.

The use of loans in the form of *rentes* to meet household demands was a crucial element in domestic economies of middling families, along with the income that a household's members generated through their efforts and the management of patrimony. Whether inheritance, land sale, or success had produced liquid capital that had to be invested, or whether demands like dowry provision or purchase of office exceeded the available resources, lending and borrowing money was a way of life for these families.

Consequently, where notarial families turned for money and for guarantors of their credit worthiness, and to whom they chose to lend constituted a crucial element of daily life. Notaries were involved as either borrowers, co-signers for loans, or lenders in more than 550 extant contracts for *rentes*. *Rentes* were a distinctively early modern French variety of credit. Borrowers could repay the loans whenever they chose, but had to offer security in the form of a mortgage on property, and often by providing co-signers to guarantee the repayment. Both creditors and debtors faced some risks. Large debts were easy to accumulate, and bad debts were difficult to collect.[42]

---

from public participation in another life-course ritual, funerals, in Renaissance Italian cities, in a pattern that contributed to and reflected larger power structures, see Strocchia, *Death and Ritual*, 10–12.

42. For an account of the development of *rentes* in the early sixteenth century and its subsequent refinements, see Bernard Schnapper, *Les Rentes au seizième siècle: Histoire d'un instru-

The risks that lenders faced encouraged them often to require co-signers, who would be ultimately liable for repayment if the borrower defaulted. Counter deeds (*contrelettres*), usually made between borrower and co-signatories (*cautions*) on the same day as the loans, identified who was the borrower of the money and who was the co-signer. The borrower promised to relieve co-signers of responsibility for the loan within a fixed period and admitted that co-signers had only entered the contract "at his request and to please him." These deeds also often added what was in any case implicitly understood: that without the added assurance of co-signers, lenders would not have released the money. To act as a co-signer was a significant gesture that entailed some risk, as lenders could pursue guarantors to seek repayment if borrowers reneged on their payments.[43]

One or more co-signers were involved in about three-quarters of *rentes*, and their importance in securing credit, and the trust involved in their agreeing to do so, make their identities key indicators of whom members of middling families felt they could turn to at moments of need. Historians' analyses of borrowing practices have ignored the role of guarantors, focusing instead on the respective identities of borrowers and lenders.[44] The pivotal role of notaries as credit brokers, seen earlier, suggests the need for caution in drawing conclusions about the implications of the extension of credit on this basis. As far as *rentes* were concerned, co-signing provides a clearer illumination of the role of personal ties in securing credit.

René Guilloteau's experiences illustrated some of the advantages and perils of co-signing. He and two other kin co-signed with his deceased wife's brother to allow the latter to borrow 1,000 *livres* in 1648. Seven years later, Guilloteau himself repaid the principal and the accumulated arrears, while declaring that he would seek reimbursement from the other co-signers. In 1649, Guilloteau himself borrowed money with the help of co-signers, and by 1657 the lender initiated legal action against his co-signer, on

---

ment de crédit (Paris, 1957). For an account of the practical workings, advantages, and shortcomings of *rentes* for all parties, see Jonathan Dewald, *The Formation of a Provincial Nobility: The Magistrates of the Parlement of Rouen, 1499–1610* (Princeton, 1980), 230–33.

43. For the development of the use of *cautions* and their liability for payment, see Schnapper, *Rentes au seizième siècle*, 213–15, 264.

44. See, for example, Dewald, *Formation of a Provincial Nobility*, 235–39; Francis Kent, *Household and Lineage in Renaissance Florence* (Princeton, 1977), 156; Jean-Paul Poisson, *Notaires et société: Travaux d'histoire et de sociologies notariales* (Paris, 1985), 247–63; Gayle Brunelle, *The New World Merchants of Rouen, 1559–1630* (Kirksville, Mo., 1991).

the grounds of Guilloteau's failure to maintain payments. Guilloteau's sister Françoise, the widow of François Rapion, stepped in on that occasion to cover her brother's obligations and save the co-signer from further pursuit.[45]

Kin were by far the most common guarantors of loans secured by members of middling families. Almost half of all the loans in which notaries were among the debtors involved kin as guarantors. The kin who allied on these occasions were usually part of the generational cohort, whether siblings, siblings-in-law, or cousins, again pointing to the dominance of this group as practical kin. Parents, uncles, and aunts were also possible resources. Moreover, when notaries themselves borrowed money, their kin were the overwhelming choice as co-signers.[46]

In the minority of instances where no guarantors co-signed for loans, husbands and wives borrowed money together more than twice as often as husbands borrowed money alone.[47] This practice suggests that spouses together were more credit worthy than husbands alone, perhaps because wives' participation added their lineage property (which could not be sold or encumbered without their permission) to the assets against which an unpaid debt could be recovered. The complaints of wives seeking separations of property because their husbands coerced them into signing loans illustrates the importance for husbands of securing their wives' participation.[48] Wives who joined their husbands in loans increased the family's access to liquid capital, thereby actively building the family's capital and prospects as well as putting their lineage property at risk.[49]

Families acted together to raise money to meet a variety of individual goals, especially to purchase offices or to fund other particularly onerous

---

45. ADLA, 4E2/1033, 29 January 1648 and 20 April 1655; ADLA, 4E2/547, 16 March 1657.

46. Of 289 loans where a notary was among the borrowers, 135 were co-signed with people who could be identified as kin (46.7 percent), and 79 were co-signed with other people (27.3 percent). Who was the borrower (rather than guarantor) among the signers was identifiable in 67 cases: the notary was the *caution* in 47 of these (70.1 percent), and the borrower in 20 others.

47. Of 289 loans to which notaries were parties as borrowers, they acted alone in only 22 cases (7.6 percent) and with their wives in 53 cases (18.3 percent).

48. Among many such complaints, see, for example, ADLA, B6125, 25 June 1620; ADLA, B6129, 1 February 1627 and 23 July 1643.

49. In 1606, Henry IV made a declaration that wives who signed contracts were commited to the obligations therein, whether or not notaries had inserted the wives' explicit renunciation of their traditional protections in acts of obligation. Francois Isambert, *Recueil général des anciennes lois françaises depuis l'an 420 jusqu'à la Révolution de 1789*, vol. 15 (Paris 1829), 302–3.

demands on an individual household's resources, as the explanations that borrowers gave for seeking loans indicated. For members of middling families the purchase of an office was expensive and frequently involved the pooling of kin resources to secure a loan. Simon Bouvier's brothers-in-law Hervé Trebillard and the merchant Guillaume Templier co-signed for the 1,400 *livres* that he borrowed to buy his office of royal notary. In the *contrelettre*, drawn up in Trebillard's house, Bouvier asserted that they had joined only "at his prayer and request, to please him and to facilitate his securing the money" that he needed. They all agreed that after paying the 1,350 *livres* that the office cost, Bouvier should keep the other 50 to cover the expenses of his reception into the office and other associated expenses. Similarly, Renée Coquet, the widow of Jean Bachelier, her brother-in-law Julien Bachelier, and her sister borrowed money on two occasions to use to purchase an office for Coquet's son. Jeanne Monnier, Pierre Granjon's widow, helped her nephew borrow the money he needed, while Jacques Bernard and Isabel Jouneaux helped their son.[50]

Kin also helped each other to borrow money to relieve many other moments of pressure on the domestic economy, whether caused by life-course transitions, ambition, or financial difficulty. François Rapion's parents helped him borrow the money to buy a house next door to his in-laws. Jean Blandin co-signed with his parents-in-law to secure the money for them to buy some rural property. Pierre Belon and Marguerite Daguin, his wife, helped Belon's brother Felix borrow 1,200 *livres* to buy merchandise for his business. Jean Bonnamy and his brother-in-law Thomas Bruneau co-signed a 2,000 *livres* loan for Bonnamy's mother, Renée Rousselet, so she could pay debts owed to two merchants.[51]

The kinds of demands that led family members to seek loans suggest why kin were the primary co-signers. At the moments in the life cycle of a family and in the life course of individuals that placed greatest pressure on the resources of a household, kin joined together to raise the capital needed to meet the challenges. For kin, such action formed another part of their ongoing role in the management of the patrimonial affairs of individual households.

---

50. ADLA, 4E2/1193, 30 April 1650; ADLA, 4E2/618, 30 April 1651; ADLA, 4E2/464, 15 August 1644; ADLA, 4E2/1209 and ADLA, 4E2/1429, both 22 June 1660. Extant notarial records of *rentes* and of the sale of notarial offices reveal many other examples of this kind of help to purchase office.

51. ADLA, 4E2/1717, 12 February 1624; ADLA, 4E2/1592, 7 September 1646; ADLA, 4E2/1157, 2 July 1646; ADLA, 4E2/94, 28 August 1629.

Members of notarial families secured loans with people who were not their kin in about a quarter of *rentes,* guarantees that sometimes seem to have been favors for friends or acquaintances, or that notaries provided as part of their role in facilitating credit in the community.[52] Pierre Belon and Marguerite Daguin twice provided the necessary security for their close friends and spiritual kin Jacques Bernard and Isabel Jouneaux to borrow money. Louis Coudret co-signed, on one occasion, for a merchant from his native parish in the *pays Nantais,* and Michel Benoist fulfilled the same role for his impecunious landlord, Julien Jouneaux.[53]

Notaries' role as key links in the circle of credit exchanges, as we saw earlier, may account for many of the contracts in which they co-signed with people who were not kin. In 70 percent of such transactions, notaries acted as the guarantors rather than the actual borrowers. In many such instances, notaries probably provided the security that borrowers needed to find a willing lender.

Rentes involved lenders as well as co-signers, and while kin constantly looked to each other to co-sign loans, they rarely lent each other money in this form. Only about one in ten loans were made entirely between kin, an illustration of the limits of kin mobilization.[54] When kin did lend money to each other, on occasion, they were meeting similar needs to those that lay behind the loans they co-signed for. Julien Lucas bought his office of royal notary by borrowing money with Françoise Leroy, his maternal grandmother, from Pierre Belon, Lucas's maternal uncle and Leroy's son-in-law. Marguerite Bernard, Claude Geneste's widow, lent her daughter 1,000 *livres* to pay for her granddaughter's reception as a novice in a convent. Guillaume Jahanneau bought his office with the help of a loan from his aunt, for which his father and paternal cousin Guillaume Penifort co-signed.[55]

The primary creditors and debtors of notarial families were elite and middling Nantais residents (see Table 7.2). In almost every case, all parties to the loan lived in the city, in contrast to the more geographically expan-

---

52. Co-signers were not kin in 79 of 314 *rentes* (25.2 percent) where the notarial families were among the borrowers.

53. ADLA, 4E2/1026, 19 May 1643; ADLA, 4E2/1423, 28 May 1658; ADLA, 4E2/1474, 19 July 1657; ADLA, 4E2/1030, 25 September 1645.

54. Of 558 loans, 57 (10.2 percent) were made entirely between kin.

55. ADLA, 4E2/1146, 13 October 1653; ADLA, 4E2/1745, 16 December 1634; ADLA, 4E2/489, 11 December 1609.

Table 7.2. Borrowing and lending patterns of notaries[56]

	As Borrowers	As Lenders
Urban elite (a)	137 (46.8%)	66 (39.1%)
Middling (b)	103 (35.1%)	69 (40.8%)
Artisans	15 (5.1%)	14 (8.3%)
Peasants	3 (1.0%)	17 (10.0%)
Religious institutions (c)	33 (11.3%)	—
No identifier	2 (0.7%)	3 (1.8%)
Total	293	169

sive parameters of elite credit networks.[57] Although most notarial families owned rural small holdings that were let to tenants, their connections did not seem to extend to credit domination, nor to relations with rural nobility, whether as debtors or creditors. The urban elite, who often held high legal office either in the royal financial court or in the city's other courts, were the lenders in almost half the loans. The middling ranks to which notarial families belonged (that is, petty legal *officiers*, apothecaries, surgeons, sundry merchants, and successful artisans) provided about another third of the loans. These two groups, together with a variety of religious institutions, accounted for almost all the lenders on whom notarial families called. Notaries' money lending followed an almost identical pattern, splitting about 80 percent of the loans they made between the urban elite and their middling peers.

Pierre Belon was personally involved in forty-eight surviving *rentes* that provide an example of the networks an individual created through exchange of credit. Only three were entirely between kin: his brother-in-law and a kinsman of his wife (perhaps her uncle) lent him money, and he lent money to his nephew. He co-signed for sixteen loans, three times with Marguerite Daguin, his wife, and seven times with other kin. The latter involved same-generation kin on five occasions and mixed-generation groups on the other two. Six loans were co-signed with non–family members: two with the same nobleman and three with Jacques Bernard, his fellow notary, spiritual

56. This table excludes the loans made entirely between kin. (a) Includes members of sovereign courts and other possessors of the honorific titles *noble homme* or *escuyer.* (b) Includes artisans with the title *honorable homme.* (c) Includes convents, monastic orders, and confraternities.

For the inclusion of *honorables hommes* in the middling milieu, see Marcel Couturier's conclusions about social structure in another Loire Valley town in his *Recherches sur les structures sociales de Châteaudun, 1525–1789* (Paris, 1969), 222. He suggested that tradespeople in this sector would include men whose situation was unclear and hardly distinct from that of artisans, except in being "chefs d'industrie . . . dont la situation est bien assise."

57. Less than 5 percent of contracts involved a nonresident of Nantes. Most of these were peasants (*laboureurs*), but the majority were involved with only one notary, Sebastien Pouetard,

kinsman, and frequent companion. The other loan was made with four bakers: the five of them had been *cautions* for Belon's stepfather in the lease of a mill, and they borrowed the money to cover the obligation that the guarantee involved when the stepfather was unable to pay. Belon also lent money by means of *rentes* on twenty-nine occasions. Nineteen of these loans were made to members of the urban elite, and ten to middlemen, three to peasants.[58]

Belon's credit exchanges using *rentes,* like those of other members of notarial families, were locally based and had a distinctive familial orientation. Although kin did not lend each other money, they were very important facilitators of capital, whose willingness to co-sign for each other enabled acquisitions that were very important in maintaining their social position.

Credit within local communities was also available in other forms than notarized *rentes,* and these more informal practices had different characteristics and established different relationships to those of *rentes.* Such exchanges are difficult to reconstruct, because they have left little in the way of records, although wills, accountings, or lawsuits occasionally provide traces of how this alternative credit network functioned.

Smaller sums of money were usually involved, and the transactions were often interest free, with kin extending credit to each other.[59] Bertrand Lucas lent his brother-in-law 39 *écus* (109 *livres*) in four *cedullas* (a kind of IOU) between October 1593 and October 1594. Jean Bonnamy noted that he owed his brother-in-law Thomas Bruneau 8 *livres* "for which there is no *cedulla.*" When Hervé Trebillard's father asked a son-in-law, a pewterer Jean Deniau, to lend him some money to pay off, as "his age and bodily indisposition" prevented him from meeting his debts, Deniau agreed, "in order to free his conscience."[60]

---

who lived outside the city on the opposite bank of the Loire, in the rural parish of St. Sebastien d'Aigné. For an analysis of the credit networks of elite merchants see Brunelle, *New World Merchants of Rouen,* 90.

58. One loan was to a person with no indication of title or occupation. Belon later transferred fourteen of the *rentes* he originally financed to other lenders, a way of freeing the capital at his discretion.

59. There were some exceptions to the small scale of these informal loans. For example, at the time of their deaths, Charles Germont owed *honorable homme* Simon Delacosse 200 *livres* in a *cedulla,* and Pierre Babin, Jean Verger's father-in-law, owed 300 *livres* and 240 *livres* in two of his *cedullas.* ADLA, B5865, 9 December 1623; and ADLA, B6130, 10 May 1630.

60. ADLA, B5898, 27 April 1598; ADLA, 4E2/94, 9 September 1630; ADLA, 4E2/131, 17 April 1638.

Kin bartered different forms of assistance and built ties of practical kinship through myriad contacts. André Tallandeau helped his sister-in-law Jeanne Davy to secure legal assent for a separation from his brother and to nullify acts that her husband had made, albeit with her consent, while she was still a minor. He also lent her small sums "on different occasions" after the act of separation. He, in turn, owed Davy rent, because he lived in part of a building that she had inherited. In the end, they were almost even.

Kin exchanges of these kinds were both essential resources and potential minefields of ill will, as the affairs of Mathurin Bruneau and his brother Pierre demonstrated. Mathurin lent 68 *livres* to Pierre's mother-in-law, or, at least, so he thought; later, Pierre's wife said that if he had lent it to her mother, he (Mathurin) should ask her for it. A nephew said that Pierre told him he had used the money to settle an account that he and Mathurin owed, as a result of their trading in grain and wine. When Pierre asked Mathurin for the rent he owed, Mathurin said he would pay it when the 68 *livres* were repaid.[61]

Informal loans like these were part of an infinitely complex system of exchanges of services, goods, and money through which practical kin were defined and mobilized as key resources in meeting daily needs. They suggested the ways in which kin were critical facilitators of each other's lives. The exactitude with which such informal and diverse exchanges were balanced suggests that they were not casual, altruistic, or given without expectation of reimbursement, but part of a web that supported a familial effort to meet the challenges of early modern life.

People outside the family were crucial sources of petty cash as well as of major borrowing, even though kin may have been more forthcoming as suppliers of informal loans than of the large obligations that *rentes* represented. François Bonnamy's will noted that he owed fourteen people money in *cedullas* and eight other people money for sundry, undefined loans, in addition to debts for goods delivered, for which he had not yet paid.

In this case, like in others, creditors for small, informal loans came from a different social milieu than *rentiers*. While notaries' middling peers were still lenders, especially on occasions when larger sums of money were involved, members of the Nantais elite were largely absent from these credit exchanges, and members of a lower social group emerged as creditors. Nineteen of the twenty-two creditors that Bonnamy listed were of lower social status than he. In addition, he owed various tradespeople, including a

61. ADLA, 4E2/1929, 21 July 1660; ADLA, B5813, 28 July 1645.

shoemaker, a saddler, a tailor, and an apothecary, for goods and services. His brother-in-law Bruneau and two other notaries had also lent money.

The small-scale informal lending and borrowing of middling families was, in these ways, oriented differently to *rentes,* but like the latter, these transactions went beyond neighborhoods and beyond people of similar social standing. Pierre Babin owed his baker for bread delivered and money lent. He also owed a cleric 100 *livres,* for which "a diamond necklace" and a silver cup had been left as security, and he owed a merchant "whose name he did not know" almost seven *livres.* Diverse services or payments were often advanced without immediate reimbursement, and delaying payment in such instances effectively coerced others into becoming creditors. Jacques Bernard, for example, owed a locksmith more than 220 *livres* for work done.[62]

Small-scale, informal credit networks also differed from the better-documented *rentes* with regard to the role of women. Widows were important creditors of *rentes,* providing the money in about 20 percent of the loans that notaries recorded, and women often co-signed with their husbands for *rentes.* However, widows and wives seemed to use these more informal loans to lend each other money. Marguerite Huet, the wife of a lawyer in the royal fiscal court, noted in her will that she had borrowed 20 *livres* from Louise Lecoq, René Guilloteau's wife, and wanted her to be repaid. She had also borrowed more than 150 *livres* from another woman. Marguerite DelaVergne, Vincent Bernard's wife, asked Jullienne Saupin, who helped do her laundry, to lend her money "for necessities" on several occasions. A kinswoman of Pierre Lebreton's told him that she had borrowed 100 *livres* from her brother's mother-in-law without her husband's knowledge.[63] Women involved in this facet of credit exchange also participated in borrowing and lending on other levels. But for married women in particular, whose ability to lend or borrow money was otherwise mediated through their husbands, an informal network of credit circulating among women was an invaluable resource.[64]

---

62. ADLA, 4E2/1195, 14 October 1652; ADLA, 4E2/1429, 2 November 1660. Innumerable other small debts of this kind existed between notaries as debtors and members of lower social groups as creditors, for both goods and cash advances. See, among many examples, the 6 *livres* and 15 *sous* that René Guilloteau owed Laurens Hubert, a *paticier;* and the sums of 61 *livres,* 11 *sous,* and 97 *livres,* 17 *sous,* and 7 *deniers* that Hervé Trebillard owed a "merchant" named Philippe Mesnard. All of these debts had to be collected by legal action. ADLA, B6123, 14 July 1618; and B6127, 4 December 1624.

63. ADLA, 4E2/1210, 8 April 1660; ADLA, B5806, 16 January 1626; ADLA, B5816, 16 January 1654.

64. Activities of this kind are difficult to document. Laurel Thatcher Ulrich, *Good Wives: Image and Reality in the Lives of Women in Northern New England, 1650–1750* (Oxford, 1980), 44–48, has noted the existence of a separate female exchange system in colonial New England.

The distinctions that existed between credit networks involved in raising formal loans and those mobilized to raise informal credit highlight some of the key priorities of early modern communities. Historians have seen credit circulation within a limited group in two distinct ways. Some have considered it a form of assistance that recognized common identification and willingness to provide help, in an epoch when demographic and financial realities increasingly necessitated widespread use of credit. Others have viewed it as a more ambivalent combination of self-interest and dependency.[65] Clarifying the differences and similarities in the kinds of credit available to early modern French families illuminates some of these issues.

Middling and elite urban families were very active participants in formal credit networks involving legal contracts and the charging of interest based around *rentes*. However, the role of notaries as central pivots of these credit networks was critical in shaping their characteristics. Notarial credit brokering may help to explain the very localized nature of lending and borrowing in this milieu. Moreover, the securing of a *rente*, as we have seen, was a commercial and impersonal transaction, when a notary arranged it, that distanced lender and borrower.

Informal credit differed from *rentes* because it did involve personal relations, with concomitant dependency and the obligation inherent in the requesting and granting of a loan. In this community, although this kind of debt was usually small scale and often interest free, it often did not come from neighbors or coworkers of similar social status providing mutual aid and economic dependency. Power relations between creditor and debtor were, if anything, more stark in these kinds of transactions.

The primary dependencies in *rentes* were between co-signers rather than borrower and lender, a difference that may explain the striking disjuncture between kin willingness to help each other borrow by co-signing for *rentes*, with the risk that involved, but their reluctance to lend through *rentes*, yet their frequent lending on a more informal basis. In both cases, kin came to the forefront to bear the brunt of the dependency and obligation created by the particular transaction. In doing so they were able to help build and protect their family's status as middling citizens, by maintaining the appearance of successful *bon mesnagement*, a pivotal value at the heart of their version of patriarchal husbandry, as we have seen. They retained critical

65. Discussions of the social and cultural implications of early modern credit relations include: Dewald, *Formation of a Provincial Nobility*, 238–239; Farr, *Hands of Honor*, 162; Wrightson and Levine, *Poverty and Piety in an English Village*, 100–101; Craig Muldrew, "Interpreting the Market: The Ethics of Credit and Community in Early Modern England," *Social History* 18 (May 1993).

patrimonial oversight within the extended family, without being forced into reliance on their peers.

Interactions over credit were elements of larger patterns that shaped kinship. The importance of lineage property in the patrimonial makeup of individual households was again critical; just as kin expected to have oversight of patrimonial affairs, the potential commitment of lineage property as security for loans gave kin mutual interests in money management. By relying on kin, these families reinforced the tendency toward mutual cooperation between households. This interdependence aligned a larger kin group with those of individual households. Although kin who co-signed entered some risk of actual loss, not only as guarantors but in the case that the debts were the responsibility of the estate to which kin might have some claim or obligation, their cooperation was part of a broad pattern of patrimonial cooperation, collaboration, and oversight.

They, too, could use the same kin, in turn, as co-signers for loans. Moreover, the "capital" of an individual family and its kin rested on the family's reputation and position, as well as on its material foundations. In all kinds of ways, from their status in the neighborhood to their ability to get more loans, kin benefited from facilitating the purchase of office or ensuring that other financial obligations were met.

The relationships that early modern Nantais fostered at moments of making marriages, celebrating baptisms, and raising loans reveal the primary actors in their everyday lives. Kinship, gender, and rank were at the heart of early modern solidarities in these urban middling families.

Extensive and bilateral ties of official kinship characterized middling families in early modern urban communities. The cooperative strategies that characterized relations between consanguinal and affinal kin were evident everywhere.[66] These expressions of kinship also had boundaries. The

---

66. The system of kinship that resulted was, therefore, quite distinctive in its construction and orientation. In Renaissance Florence, for instance, the patrilineal orientation of kinship emphasized kin ties within the lineage, and women were only temporarily part of their spouse's family, rather than serving as key integrators. "Houses [kinship groups] were made by men. Kinship was determined by men." See Christiane Klapisch-Zuber, "The 'Cruel Mother': Maternity, Widowhood, and Dowry in Florence in the Fourteenth and Fifteenth Centuries," in her *Women, Family, and Ritual*, 117–20. In early modern Germany, David Sabean has suggested, while partible inheritance practice encouraged cooperation between brothers-in-law, affines were a focus of enmity as well as of support, because of the threat they posed to the patrimonial estate. See Sabean, "Young Bees in an Empty Hive," in Medick and Sabean, eds., *Interest and Emotion*; and David Warren Sabean, *Power in the Blood: Popular Culture and Village Discourse in Early Modern Germany* (Cambridge, 1984), 31–32, 108.

widespread reluctance of kin who gave advice about the appointment of a guardian to accept that role for themselves may be explained in part by the perception that a boundary demarcated the extent of their obligations. Perhaps official kin felt that such a responsibility was beyond the call of duty for them, and that it should fall to those who were effective kin.

Practical kinship—that is, relations mobilized in myriad ways—was more narrowly delineated around some kin among the same-generation cohort who became primary actors in the everyday lives of their relatives. Ties with collateral kin—from siblings, their siblings-in-law, cousins, to even second or third cousins—were affirmed in many common activities. Practical kin called on each other to participate in overseeing occasions when household patrimonial issues were at stake, to help each other borrow money, and to provide companionship, as well as material support.

Among middling families, practical kin and friends had similar profiles but served quite distinct roles, at least for men. Friends were likely to be residents of the same parish, although not immediate neighbors, and to be of similar socioeconomic rank. Parishes were powerful parameters of urban space, in the social and spatial horizons of families.[67] A noteworthy absence was that of occupational bonding, apparently. Although kin who were also notaries were often frequent companions, notaries' companions otherwise rarely included other notaries. Friends neither provided nor guaranteed loans, nor did they oversee patrimonial matters or, normally, provide a pool from which future kin might be drawn as marriage partners. They were, instead, companions who shared in public life in the parish. In moments of crisis, kin rather than friends were the source of material help of whatever kind.[68] Women's own networks, albeit difficult to recover in the same detail, were equally gender specific, but women may have expected support, help, and sociability from friends as well as from kin.

67. Recent historiography, at least of the eighteenth century, has tended to downplay the importance of the parish as a social or spatial domain, in favor of emphasis on the smaller unit of the neighborhood. For an example of the emphasis on neighborhood over parish, see David Garrioch, *Neighbourhood and Community in Paris, 1740–1790* (Cambridge, 1986), 157–60. In a recent book, however, Garrioch argues for the importance of parish ties. See Garrioch, *Formation of the Parisian Bourgeoisie.*

68. In an illuminating discussion of friendship in the seventeenth-century French aristocracy, Jonathan Dewald has suggested that at this time, friendship complemented family relations by providing a haven from the complicated obligations and negotiations of kinship. His analysis resonates with the separate domains of friendship and kinship occupied for middling urban men. However, for middling men, unlike for aristocrats, friendship also remained as part of public life, rather than as a private refuge from civic obligations, as the next chapter will illustrate. Dewald, *Aristocratic Experience,* 104–45.

Women linked a bilateral practical kin network that emphasized relations between collateral kinsmen, a position derived from women's claim to property through partible inheritance. Yet in public expressions of those relationships, women's participation was often hidden. The centrality of women in the construction of kinship was disguised by practices that emphasized the bonds between men as patrimonial managers, as guarantors of loans, as public social contacts, and in myriad other roles.[69] Such practices reflected and perpetuated public hierarchies of authority that allowed networks of patrimonial management, credit, kinship, and sociability built up by both men and women to materialize in public form without the women who provided the links within them.

The relationships that people created in meeting the needs of their personal lives were also intrinsic parts of other aspects of early modern life. Men who were kin or friends associated with each other not only at baptisms and in their own households, but in the local militia and in meetings of members of their parish church. The narrow social spectrum from which kin and friends were drawn among these middling families found its public identity in all these places, where notaries, with their kin and their friends, participated in events that constituted the social basis of the parish as a unit, and where men working as notaries continued their negotiation of the bases of household authority.

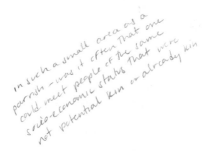

in such a small area as a parish – was it often that one could meet people of the same socio-economic status that were not potential kin or already kin

---

69. It is difficult to draw conclusions for the early modern period about whether men or women were more active in maintaining kin ties. Work on kinship in nineteenth-century cities has shown that women had central and active roles as "kin keepers" in the making and maintaining of kin ties. On the other hand, in some nineteenth-century rural communities, men played an equal role in maintaining kin ties. Discussions of the gendering of the keeping of kin ties include: Micaela di Leonardo, "The Female World of Cards and Holidays: Women, Families, and the Work of Kinship," *Signs* 12 (Spring 1987); Davidoff and Hall, *Family Fortunes*; Hareven, *Family Time, Industrial Time,* 105–6; Nancy Grey Osterud, *Bonds of Community: The Lives of Farm Women in Nineteenth-Century New York* (Ithaca, N.Y., 1991), 248.

8

Public Life in the City

One night in April of 1616, a militia squad was keeping guard at a Nantes city gate. The corporal, notary René Lebigot, and his seven men were probably, as on many other nights, playing cards, gambling, drinking, and enjoying the company of friends. The squad included three other notaries besides Lebigot: Etienne Poullain and the cousins Simon Ertaud and Simon Aubin. The routine of the evening was disrupted when an unidentified man fell to his death from a platform on the watch tower. In the subsequent inquiry, the men keeping watch staunchly claimed to have been inside the tower when the incident occurred, and they denied that any dispute among themselves had caused the accident.[1]

This tale of a night watch gone awry points to one of the possibilities for participation in public life for middling men and to some of the attractions of such activity in a provincial city. Service as a rank-and-file militiaman was

---

1. Eight squad members signed the declaration describing the accident. Besides the four notaries, two *procureurs* were present. The occupations of the other squad members are unknown. A surgeon called to the scene speculated that the man had been looking for the latrines and fell accidentally through a hole where planks were missing. ADLA, B6122, 5 April 1616.

perhaps the lowest institutional outlet for civic activism, but notaries also took part in other local public institutions. Many of them attended general assemblies of the municipal council, took part in the administration of their parish churches, and ran the Nantais poorhouse.

Historians analyzing the political culture of early modern France have focused in large part on the behavior and ideology of elites, whether at the court or in the provinces, or on popular outbreaks of contentiousness and their eventual mitigation.[2] These analyses have as yet done little to suggest the ordinary political activities of people below the elite, that is, outside of the exceptional moments of revolt, riot, and civil war that are beyond the scope of this study. At the same time, historians of the late eighteenth century have suggested that middling men and their superiors created a politically influential "public sphere" at that time in which gender became a key constituent of engagement, and through which women were largely excluded from political culture.[3]

Yet at a much earlier time, the participation of middling men like notaries in the institutions of urban life helped to build the highly gendered patterns of association that were pillars of early modern local urban political culture.[4] Why notaries chose to pursue public activities when many of their peers did not, and why they preferred some of these activities over others, suggests how the involvement of middling men shaped the forms of local politics in early modern French cities. The local issues in which mid-

2. The literature on the political culture of early modern France is vast. To start, see William Beik, *Absolutism and Society in Seventeenth-Century France: State Power and Provincial Aristocracy in Languedoc* (Cambridge, 1985); and Sharon Kettering, *Patrons, Brokers, and Clients in Seventeenth-Century France* (Oxford, 1986).

3. Key studies of the role of gender in the creation of the eighteenth-century public sphere include Joan Landes, *Women and the Public Sphere in the Age of the French Revolution* (Ithaca, N.Y., 1988); and Sarah Maza, *Private Lives and Public Affairs: The Causes Célèbres of Prerevolutionary France* (Berkeley and Los Angeles, 1993).

4. A very important exception to the neglect of nonelite political life is David Garrioch's *The Formation of the Parisian Bourgeoisie, 1690–1830* (Cambridge, Mass., 1996). See also the assertion that *gens du bien* (men like shopkeepers and artisan masters) were the "frontier of order" in early modern French civil society, in James B. Collins, *Classes, Estates, and Order in Early Modern Brittany* (Cambridge, 1994), 17–18.

Considerable work on early modern England has recently sought to highlight the importance of the political role of such middling men and the local issues with which they were involved. See, for example, Matthew Boulton, *Neighbourhood and Society: A London Suburb in the Seventeenth Century* (Cambridge, 1987); Steve Rappaport, *World Within Worlds: Structures of Life in Sixteenth-Century London* (Cambridge, 1987); David Harris Sacks, *The Widening Gate: Bristol and the Atlantic Economy, 1450–1700* (Berkeley and Los Angeles, 1991); Linda Colley, *Britons: Forging the Nation, 1707–1837* (New Haven, Conn., 1992).

dling men were involved—while often lost in the midst of religious wars, sieges, and tax revolts that have seized historians' attention, and that, even for contemporary men at the centers of power, were hardly blips on the horizon—were of critical import to them and to their communities. The mediations of their concerns were the foundations that underpinned urban political culture in early modern France.

Municipal assembly, militia duty, parish meeting, and poorhouse administration provided contexts where the issues of property, sociability, and the securing of order in the larger context of the city were negotiated, joining the personal lives and the public work of the notariat in the many sites where authority was constructed on a day-to-day basis. By examining the public lives of middling men in ordinary times, their attitudes toward and their roles in building urban political culture emerge.

Notarial Horizons: The City and the Nation

Middling men like notaries had little direct role in public life on a national, provincial level, or even on a city-wide level, but where they did choose to give their presence, energy, and attention suggests how they perceived the sources of authority around them. The narrowness of notaries' horizons and their limited prospects did not mean that notaries or other men of their rank were apolitical or detached from governance.

Few hints survive that shed light on the attitudes of these middling families toward—or on the impact on them of—the political and religious disturbances that play such a prominent role in the historiography of early modern France. Notaries in the neighboring Breton city of Rennes, for example, were thought by some, at least, to be loyal to the crown and "very good servants of the king" during the struggles between royalist and Catholic League factions in the 1590s.[5] Evidence on these kinds of issues remains, however, elusive.

Certainly a persistent localism, generally, characterized notaries' experiences and perhaps their concerns. Nantais notaries, as we have seen, over-

---

5. Although Nantes declared for the League in 1589 and remained Leaguer until the peace of 1598, the city council opposed the Leaguer affiliation, and its composition remained separate from that of the institutions controlled by the Leaguer governor of Brittany, who made his headquarters in the city. Robert Harding, "Revolution and Reform in the Holy League: Angers, Rennes, and Nantes," *Journal of Modern History* 53 (September 1981).

whelmingly came from the city itself or from its immediate environs, and, unlike the sons of elite families, they did not attend university. Despite occasional exceptions, such as René Germont's experience as a young man when he was captured by pirates in the Mediterranean and held hostage in Algeria for a couple of years, most middling men had little broader experience than the odd trip across Brittany to Rennes.[6]

By the later seventeenth century, royal notaries as a group did seek, on occasion, at least, to demonstrate a relationship with the larger polity. To secure prayers for the king's recovery during his illness in early 1687, for instance, thirty-seven of the forty-six Nantais notaries contributed to a collection that paid for a mass in the church of the Jacobins (decorated for that day by a *marchand tapissier* hired by the notaries) and for a distribution of bread to the poor of the city a week later. Some of them participated as a group in the religious ceremony, and twenty-three notaries afterward attended a catered dinner.[7]

This attention, however, may not have predated the emergence of major issues of contention between notaries and the French state from the 1670s. Beginning at that time, notaries faced increasing taxation, repeated efforts to reduce their number, and tighter government scrutiny and regulation, such as the introduction of a requirement that notaries maintain repertories of all the acts they made. Such initiatives combined to galvanize notarial companies in many cities to organize more cohesively, in order to defend themselves against the crown. The evidence of Nantais notaries' efforts to meet more regularly starting in the 1680s suggests a similar evolution in their attitudes.[8]

Notaries played little part in political leadership in the city. Nantais notaries did not rise to attain city-wide positions such as that of mayor or of governor of the poorhouse. Other high-ranking offices such as alderman (*échevin*) or militia captain were also virtually beyond reach. Between 1560

6. For the efforts of Germont's "very poor and needy" mother, Louise Lucas, the widow of Charles Germont, to send money for the release of her son, see ADLA, 4E2/1758, 27 January 1637; and ADLA, 4E2/1760, 14 September 1639. Similar conclusions have been drawn about the local orientation of middling men in England. See the works cited in note 4.

7. ADLA, 5E, Corporations 26, Compte de Syndics, 1673–1788.

8. See ADLA, 5E, Corporations 4, 5, 13, and 26, for disputes over taxation and the number of notaries in the late seventeenth century. For the evolution of disputes from the later seventeenth century, see Jean Gaston, *La Communauté des notaires de Bordeaux, 1520–1791* (Bordeaux, 1913; reprinted Toulouse, 1991); Maurice Garsonnin, *Histoire de la communauté des notaires au Châtelet d'Orléans, 1303–1791* (Orléans, 1922); Ludovic Langlois, *La Communauté des notaires de Tours, de 1512 à 1791* (Paris, 1911); Monique Limon, *Les Notaires au Châtelet de Paris sous le règne de Louis XIV: Etude institutionelle et sociale* (Toulouse, 1992).

and 1660, only three notaries became aldermen and only four served as captains of militia companies, and only one of these positions was gained after 1600. As in other cities, elites dominated high public office.

Nevertheless, notaries seem to have seen their public and personal lives converging in a local context. A handful of early modern French notaries took it upon themselves to write narratives of episodes in their towns' histories, an interesting intersection of personal and public lives. In writing personal civic narratives in this form, they made records of the events that served rather like the *procès-verbaux* that they made for individuals in their notarial capacity.[9]

Moreover, at least from the mid-sixteenth century, a few notaries were formally involved in the public life of their cities, albeit as recorders and facilitators rather than as makers of governance. In Nantes, some men who worked as notaries participated in these ways in the city's formal political institutions. In 1588 Bertrand Lucas was paid to take the correspondence of the city to the king.[10] A series of notaries held the position of city clerk (*greffier de la ville*) for the municipal council continuously during the period from 1560 to 1660, and effectively worked as the notary of the municipality in that position, keeping the records of the council's activities.[11]

In January 1582, Guillaume Bodin had just taken over as city clerk from his predecessor, Jean Bizeul, when he was involved in an incident that provided a rare insight into how notaries perceived their place in the potentially competing polities around them. At the end of January, Nantes's royal judge (the *sénéschal*) asked Bodin to hand over the city's records, but Bodin refused, declaring that the request was contrary to usual practice. In the dispute that ensued, the judge maintained that by virtue of his rank, he was entitled to request the records without giving reason or justification, while Bodin maintained that as a municipal official, he could not hand them

---

9. Published versions of these accounts include: *Mémoires de Eustache Piemond: Notaire royal-delphinal de la ville de Saint-Antoine en Dauphine, 1572–1608* (Valence, 1885; reprinted Geneva, 1973); Charlie R. Steen, ed., *The Chronicles and Memoirs of Pasquier de la Barre of Tournai, 1559–1567* (New York, 1989); "Le Livre de raison du notaire Etienne Borrelly, 1654 à 1717," *Mémoires de l'Académie de Nîmes* (Nîmes, 1885). I thank Professor James Amelang for these references. Other similar narratives were no doubt made but have not been published. See, for example, "L'Extrait d'un Mémorial Rédigé par le Sieur Nicolas Herpin Notaire et Procureur à Saint Martin, Ile de Re," 1581–1603, Bibliothèque Municipale de La Rochelle.

10. AMN, BB20, 24 May 1588.

11. Indeed, just as witnesses were called to attest to the character and experience of men wanting to be notaries, the same requirements and language were used to determine the suitability of a candidate for *greffier*, who had to provide witnesses of his "bonne vie, moeurs, conversations et religion catholique, apostolique et romaine . . . et de la suffisance expérience et dilligence et capacité au fait de practique." AMN, BB18, 4 January 1582.

over without an order from the city council. Finally the judge insisted that Bodin had a responsibility to obey him. Bodin responded that as a royal notary, he should obey the royal judge and would show him the acts he had made in that capacity, but as *greffier* of the city he would not show the judge the town's records without an order from the city council. The judge promptly threw Bodin into prison. The city council supported Bodin's refusal, saying that the judge could review the records in its archives but could not remove them.

This episode marked but one in a long series of struggles between royal and municipal authority that took place all over France beginning in the late sixteenth century, but it offered a rare contemporary perspective on how notaries perceived their place in early modern political culture. Bodin clearly differentiated between the authority of the state and the authority of the city. While he associated his own responsibility as a royal notary with the power of the crown, as the recorder of the city he upheld its rights and privileges. In this contest over authority, the archives were sacrosanct. In allowing the royal judge to look at the municipal records in the archives but not permitting him to remove them, Bodin and the municipal council emphasized the role of the archives as the symbolic safeguard of the town's authority.

Both royal judge and municipality, though, seemed anxious to avoid confrontation over the issue of Bodin himself, indicating perhaps the lowliness of his status. The judge asserted that he was imprisoned not for refusing to hand over the records but for contempt and insolence; the city council responded that as long as Bodin had been imprisoned "as a private person" (as opposed to in his official city capacity, presumably), it "did not want to prevent justice."[12] Thus they seem to have agreed to view the matter of Bodin's imprisonment as a personal rather than a political or principle issue.

Notaries and their middling peers did have the opportunity to attend assemblies of the city council, so they were not were not entirely excluded from the process of urban governance. The municipal assemblies that were held to discuss city business and conduct elections for municipal offices were, in theory, open to all heads of household, but in practice, only a small proportion of the Nantais population attended these gatherings. Although the number of men present varied from assembly to assembly, the biggest gathering of the year was usually on 1 May, when candidates for offices were nominated. At that time, perhaps one hundred or so men were present in addition to the officers.[13]

12. AMN, BB18, 27, 28, and 29 January 1582.
13. Lists of the names of those present at every general assembly were kept in the deliberations of the municipal council, now held in *série* BB of the AMN. These records are not perfect

Notaries tended to be enthusiastic participants, although attenders did little other than observe at general assemblies, and assemblies were held less frequently and enjoyed less discretionary authority after the end of the Wars of Religion. They and other minor legal officials were stalwarts among the few who exercised their rights to take part in deliberations on urban governance. Of the twelve men named as attending an October 1597 general assembly, two were notaries, and the few attenders led the mayor to complain that the good of the city would be better served if more city residents attended. At the larger assemblies every 1 May, notaries were regularly among the best-represented occupations. A historian of Nantais municipal life noted the "very average" socio-professional status of the members of the assembly and observed that men who were "only auxiliaries" in the city's legal tribunals dominated its general assemblies. Indeed, lawyers were even more numerous than notaries at these assemblies.[14]

The attractions for notaries of going to these assemblies seem to have been social and professional. Participants associated themselves with sources of civic and social distinction, allowing middling men the chance to differentiate themselves more clearly from the ranks below them and to borrow the status that was attached to involvement in municipal governance. Moreover, notaries' particular association with public order, a goal they were supposed to realize for their contemporaries in daily life by their enactment of legal deeds, perhaps made them likely participants in other institutions that pursued similar ends. While assembly attenders could not have failed to realize that they were not key political players, they may have liked occasions to demonstrate an association with governance and with public confidence.

Parishes and Public Life

For middling men like notaries, participating in the local organizations based in their parishes, and perhaps even becoming office holders there, provided a key means of establishing their own local social prominence

---

guides to participation, as, after listing the names of the "habitants et manants" present, they usually ended vaguely, with the signification "et plusieurs autres," but they remain a useful guide to who was present.

14. AMN, BB22, 10 October 1597; Guy Saupin, "La Vie municipale à Nantes sous l'Ancien Régime, 1565–1789" (thèse pour le doctorat de troisième cycle, 2 vols., Université de Nantes, 1981), 243–50. Saupin observes that a significant change in attendance patterns did not occur until the late seventeenth century, when artisans began attending in much greater numbers.

and of having some political voice in the day-to-day running of their immediate communities.[15] Notaries' main reference for public activity was in the localized context of parochial organizations, such as parish assemblies and militias. In the more limited context of their church meetings and militia companies, middling men could go beyond observation to active participation in decision making, and could even aspire to take their turn as leaders and holders of positions of local offices.

Service in the militia bridged the gap between civic and parish public life, as militia companies were part of the city's efforts to maintain public order and took part in many civic ceremonies. But they were organized on a parish basis, and their usual duties involved keeping watch over their individual parishes. All the town's inhabitants were, theoretically, obliged to serve in the militia, but, except in times of crisis, participation was practically limited to a relatively small number of men. Indeed, when a larger militia turnout was needed because of disorder or external threat, the municipal council frequently complained about the difficulty of getting the population en masse to observe the obligation to serve.

Militia life was based in the parishes. Each *quartier*—roughly based on parishes—of the city provided men for a company under the leadership of a captain, lieutenant, and ensign, and every company was divided into smaller squads, each headed by a corporal. The number of companies varied from perhaps eight before 1598 to about fourteen afterward.[16] The importance of the parish basis was shown, for example, in 1649, when the lieutenant of a militia company and Julien Belute, as the "representative of the company," appeared before the municipal council. Belute requested, "for himself and for the other residents of the parish following the charge he carried," that the newly appointed captain of their company, who was not resident in the parish and had declared so at mass to avoid paying a lo-

15. David Garrioch has argued that for middling men in the eighteenth century, parish office holding was "central to the identity of the middle classes" and was "a central facet of social identity and social power." Garrioch, *Parisian Bourgeoisie*, 7.

16. Saupin, "La Vie municipale," 64–65. Saupin estimates that the number of companies grew from six or seven in the late sixteenth century to fourteen or sixteen in the late eighteenth century, thereby increasing the number of men involved from 600 or 700 in the mid-sixteenth century to 3,500 in the mid-eighteenth century. He may underestimate the numbers involved for the earlier period, though. Lists of militia captains (and therefore companies) from meetings of the municipal assembly in the 1580s and 1590s regularly named 12 or 14 men (although it is possible that extra militia companies were temporarily added during these difficult years). A history of the Nantes militia lists fourteen militia companies from the time of Henry IV's reorganization of the militia in 1598, and notes that beginning in 1611, each company was divided into five *escouades*, each headed by a corporal. See also Camille Mellinet, *La Commune et la milice de Nantes*, vol. 3 (Nantes, 1844), 57–86.

cal tax, be removed. The captain "could not and must not" carry out his charge if he was not a parish resident. The captain argued that he was a Nantes resident who had houses in the company's district and elsewhere, but promised that to avoid greater conflict, he would in future reside in the parish. The municipal council confirmed his appointment "as long as he lived" in the parish.[17]

Notaries and men of their rank apparently dominated the Nantes city militia during times of peace, a pattern common to other city militias.[18] The very designation "bourgeois militia" (*milice bourgeoise*) implies that the guard was kept by men of property, in the early modern sense of *bourgeois*. Occasional lists of militia company members from the late sixteenth century confirm the orientation suggested by Lebigot's squad of notaries and lawyers. A 1580 list of one company named 107 men, including 8 notaries, 6 men who were both notaries and lawyers, and 8 other petty legal officials. The company also comprised 22 artisans, as well as various members of the urban elite.[19] A 1569 list for a company of the parish of St. Croix and environs listed 144 men, only about 1 in 7 or 8 of the adult men resident in the area that the company covered, at least a third of whom shared the designation *maître* with notaries.[20]

17. AMN, 22 April and 29 April 1649.

18. It is very difficult to establish who served regularly in the guard, but evidence suggests that middling men ordinarily filled the ranks. The actions of the town council in extraordinary times seem to illustrate this pattern. In 1625, for example, Nantes was experiencing a period of civil unrest and an epidemic. The municipal assembly, as a result, was temporarily very preoccupied with militia affairs; it reasserted again that "all kinds of inhabitants" were required to serve, instigated a reform of the militia rolls, reasserted the fines that defaulters would face, and provided money and provisions to help with expenses. A few months later, militia officers were still complaining that most of the town's population had left the city to get away from the epidemic and without naming a substitute for the guard, leaving the town in danger if faced by a surprise attack. All these efforts seem to suggest that in less-threatening times, the militia was manned by only a small part of the population. AMN, BB30, 9 and 21 January 1625; BB31, 25 August 1625.

Analysis of other urban militia companies is scarce. For the most recent overview, see William Beik, *Urban Protest in Seventeenth-Century France: The Culture of Retribution* (Cambridge, 1997), 79–84. Militia service in La Rochelle was limited to heads of "bourgeois households," implying a similar function of differentiation. About two-thirds of members of a Rouen militia company in the late sixteenth century were artisans, and one-third were minor officials and other men of similar rank to notaries. Kevin Robbins, "The Families and Politics of La Rochelle, 1550–1650," (Ph.D. diss., Johns Hopkins University, 1990), 190; Philip Benedict, *Rouen During the Wars of Religion* (Cambridge, 1981), 43. See also Bernard Chevalier, *Les Bonnes Villes de France du quatorzième au seizième siècle* (Paris, 1982), 118–121.

19. AMN, EE31 (no date; "vers 1580" added in different hand).

20. AMN, EE 31, 1569. The proportion of adult men given here is estimated on the basis of figures in 1600 from Alain Croix, *Nantes et le pays Nantais au seizième siècle: Etude démographique*

The social parameters of militia service had upper as well as lower boundaries, suggesting that while middling men were drawn to militia service to affirm their status, elite men sought other more satisfactory symbols of theirs. Elite men who were not officers were far more likely than others to ignore the duty and pay the resulting fine, as a 1580 list of men who were defaulting from their militia obligation showed. Twelve of the twenty-five defaulters had elite titles, and they included the *juge criminel* of the city. Moreover, in 1634, a wealthy merchant named Mathurin Sublard refused to join a guard being formed to accompany the arrival in the city of the governor of Brittany. Sublard told the lieutenant of his neighborhood company that, besides having other business, "he was more than those in arms . . . that there were others who were not more than him who had not gone and that when they went he would go."[21]

Militia service involved two kinds of obligations: to take part in the ceremonial life of the city and to maintain watch in the different areas of the city. Militia companies provided the escorts at major civic functions, such as the yearly installation of a new mayor, or the general assembly of the town for the opening of the letters of the king. A 1636 visitor to Nantes described the new mayor's inauguration: "All the companies of the town or parts of them are in arms and accompany the new mayor from his lodging, through the streets, in arms, drum beating, flags waving, until [they reach] Notre Dame, where mass is heard with organ and music." The procession then continued to the cathedral before returning to the town hall, "where dinner is had at the expense of the town."[22]

Militiamen who took part in public festivities like these shared the privileges and special distinctions that affirmed their differentiation from the mass of the city population. Indeed, as the role of the militia became in-

---

(Paris, 1974), 206. Titles and occupations were not always recorded accurately, so more of the men may have been of the rank of notaries. Jean Minquet, for instance, was listed without any title, although he was a notary and lawyer and, as such, would usually have the designation *maître*.

21. AMN, EE33, 19 August 1580; AMN, BB37, 19 November 1634.

22. Dubuisson-Aubenay, *Itinéraire en Bretagne en 1636* (Nantes, 1902), 99. Similarly, for meetings of the municipal assembly on ceremonial occasions, the captain of each company was instructed to select a few of the "most apparent and best equipped" men under his command to assist at these functions. The minutes of the municipal assembly confirmed the customary participation of the militia companies, together with trumpets and drums. See, for example, AM Nantes, BB35, 19 August 1635. The precise number of men varied. In 1616, each captain was to choose "10 to 12" men for such a function, while in 1617, each was to choose "12 to 15." AMN BB28, 18 August 1616 and 6 July 1617.

creasingly ceremonial with the end of the Wars of Religion, the honor of involvement may have become an important factor in attracting the participation of men like notaries and their middling peers, whose status was in many other ways precarious at this time, and who had few other opportunities for civic distinction.[23]

Militia duty may also have helped notaries to reassert their official role as guarantors of public confidence when they also served that role as militiamen. Civic participation could, perhaps, counteract their other activities (whether as credit brokers or card players) that potentially eroded their position as either notaries or good middling-order citizens.

Moreover, militia service offered middling men another avenue for local prestige, by providing the possibility of becoming minor officers of company squads as well as of participating in the public ceremony of the city. Notaries, who had almost no chance of achieving city-wide preeminence as captains of militia companies, could aspire to the lesser offices of lieutenants, ensigns, or corporals within a company. At least twenty-two notaries were (not always successful) nominees for the positions of lieutenant or ensign between 1580 and 1660, and many others held more minor posts as corporals of the squads. A 1569 company roll for the parish of St. Croix listed 144 men divided into eight districts, three of which were headed by notaries.[24]

The main duties of militiamen, however, entailed that each squad of a company keep watch at one of the city's towers for one night a week. In this regard, the issues of property oversight, regulating a particular vision of public order, and sociability were paramount as notaries' personal lives came together with their public lives.

23. Although the Nantais militia was, on occasion, mobilized in larger numbers for serious matters after the end of the Wars of Religion, such as during the urban disturbances of the 1630s, the deliberations of the bourgeois assembly (AMN, *série* BB) indicate that its role was far more routine after 1600 than before, when discussions of militia activities dominated the records and militia officers were often present. Militia companies in other cities apparently experienced similar transitions beginning in the late sixteenth century. See, for example, Benedict, *Rouen During the Wars of Religion*, 191.

24. Captains, like other city officials, were, on the whole, drawn from the leading mercantile and legal families of Nantes. Pierre Belon, whose exceptional status was signaled by his election as *échevin*, was the captain of a militia company in the 1650s. Jean Lemoyne and Jean Blanchard were militia captains in the early part of the seventeenth century and in the 1580s, respectively.

The only other notaries to come close to this status lived outside the city walls. Mathurin Boutard, who lived in the *faubourg* of St. Clement, became a militia captain, and Pierre Delacroix, who lived across the Loire in the parish of St. Sebastien, was nominated as captain of that company but only became a lieutenant. AMN, BB35, 21 December 1631; AMN, BB41, 1 May 1649; AMN, BB39, 1 May 1641; AMN, BB41, 1 May 1648; AMN, EE31, 1569.

The evenings of militia watches were primary opportunities for sociability. Membership in the same squad was assumed to be an indication of friendship among men.[25] Militia duty, on the majority of nights, offered occasions for rowdy entertainment that potentially contradicted the militia's responsibility to maintain order. The haste with which the militiamen insisted that the fatal accident during their watch did not result from any "disorder" among themselves suggests this tension. Individual militia watches, like individual households, did not always live up to the standards they were supposed to perpetuate.[26] Yet while the social aspects of militia duty were attractive, the same male sociability reinforced the ties between men by which they asserted their claims to authority.

Through the duties of militiamen on guard, notaries and their peers upheld in this civic institution the principles of orderliness (in their readiness to prevent threats to the peace of the night), financial probity (in stopping goods from leaving or entering the city illegally), and keeping good company, all of which were at the essence of household government, for them. Although we know little of the day-to-day actions of militia companies in peacetime, in Paris, for instance, militiamen exerted discipline and protected property in their neighborhoods.[27]

The middling men who were militia stalwarts had other opportunities, too, to espouse their particular formulation of values in ways that shaped the tone of urban political culture, as, for example, in their debates over the selection of minor militia officers. The men of one militia company asked the city council in 1634 to remove an officer for reasons that illustrated the qualities that rank-and-file militiamen thought were necessary attributes of authority. They explained that when a militia office was vacant, "the remaining officers and members of the company have customarily met and deliberated among themselves about those who are the most capable of serving the king in such a position."[28] The neglect of this process was one of the grounds for the officer's dismissal.

The men based their dissatisfaction, however, on a sense of the violation of their values that went beyond procedural wrongdoing. They alleged that the officer they sought to remove could not carry out his charge adequately

25. See, for instance, ADLA, B6652, 10 [illegible] 1626.

26. For discussions of militia companies and guard rooms as foci of sociability, see Philip Benedict, *Cities and Social Change in Early Modern France* (London, 1989), 18; Orest Ranum, "La 'Colonne' de miliciens bourgeois du faubourg Saint-Germain pendant le blocus de 1649," in *La France d'Ancien Régime: Etudes réunies en l'honneur de Pierre Goubert* (Toulouse, 1984).

27. Orest Ranum, *The Fronde: A French Revolution* (New York, 1993), 147–71.

28. They then presented a list to the town council, who might adjust it as they saw fit before presenting it for nomination. AMN, EE62, May 1634.

because: "In the first place [he was] of so unsociable a temperament that he could never secure the affection of his men, in the second place he is accused of various crimes . . . [including] violences and excesses committed to the house and person of one of the residents . . . and in the house where he lives much disorder occurs." They would not serve him "because of the small trust between him and his men who do not judge him either worthy or capable of commanding them nor would they follow him willingly."[29] These militia enthusiasts found their lieutenant unacceptable in part because he had fallen down on his duties as a patriarch. By failing to direct his own household appropriately and disturbing someone else's, he showed himself incapable of commanding others. A man who could not observe the tenets (of maintaining order, financial and otherwise, and keeping good company) that were at the heart of organizing authority in daily life for his men disqualified himself as their leader.

Militia service, like attendance at the general assemblies of the town, gave notaries an opportunity to associate themselves with the process of governance. The mayor was the colonel, the commanding officer, of the militia, as well as heading the city council. Notaries' participation in militia duty confirmed their status and distinguished them from the mass of urban dwellers; it also gave them the chance to take up positions of leadership in their parish communities. As militiamen, notaries upheld in this public forum the values they endorsed as middling men that were essential to their occupational identity, but that all too often were lacking in practice.

General meetings (*chapitres*) of parishioners, held regularly after mass on Sundays, were forums for local governance of a different kind.[30] Typically, a group of parishioners met "*en corps politique*" in a chapel of the church after mass, to "discuss the affairs of the parish." Those present, always all men, were routinely described as "being the best and soundest" part of the parish, implying that (as with militia service) attendance provided an opportunity to participate in the governance of the parish from a position of local leadership. Men who attended were listed by name and occupation, and these men added their signatures to the end of the record.

Although, as in the case of city assemblies, any parish resident could theoretically attend, in practice, again only a small proportion of residents attended these meetings. Most of these Sunday meetings were small, attracting about twenty or thirty men, as a rule. Although a few nonsigners may

29. Ibid.
30. These parish assemblies, distinct from the meetings of vestrymen, have received little attention from urban historians. An exception is Jacques Maillard, *Le Pouvoir municipal à Angers, de 1657 à 1789,* vol. 1 (Angers, 1984), 75–86.

also have been present (as indicated by the proviso sometimes added to the list of names "and several others," or "were present among others"), they must have been a small group. This can be inferred because, for instance, when a crowd of fifty men attended a meeting in St. Croix in 1635, it was so exceptional that the record noted the "great numbers" of parishioners who had congregated.[31]

Middling men usually formed the bottom rank of attenders singled out by name at such occasions. They were first listed at the start of the act, and then added their names at the end, after any nobles or other members of the Nantais elite who were their superiors. Artisans or other men of lesser rank were rarely present. At a typical St. Croix *chapitre* attended by thirty-one men, apart from the parish clergy, in 1621, the first names were those of six men who, by virtue of the high positions they held in the city courts, were part of the urban elite. Others present included ten lawyers and four notaries, along with a bailiff, a man with the title of *maître* for whom no occupation was given, a surgeon, and seven *honorables personnes,* designated generically as merchants.[32]

Beyond the small elite group, most active members of the meetings seem to have been men who shared many of the characteristics of notaries. In the commercial parishes of St. Saturnin and St. Nicolas, where few elites resided (although some very wealthy merchants did), men below the middling rank were as unlikely to take part as they were in other parishes.

Notaries seem to have been as enthusiastic about participating in their parish governance as they were about attending city assemblies. At these parish meetings, the prominence of middling men like notaries, the lawyers who were usually given precedence over them in these accounts, and men designated as *honorable hommes,* repeated on a local level the pattern of city-wide assemblies at the town hall.

Although Nantais parishes do not seem to have engaged in larger political issues, either by sending deputies to the town council or in other ways, their efforts to have their sessions recorded with the public and secular instrument of a notarial act suggest that they perceived themselves as a governing unit. Like other meetings that notaries recorded, no references to such acts like parish assemblies existed in contemporary printed notarial handbooks, that is, such acts were not part of the traditional repertoire of the notary. Rather, the using of a notary to record the meetings reflected

31. ADLA, 4E2/126, 14 January 1635.

32. ADLA, 4E22/1714, 14 November 1621. The St. Croix population in 1600 is taken from Croix, *Nantes et le pays Nantais,* 206.

the effort of the communities to use the authority and form of a public instrument. In these cases, such documents were closely modeled after the
manner of municipal deliberations, to legitimate their own role as an organ of governance and public order.[33]

What parish assemblies did do was deliberate over the management of
the temporal affairs of their church. They made decisions about parochial
finances, maintenance of the fabric of parish buildings, and personnel issues such as the selection of new priests. In these forums, parish clergy and
the parishioners who were serving as church wardens brought matters to
which the parish needed to attend to the other parishioners.

The political as well as managerial quality of their decision making became evident when, for example, the gathered parishioners and their leaders in the vestry, on occasion, contended with the clergy over who had authority in the running of the parish. The extent of participation exercised
by the men who attended is difficult to assess, as meeting records typically
noted that "the matter was introduced for discussion between the rector
and parishioners," and records noted only that decisions taken were made
"unanimously," rather than transcribing discussions.[34] Yet the gathered
parishioners did not simply endorse the actions of either their lay leaders
in the vestry or the clergy.

Parishioners attached great importance to the holding of chapters to decide parochial matters. When they felt that their right to this participation
had been ignored, they were quick to reassert it. The parishioners of St.
Croix met in November 1621 to consider a request from one of their priests
that he be excused from his duties for a few months, while he went to take
care of his affairs in a rural parish. He put forward a replacement to fulfill
the obligations of the chaplaincy that he held, and the chapter agreed, but
only with the rider that "in the future," no presentation of a chaplaincy was
to be made without a parish meeting being held. The parishioners also
asked their church wardens to consult the "archives of the vestry," in order

33. Maillard, using evidence from a later period, finds evidence of parochial involvement in
larger political issues in the parish assemblies of Angers. For the uses of notaries to record the
meetings of community groups, see Laurie Nussdorfer, "Writing and the Power of Speech: Notaries and Artisans in Baroque Rome," in Carla Hesse and Barbara Diefendorf, eds., *Culture
and Identity in Early Modern Europe, 1500–1800: Essays in Honor of Natalie Davis* (Ann Arbor,
Mich., 1993); and Laurie Nussdorfer, "Notarial Inscription and Artisan Collectivities in Seventeenth-Century Rome," paper presented to the annual meeting of the American Historical Association, San Francisco, 1994.

34. The particular language here is taken from the record of a *chapitre* in St. Croix to
choose a new priest. ADLA, 4E2/1691, 19 May 1637.

to make a list of the titles and holders of the chaplaincies in the parish's gift that would clarify the assembly's control of these positions.[35]

Parishioners asserted their right to determine such matters by actions as well as rhetoric. A week earlier, the St. Croix chapter had removed a priest who, they claimed, had acquired his chaplaincy by "a fraud" that went "against the accustomed forms," rather than by the behest of the parishioners. They replaced him with a person of their own choosing. On another occasion, the parishioners of St. Saturnin took their church wardens to court over a chaplaincy that those lay leaders had filled, thereby ignoring "the right of the parishioners who are the true and legitimate patrons" of the contested chaplaincy. They demanded that a chapter be held of parishioners and churchwardens, "together and conjointly," to make such decisions, and the settlement reaffirmed that the vestry could not, then or in the future, assume the right of patronage of the chaplaincy, nor of other church services.[36]

In these ways, parishioners attending parish assemblies claimed their right to a role in the governance of a key local institution, and they expected that governance to be based on the same principles as those that were operating in their own households. The patterns of kin oversight that played such an important role in the lives of individual households were replicated in the demands that the parishoners made for consultation of the "household" of their parish church.

Pragmatism as well as principle lay behind the desire of parish activists to assert their right to participate in determining parochial affairs. For fathers of middling families, protecting patronage rights in their parish church also ensured that opportunities were safeguarded for their own kin, in a milieu where it was very common for one son to become a cleric. The links between familial and parochial interests became clear when parish assemblies insisted that priests who were natives of the parish were to be preferred to all others for appointments over which the parish had discretion.[37]

Sunday gatherings after mass also provided another site for the rank- and gender-specific sociability and decision making that characterized so many parts of the lives of the men who attended them. The same parameters of kinship and occupation bonded participants in these assemblies as they did in other aspects of daily life for notaries and their families. Pierre Belon encountered many of the men, at these meetings in the St. Saturnin parish

---

35. ADLA, 4E2/1714, 21 November 1621.
36. ADLA, 4E2/1714, 14 November 1621; ADLA, 4E2/1654, 5 December 1654.
37. See, for instance, ADLA, 4E2/1714, 21 November 1621.

church, who were his most common companions on other kinds of occasions, including several of his wife's kinsmen and his spiritual kinsman the
notary Jacques Bernard, as well as the merchant Pierre Chastelier and the
apothecary Bonnaventure Papin.[38] The gendered sociability of early modern society with the boundaries around processes of power, decision making, and authority that it implied was reinforced again on these occasions.

Women parishioners often left church together in small groups after
Sunday mass; even widows were not among those who participated in the
assemblies.[39] Women's roles in the governance of the parish community
took a limited and contingent form. Sporadically, in late-sixteenth-century
collections of poor relief, the wives of the Nantais elite were sometimes
named as collectors, but even then they were identified by their husband's
names ("wife of") rather than by their own, as was usually the case for early
modern women.[40] Middling women, in any case, had no such role in the
life of the parish.

Parish assemblies also provided opportunities for attendees to identify
themselves as part of a leadership group in the parish. Middling men found
themselves in meetings with the leading members of their parishes, and indeed, on occasion, with some of the most prominent men in the city. For
notaries, whose status, both occupational and socioeconomic, was often
challenged, parish assemblies offered chances to differentiate themselves
from other parishioners while associating themselves with parish elites, and
to assert their own values in a public site.

Some middling men, including some notaries, moved beyond participating in general meetings of parishioners to become members of the vestry
as churchwardens, each of whom served for a year. For men like notaries or
apothecaries, the vestry offered a rare opportunity for access to the holding
of a local office that marked them as social and political leaders, at least in
their neighborhoods.

Several factors facilitated middling men's access to seats on the vestry.
Nantais parishes had very distinctive socioeconomic characteristics, which
meant that most of the city's social elite were concentrated in a few
parishes. As a result, competition from elite men for parish leadership was
relatively limited. Moreover, even in parishes like St. Croix or St. Denis,
where the city's elite attended the general parish meetings, on occasion,

38. For St. Saturnin *chapitres,* see, for instance, ADLA, 4E2/244, 30 June 1647; ADLA,
4E2/1193, 15 May 1650; ADLA, 4E2/173, 29 November 1654.
39. For some examples of women talking about leaving church together in small groups,
see ADLA, B5807, 11 August 1628; ADLA, B6664, 27 June 1647; ADLA, B6667, 27 April 1654.
40. See Collins, *Classes, Estates, and Order,* 99–100.

such men rarely seem to have been interested in bothering themselves with vestry responsibilities. Middling men, however, had few outlets for their civic ambitions. Additionally, notaries shared with other middling men literacy and a familiarity with record keeping that made them obvious candidates for these positions.

Through their parish activism, in militia service, and in the running of their churches, middling men brought into the public world of political culture the values and understandings that underpinned their own households and family lives. When notaries and their peers took part in the militia and in church assemblies, they shared sociability and reemphasized the importance of the parish as a focus within the city. However, when they asserted their right to advise on the management of church personnel and finances, or to have their say in selecting the officers of their militia companies that were charged with keeping order in the city, they also began to bridge the gap between household and polity. They expected that, as on the terms of their personal experiences, competence and oversight were also appropriate elements of orderly parochial life.

Poorhouse Governance

Notaries and their peers were also active in the management of the city's poorhouse (*Hôtel-Dieu*), an institution overseen by the municipal council and one that was also crucial to the maintenance of public order in the city. Successful management of the poorhouse was an important political matter. It removed its charges from being potential sources of disorder in the community. Claude Geneste noted the "great scandal" caused when for lack of money, he turned poorhouse occupants out onto the street.[41]

Administering poor relief also could be construed as part of the civic and Christian charitable obligations that demarcated respectable subjects of the city from the masses below them. In 1586, Gilles Thomin refused to contribute to poor relief on the grounds that he was already the poorhouse administrator. By 1587, when an influx of poor had created an unprecedented strain on the town's resources, the city council created a new and separate position of annuity collector that was later formalized and was held by a succession of notaries. Claude Geneste, who was appointed to fill

41. AMN, BB20, 16 April 1587.

the new position, was unenthusiastic but accepted, as he stated, "out of charity for the poor."[42]

The rationales and strategies for running the poorhouse mobilized the household basis of social organization on individual and community levels that operated in other areas of middling men's lives. The designation of the institution's governors as the "fathers of the poor" suggested this association explicitly. Moreover, at the *Hôtel-Dieu*, as in other households, successful *mesnagement* entailed obligations for both spouses. As Guillaume Thomin argued in 1581, poorhouse administration depended "rather on the diligence of a woman than a man," and so he should be excused, because his young wife was pregnant and little experienced "in such matters."[43]

Although notaries were quick to seize other kinds of opportunities for involvement in public affairs, they, like other candidates for the poorhouse administration, were sometimes reluctant to accept this duty. On the surface, the patterns of the personnel involved in the poorhouse were similar to those in other of the city's political arenas. The urban elite, who acted as aldermen and militia captains, also governed the Nantes poorhouse, and again, this top level was beyond the reach of notaries or other middling men. The city council, though, chose two administrators annually to serve one-year terms as managers of the day-to-day affairs of the poorhouse, and, as in the other cases, notarial involvement occurred at this more mundane level. Despite these apparent similarities, middling men were quick to recognize that not all forms of civic activity conferred the same advantages or distinctions.

Notaries' frequent ambivalence about involvement in the poorhouse highlights ways in which their roles there differed from their other kinds of public activities. While parish leadership and militia duty attracted middling men, in part, at least, because it identified them with local distinction, the task of poorhouse administration clearly fell to men who were below the elite. Elite men were eligible to be administrators, and a 1556 royal ordinance enjoined all Nantais who were asked, and especially men "of the long and short robe," to accept the charge.[44] However, men who could afford to usually gave money to the poorhouse in lieu of accepting the office.

---

42. Tax roll for St. Croix, 20 June 1586; AMN, GG725, 1587. Unfortunately, the *Hôtel-Dieu* records are very poor after 1600. Fragmentary evidence shows Raoul Boucaud, for instance, as *receveur des rentes* in 1616. Hervé Trebillard was appointed permanently as a salaried *receveur* in 1647, to avoid the "abuses and losses" caused by changing *receveurs* every year. AMN, BB28, 23 June 1616; AMN, GG303, 30 August 1647.

43. AMN, BB17, 19 June 1581. Thomin was excused for a year.

44. Cited in Alain Croix, *La Bretagne aux seizième et dix-septième siècles: La Vie, la mort, la foi* (Paris, 1981), 590.

This practice was technically illegal, and men appointed sometimes re-ferred bitterly to "the richer" men who successfully avoided the duty. In 1586, Gilles Thomin complained of his own "poverty," and made "other ex-cuses much more pertinent" than those of men who had been excused.[45]

Appointment as administrators suggested the mediocrity of notaries' own status in the city, as a whole, and reinforced their association with the milieu of artisans. Artisans, in the provisioning trades or other crafts, and petty merchants were men on the bottom edge of the narrow social world that no-taries generally lived in. In the late sixteenth century, a clockmaker who was nominated sought exemption not only because he was usually out of town and his wife was old and ill, but also because he was not the owner of a resi-dence and could not read or write. Many of the nominees had only "sire" as their title, indicating that they were assigned lower status than notaries.[46]

To notaries' apparent frequent mortification, the municipal council seemed to find them particularly attractive candidates for poorhouse ad-ministration. Notaries were significantly overrepresented among the men the municipal council considered for nomination, and many notaries be-came administrators. A 1580 list of sixty men who were "appropriate" as ad-ministrators of the hospital included ten notaries.[47] One administrator usu-ally came from the mercantile-artisan ranks, while the other from the lowest echelons of the legal profession.[48] Just as artisans or merchants could help to supply the institution with provisions, the occupational skills of no-taries were valuable. They were expected to be good record keepers and might encourage their clients, especially in wills, when souls were at stake, to make bequests to the hospital.[49]

Moreover, poorhouse administration was not only menial in terms of city

45. AMN, GG701, 23 July 1586. For discussions about gifts of money in exchange for ex-emption, and expressions of resentment, see, among others, AMN, GG702, 25 May 1577; AMN, GG702, [illegible] 1583; AMN, GG702, 18 July 1578; AMN, GG701, 25 October 1586.

46. AMN, GG702 (no date, but after 1597). The 1580 list of potential candidates included sixty names, but only twenty-two were distinguished as *maître*, like notaries. AMN, GG702, 26 May 1580.

47. AMN, GG702, 26 May 1580.

48. Among many examples of the consistent pattern of selection, see, for instance: Maître Jacques Delalande (notary) and Sire François Barbier (merchant) in 1577; Maître Pierre Fournier and Sire Guillaume Mesant in 1578; Maître Charles Demons (notary and *procureur*) and Durandeau (merchant) in 1579; Guillaume Davy and a "merchant" in 1580. AMN, GG702.

49. Jean-Paul Poisson, "Pour une étude de la fonction notariale dans l'assistance sociale et charitable sous l'Ancien Régime," in Poisson, *Notaires et société: Travaux d'histoire et de sociologies notariales*, vol. 2 (Paris, 1990), 385–90.

status, but, in contrast to other forms of civic life, it could be burdensome and relatively solitary. Running the poorhouse was an onerous task. It included the day-to-day management of the hospital (overseeing the personnel and buying items needed, like bread and wine, in large quantity), the maintenance of the building, the management of the hospital's funds, and decisions about admissions.[50] In 1579, Charles Demons asked to be exempted, "it being impossible for him to carry out the said charge because of his other business, duties and offices of lawyer and royal notary and other urgent matters." Poorhouse administration was shared formally with only one other man, and informally with spouses, neither of whom offered the potential sociability that other public activities did. In the starkest expression of the difference, Jacques Delalande claimed, in fact, that he was "a mortal and capital enemy" of the merchant who was nominated with him.[51]

The financial structure of the poorhouse was probably, however, a more decisive factor behind the reluctance of men to act as administrators and the proclivity of the town council to appoint notaries. Administrators had to pay out of their own pockets any costs they incurred that exceeded the hospital's revenues and were reimbursed later by the city council. *Rentes* created in favor of the *Hôtel-Dieu* were its main source of funds, but the complaints of administrators to the city council suggest that these annuities were notoriously difficult to collect.[52] The hospital would soon have been in dire straits without administrators who had access to cash, so men had to be appointed who were expected to have enough cash on hand, or sufficient cash flow, to advance the money needed to run the poorhouse.

The need to make advances and the difficulty of reimbursement, which in large part made the job of administering the poorhouse onerous, made notaries attractive candidates to the municipal council. Although notaries were far from wealthy in their own rights, their community role as credit brokers made them seem likely to have the liquidity to advance from the

50. Croix, *La Bretagne aux seizième et dix-septième siècles*, 587. The duties must have been especially heavy in the difficult years of the Wars of Religion, during which the numbers of poor in the city rose precipitously, on occasion.

51. Demons offered successfully to pay a *rente* of 10 *livres* a year during his lifetime instead. AMN, GG702, 1 June 1579; AMN, GG702, 25 May 1577.

52. See, for example, the request of Guillaume Davy and Sire Jean Minquet in 1581 for the *rolle* of the *devoirs et rentes* owed to the hospital to help collection. The difficulties in managing the financial affairs of the hospital were apparently compounded by power struggles between the administrators, governors, and municipal council members. Their request was turned down, although the council instead decided to send the roll to the governors. AMN, BB17, 22 June 1581.

funds that they held the money needed to run the poorhouse, during their terms in office.

For notaries, however, the charge of administrator entailed significant financial risks that their personal finances could ill afford. The requests for exemptions that multiplied in the 1570s and 1580s, as the number of Nantais poor grew in the midst of the disruptions of the Wars of Religion, were probably correlated to the increased monetary penalties that administrators seemed likely to incur. By the standards of notarial families, large amounts of money were involved.

François Maillard argued against his appointment in 1583 on the grounds that he "did not have the means to amass any *deniers.*" He was not excused, in part, perhaps, because of the opportunities that his notarial occupation seemed to offer for liquid funds. Three days later, Maillard asked for reimbursement of expenses of 210 *livres,* as "he did not have the means to make any advance." The council responded unsympathetically that they would forward him some money the next Saturday, and 400 *livres* more as soon as possible, so Maillard had no excuse "not to do his duty." By 1586, Maillard and the apothecary who was his fellow administrator in 1583 had started legal action against the city council to secure reimbursement for the 1,341 *livres* they had spent out of pocket.[53]

Nor was Maillard alone. The next year, Guillaume Davy complained that he had outstanding out-of-pocket expenses totaling 1,500 *livres.*[54] Poorhouse administration, especially in difficult times, in this way threatened the ability of notaries or their peers to steward their own household resources and to maintain their personal authority.

Notaries' involvement in the circulation of credit may have led the city council to view them as good candidates to administer the poorhouse, but from notaries' perspective, the position emphasized a side of their business activities that tended to undermine their official roles as guarantors of public confidence. While notaries usually eagerly embraced public activities that reinforced their positions in their own households, in their work, and in the city, administering the poorhouse drew attention to activities that

53. AMN, BB19, 20 and 23 June 1583; AMN, CC340, 2 June 1586.
54. AMN, BB19, 27 October 1583; AMN, BB20, 25 June 1587. In 1587, the council reimbursed Thomas Lemoyne and his former co-administrator 90 *écus* (about 270 *livres*) for the costs they had incurred in that position. Other candidates also sought exemption, on the grounds of insufficient access to the necessary resources. See, for example, the request of Jean Magdeleneau in 1585 to be exempted "for reason of the several losses he had recently suffered." AMN, GG702, [illegible] 1585. By 1587, Gilles Thomin, the incumbent administrator, was refusing to collect the revenues because of the difficulty of doing so.

notaries carefully elided in constructing their public identities, as well as emphasizing their distance from the elite. While all of Nantes knew how notaries tried to generate business, notaries themselves were reluctant to accept the public affirmation of this side of their affairs that poorhouse administration entailed.

Notaries' ambivalence about poorhouse administration pointed to the extent and limits of public life for middling men. On one hand, poorhouse administration gave notaries another public opportunity to define their status and to accept the obligations and duties that accompanied the possession of authority and status. As in the other sites, property was at the heart of the issue for the administrators as well as for their inmates. On the other hand, poorhouse administration lacked the attributes of sociability and status enhancement that the other public activities of middling men promised, and, in hard times, threatened the administrator's personal resources.

The public lives of middling men like notaries, in their choice of activities and in the values espoused in those locations, highlight a very elusive aspect of political culture, that is, how, at local levels, middling men constructed and maintained concepts of authority and ways of ordering society in everyday life.[55] Revisionist interpretations of the conditions of French royal sovereignty have increasingly emphasized the mutual exchanges and negotiation that the crown's accrual of power involved. The small matters in which middling men were involved were far from such great stakes, but they too were critical in consolidating the formulation of a political culture sympathetic to a climate in which royal oversight and regulation was increasingly legitimated.

The many sites in which urban political culture took shape in Nantes illustrate that men outside of the elite were participants and builders, as well as spectators and consumers, of formulations of authority, even within the context of an emerging sovereign monarchy in early modern France. Notaries actively took up political issues that may seem minor and mundane, in the context of the great political dramas that have taken center stage in early modern historiography. The horizons of public life, for these notaries, and no doubt for their middling-order peers, hardly stretched be-

---

55. Other types of associational public life also existed, of course. Notaries, like other middling men, were also members of religious confraternities, for example, but unfortunately, the Nantais records of these organizations are too scant to allow useful analysis.

yond the city. They apparently had little concern for larger political debates outside the city gates.

Nevertheless, their involvement in local issues illustrated how members of early modern communities constructed and understood particular forms of authority. Notaries built a public life that not only allowed them to align themselves with the activities of the city's elite, but that shared in the building of a social and political order founded on the idea of a household patriarchy operating on many levels. They asserted, in the public domains of militia, parish meeting, and poorhouse, their values of order, financial management, oversight, and good company. As *Hôtel-Dieu* administrators, notaries fulfilled in that larger household their duties on behalf of the community. As militiamen and parish activists, as well as in their work as officials of the state, notaries and their peers upheld the qualities of hard work, *mesnagement,* and keeping good company that were, for them, the essence of households' writ, large or small. In their public as well as personal lives, they understood the need for community oversight of the internal affairs of "households," on whatever scale, and for community intervention in a wide variety of forms, should the management of any "household" fail.

Notaries, as participants in public life, were political actors who helped to maintain order in the larger community, as well as in their own households. Notaries were charged with securing public order and civil society by guaranteeing the transactions that their peers made, and the form of the acts that they produced sought to preserve that role. In their other public activities, they reinforced their prescriptive function as guarantors of public order by upholding the values that were central to patriarchal order for their milieu.

In the decades of the later seventeenth and eighteenth centuries that followed, the influence of militias, parish governance, and municipal authority would be eroded, leaving middling men without the space in which they had traditionally participated in local governance and public life.[56] Like their eighteenth-century peers who began to create associations of their own as new sites in which to take part in political culture, middling men of the later sixteenth and seventeenth centuries already monopolized local public life. Unlike their descendants, however, they were able to join groups whose alignment with the centers of authority, whether parochial or civic, placed them within the parameters of the prevailing political culture, rather placing them in opposition to it.

56. The eighteenth-century process is traced in Garrioch, *Formation of a Parisian Bourgeoisie.*

Conclusion

The Practice of Patriarchy

The personal and public lives of notaries and their families shaped urban political culture and suggest some of the parameters of gender and authority as elements of daily life in early modern France. The maintenance of intertwined hierarchies of gender and authority, as a cultural process, entailed the negotiation of gender roles, of property relations, of civic opportunity and obligation, as well as of royal authority and subjects' obedience. In practice, the intertwining between the creation of gender hierarchies and the location of authority involved men and women in a complex topography of power.

René Guilloteau's flight from Nantes and Louise Lecoq's efforts to deal with its consequences, the episode with which this book began, involved many facets of the processes inherent in urban political culture. The threads examined separately in this book were woven together in that affair, as they always were in people's daily lives. All the essential ingredients were present: the interests of the state, represented by provost and prosecutor; the interests of clients in the community; the work of notaries, as producers of public instruments and brokers of credit; the blurring of the domestic and political economies of a household; and the involvement of kin.

The provost and prosecutor, whose charge was to maintain public order, articulated their intervention in uncovering any wrongdoing on the basis of the public "interests" at stake, suggesting the link that they perceived between the state, notaries, and subjects. For the Nantais court officials, notarial fraud threatened public confidence, and thus it held the potential to be a source of disorder in the city that they were charged with regulating.

Some of the diversity of notarial work became clear in the course of the investigation. Notaries recorded private deeds, and, by transforming them into public instruments, offered clients legality and security, but they also were very active as credit brokers, a pursuit that met their own need to enhance their income and the necessity of their communities to develop mechanisms for the circulation of credit.

Lecoq's situation pointed to spousal relations in households. The clients and officials who came to her expected her to have some familiarity with notarial work. Husbands and wives worked together in building and protecting their interests, but Lecoq's actions suggested that individual family members could also see their own interests, epitomizing the tensions in households.

Guilloteau and Lecoq's household was literally embedded in a kin network that provided both support and oversight. Their immediate neighbors were his sister Françoise, herself the daughter and widow of notaries, and Lecoq's sister Jeanne and brother-in-law, another notary, Mathurin Coustans. The links between their households had been multiple, as, for example, when Coustans and Guilloteau frequently co-signed acts the other made.

The public behaviors of these kin were quite different, however, in the aftermath of Guilloteau's departure. From the second day of the investigation, Françoise was present, while Coustans was consistently absent. Yet these differences concealed a complicated and perhaps coordinated effort to protect Lecoq and Guilloteau's interests as well as their own. Françoise engaged in a well-timed effort to stall the process, on occasion, and her presence may have provided her sister-in-law with welcome familial support. Coustans's public absence may have been, in part, motivated by a need to preserve his own notarial business and household, but he seems to have maintained close and prolonged involvement in other less-visible ways. From the earliest weeks of Guilloteau's absence, Coustans had full knowledge of the situation, because he made a copy for Lecoq of the power of attorney that her husband had sent her. In subsequent years, he repeatedly served as Lecoq's notary when she made transactions, and he attended the marriages of her children and the baptism of her grandchildren.[1]

As this episode reveals, early modern political culture was created and maintained not only in the grandeur of the royal palaces or in the august, monumental settings of law courts, but on the front steps and in the back room of a notary's house, and within and between individual households.

1. See, for example, ADLA, 4E2/547, 24 March 1657, 28 June 1657, and 20 February 1659.

Structures of authority and hierarchies of power were contingent upon the outcome of myriad negotiations and contests. The perpetuation of particular formulations of power rested on the energy and effort of many different groups and individuals outside national elites, in their personal and public lives, who did not always concur in their own construction of its meanings. Resistance or alternative interpretations and actions were always possible.

Gender and family were central constituents of early modern political culture. The personal and familial have a symbiotic relationship with the public and political, as a variety of commentators have recently emphasized.[2] This relationship was never clearer than in early modern societies, where kings were equated with fathers, realms with wives, and subjects with children. The impetus that rulers and elites drew from as well as contributed to this relationship was, however, matched by that of ordinary people. The personal, public, and working lives of men and women of every rank were sites where power was negotiated through the interactions between individual encounters and choices and larger structural imperatives. The gendering of authority in day-to-day life was not only produced through political rhetoric or law-court decisions, but was continuously defined and refined in the to-and-fro between public and personal, friends and family, political and patrimonial, in towns like Nantes and among households like those of Guilloteau and Lecoq.

Like Guilloteau and Lecoq, notarial families and their middling peers in Nantes were participants and builders, as well as consumers and spectators of early modern political culture. Although they were objects of the newly invigorated patriarchal impulse of the crown from the late sixteenth century, other factors were just as significant in shaping their daily lives. The responses of family members to the configuration of opportunities and challenges that they faced also combined at a grassroots level to create a culture of power.

Notaries' work was essentially artisanal, in many aspects, and they engaged in a variety of activities beyond the production of documents to maintain adequate incomes. Notaries actively participated in the vast ex-

---

2. See, for example, the methodological comments of: Elinor Accampo, "Gender Relations in the City: A Response," *French Historical Studies* 18 (Spring 1993); Joan Scott, "Gender: A Useful Category of Historical Analysis," *American Historical Review* 91 (December 1985); Katherine A. Lynch, "The Family and the History of Public Life," *Journal of Interdisciplinary History* 24 (Spring 1994). For empirical work exploring these links in other early modern societies, see, for instance, Susan Amussen, *An Ordered Society: Class and Gender in Early Modern England* (London, 1988); Lyndal Roper, *The Holy Household: Women and Morals in Reformation Augsburg* (Oxford, 1989); Mary Elizabeth Perry, *Gender and Disorder in Early Modern Seville* (Princeton, 1990).

pansion of credit that took place in the decades after the early sixteenth century, by brokering loans to the extent that credit transactions quickly dominated notarial productivity. Yet in taking advantage of the opportunity that arranging credit gave them to drum up notarial business, notaries accentuated contemporary anxieties about fraud and deception, because credit itself was a source of considerable unease.

Notarial acts, though, continued to help to mediate the social, economic, and political uncertainties of notaries' own lives and those of their contemporaries. The forms of notarial documents represented more reassuring versions of early modern life—when notaries were neutral and authoritative, when loans were face-to-face, concrete transactions made between parties who were present in one place at the same time. Notaries had to meet the needs of clients to keep their business going, and they responded pragmatically in drawing up acts that clients wanted, like recording meetings, for instance.

Although notaries' relationship to the French state was in many ways remote in this period, they did help assert structures of authority in daily life, both for the state and for their communities. Women might be able to do a variety of work in and out of their households, but to make a notarial contract, they needed the permission of their husbands. Likewise, a notarized marriage contract not only firmly declared that the spouses married with the consent of their parents (and kin), but that they made that marriage a public affair.

Compared with the regulatory and oversight apparatus available to modern states, early modern monarchies had relatively few means of ordering their populations. While the threat of coercion did provide a tool for states, rulers also needed to seek other means of pacifying, negotiating, and appropriating the at least tacit support of their subjects.[3] Notaries were a link between king and subject, and their acts were central in the web of laws and social relations that perpetuated gender, power, and authority hierarchies.

The individual household, the building block of patriarchal political rhetoric, was an important site for the ordering of family life, where the re-

---

3. This has been shown in recent work on the success of royal authority, in the seventeenth century, in gradually overcoming elite provincial opposition and securing noble support. See William Beik, *Absolutism and Society in Seventeenth-Century France: State Power and Provincial Aristocracy in Languedoc* (Cambridge, 1985); Sarah Hanley, "Engendering the State: Family Formation and State Building in Early Modern France," *French Historical Studies* 16 (Spring 1989); and Sarah Hanley, "Family and State in Early Modern France: The Marriage Pact," in Marilyn J. Boxer and Jean H. Quataert, eds., *Connecting Spheres: Women in the Western World, 1500 to the Present* (Oxford, 1987).

alties of gender and authority were negotiated and given meaning in daily practice. Patterns of sociability were gendered even within households, providing one base for the maintenance of order through the alliances of men of different households.

The emphasis of middling families on appropriate *mesnagement* as a key to household authority was at the heart of the construction of gender, creating obligations as well as rights and privileges for household members. Male household heads were not immune from criticism or restraint if they failed to meet the requirement that heads of households maintain order, financial as well as otherwise, as a prerequisite for enjoying authority. Women as well as men took responsibility for the maintenance of household economies in middling families. Their dowries and labor made important contributions to the financial health of the household, and they had an essential role in the creation of a distinctive sociability based on hosting. Moreover, financial disorder, more than anything else, attracted outside intervention in the affairs of the household, as kin stepped in to prevent the dissipation of resources. The priorities and values of middling families gave women spaces to exert their own power and influence and to seek protection against spousal excess.

Moreover, middling families employed an inheritance system where customary law and practice profoundly committed parents, as well as children, to equal provision among heirs and to kin oversight of household patrimonial management. They scrupulously observed the strict partibility of Breton customary law in practice. In the seventeenth century, at least, they faced a threat to their socioeconomic position that they often chose to resist, by trying to provide for all children, in the hope that all would secure middling-order status even if none would rise beyond it. The complexity of the early modern French legal system meant that royal decrees did not work in a vacuum—they had to mesh with an already well-established customary law whose precepts were deeply imbued in local populations.

The imperatives of Breton customary law and practice in many ways countered the power of fathers and husbands over their children and wives, power that the royal decrees of 1560–1630 so increased. The emphases of customary law, rather, fostered kin consultation and oversight of with the advocacy of kin consultation and strict partibility.

These emphases also fostered the central part that kin played in negotiating the challenges of daily life. The collective strategies that inheritance practices encouraged among heirs also facilitated ties between men who were related through their wives and sisters. Resulting kinship structures, especially those that were practical rather than official, were neither patrilineal nor focused on conjugal family. Instead, bilateral, same-generation male kin predominated in family ties of any one individual notary. The families of both spouses were equally important sources of a broadly based kinship. Same-generation kin, above all, constantly mobilized their ties in myriad ways.[4]

The locus of gender and authority in daily life was focused more broadly than on individual fathers and husbands, as middling urban families were enmeshed in relations of diverse kinds between households that played a critical part in shaping and maintaining power relations in particular forms. Kinsmen together adopted practices of property management and daily sociability that were profoundly patriarchal in their implications. Structures of authority in middling families, in contrast to the royal rhetoric that emphasized the supremacy of the household patriarch, rested largely on cooperation between male kin of different households. The inability of widows to take advantage of the opportunities that were legally available to them illustrated the continuing disabilities that women encountered in practice. Women as much as men built the kinship system, but, at least in its public manifestation, women's partnership was elided.

Links with households with whom no kinship relation existed were also important resources for men and women. Women's alliances with other women, while very difficult to recover, seem to have provided friendship, support, and material aid of various kinds. Sociability bound men of middling households together in bars, militia guard rooms, parish meetings, and baptismal celebrations. For them, the parish marked an important divider of urban space and a key site of community organization. Men of a closely knit group of notaries, apothecaries, and their ilk, whose lives precariously straddled the line between the artisanat and the bottom ranks of the professions, formed a cohort whose sociability encompassed not only entertainment, but also the public expression and representation of their vision of a civic order.

The active participation of these middling men in the affairs of their parish community helped to shape the meanings of public order in their

4. Although most studies of northern Europe have minimized the importance of kinship in nonelite groups, its role as a resource and in structuring relations of power has been shown in studies of the Renaissance Italian elite. For an exception that emphasizes the role of kinship in middling families in eighteenth-century Paris, see David Garrioch, *The Formation of the Parisian Bourgeoisie, 1690–1830* (Cambridge, Mass., 1996). For Italy, see Diane Owen Hughes, "Representing the Family: Portraits and Purposes in Early Modern Italy," *Journal of Interdisciplinary History* 17 (Summer 1986); Sharon Strocchia, *Death and Ritual in Renaissance Florence* (Baltimore, 1992).

world. Many were keen attenders at the Nantais municipal assembly, active in parochial affairs, and energetic as militia members. In all these sites, they brought the values of their middling rank into play to contribute to the working out of patriarchal order in practice.

Public life had other attractions for middling men like notaries, whose socioeconomic position was under threat. It provided them with rare opportunities for distinction, perhaps as vestrymen or militia officers; it associated them with the city's elite, rather than with the ranks below them; and it was a site for rank-appropriate sociability.

In these ways, a distinctly middling worldview emerged. The emphasis on husbandry, thrift, and *bon mesnagement* may have been part of the new necessity of engaging with an expanding money economy and its credit relations, but the reaction of the urban middling ranks to this economic evolution was in sharp contrast to the monetary flamboyance favored by the contemporary aristocracy. Other ways in which middling families managed the challenges of early modern daily life may have been similarly distinctive: their emphasis on lineage property, on provision for all children over the protection intact of patrimony, and on bilateral collateral kin ties. The patterns of authority that were espoused in such families were fraternal as well as paternal.[5]

Such differences allowed a broad spectrum of early modern society to agree on a gendered authority as the basis of social and political order, without achieving consensus as to what, exactly, the implications of such an order would be. While the desire for "order" was widespread, it was not a stable concept, because different interests maintained different ideas about how it should be realized.

This contingency permitted, for example, the capacity for criticism and opposition to the government that characterized some of the most eye-catching moments of the seventeenth century, moments that took place under the umbrella of household patriarchy. While kings and elites emphasized paternal authority and extensive sovereignty, middling families fa-

---

5. For noble values of the same period, see Jonathan Dewald, *Aristocratic Experience and the Origins of Modern Culture, France, 1570–1715* (Berkeley and Los Angeles, 1993). The distinctiveness of the identities and mores of middling families addresses one of the great issues of early modern French historiography, clearly pointing to the existence of horizontal as well as vertical solidarities in early modern communities. For particular patterns of gender and kinship as key elements of class identity in the modern period, see, for instance, Leonore Davidoff and Catherine Hall, *Family Fortunes: Men and Women of the English Middle Class, 1780–1850* (London, 1987); Mary Ryan, *Cradle of the Middle Class: The Family in Oneida County, New York, 1790–1865* (Cambridge, 1981).

vored kin advice, supervision, and obligations having to do with *mesnage-ment*.

The centrality of *mesnagement* as a source of authority in these families may have had larger political implications too, in terms of the families' perceptions of the meanings and parameters of royal sovereignty in the seventeenth century. Opposition to the crown along the lines of criticism of the failure of *mesnagement* by the crown or its representatives did occur. During the Fronde, as Jeffrey Merrick has shown, pamphleteers opposed to the king focused attention on the shortcomings of the mid-century royal household, with its adolescent king, female regent, and chief minister, Cardinal Mazarin, whose behavior contradicted all the tenets of *bon mesnage-ment*. These critiques of the crown did not challenge the principle of royal sovereignty, but justified their opposition on the grounds that the crown, at that moment, was not managing its affairs satisfactorily.[6] The political language of the Mazarinades, pushing for the recognition of the obligations as well as privileges of leadership and the need for oversight, could easily resonate with the perspectives of middling subjects. In the revolutionary remaking of French political discourses of the late eighteenth century, the fraternal emphasis came, in fact, to usurp the paternal.[7]

The knitting of cultural processes that made household patriarchy writ, large and small, a central feature of early modern life was a complex and often challenged process. In daily life, every individual encountering another could and did frequently chafe at, temper, or actively resist the hierarchies of power that enmeshed them. The shift from the internal dynamics of the household that was suggested at the signing of marriage contracts (when women's contributions to the production of wealth and kinship were acknowledged) to the public community affirmed at baptisms (which represented an almost exclusively fraternal kinship in which women's role was elided) shows the multilayered, contingent character of gendered authority.

This dynamic explains one of apparent contradictions of early modern political culture, that is, that in a society that was ideologically and rhetorically fiercely patriarchal, many individual instances show that women and subjects had considerable room to maneuver. In practice, women had re-

---

6. For evidence of this political application of patriarchy allowing an oppositional culture to develop, see Jeffrey Merrick, "The Cardinal and the Queen: Political and Sexual Disorders in the Mazarinades," *French Historical Studies* 18 (Spring 1994).

7. Merrick, "The Cardinal and the Queen"; Lynn Hunt, *The Family Romance of the French Revolution* (Berkeley and Los Angeles, 1992).

sponsibilities and men were assigned obligations, making a context where, within individual households, men and women could build their lives together. These individual household situations, however, were part of the process by which household patriarchy became a pillar of early modern political culture, rather than a threat to its foundations. In almost all public representations and formations, men's authority was highlighted and reiterated, while women's contributions were assigned little value. The continual reiteration of this pattern at the ground level, as well as political rhetoric and royal edict, contributed to legitimizing and authorizing the sovereign claims of the kings of France, even while it allowed individuals and subjects room to frame their opposition to their father-king.

Bibliography

Abbreviations

ADLA   Archives Départementales de Loire-Atlantique
AMN   Archives Municipales de Nantes

Note on Usage
All men named without any other reference to occupation were notaries, and all
    women named without additional identification were wives of notaries.

MANUSCRIPT PRIMARY SOURCES

1. Archives Départementales de Loire-Atlantique, Nantes

Court of Nantes

(Includes records of the *sénéchausée* and the *prévôte*)
B5646–5698:   Scelles, Inventaires et Vantes de Meubles, 1553–1660
B5801–5818:   Serments d'Experts, Enquêtes, Rapports, Procès-Verbaux, 1600–
                1660
B5865–5874:   Saisies et Successions, Beneficiares, Bannies, Adjudications, Sépara-
                tions, Démissions, et Ordres
B6370–6378:   Minutes de Sentences Relatives aux Tutelles et Curatelles, 1609–
                1660
B6112–6144:   Audiences Ordinaires: Sentences sur Requêtes, 1590–1660
B6648–6669:   Police Municipale: Minutes des Plaintes, des Procès-Verbaux, des In-
                formations, et des Sentences, 1600–1660
B7207–7233:   Tutelles, Curatelles, Procédures Civiles (in alphabetical order), dix-
                septième et dix-huitième siècles

Notarial Records

Série 4E2: 416 *liasses* comprising all extant minutes, 1560–1660

Parish Registers

Série J sous série 25j: Dépouillement sur Fiches Manuscrites des Registres Parois-
seaux par le Vicompte Paul de Freslon

Parish Records

G468: St. Croix
G480: St. Denis
G507: St. Saturnin

Corporation Records

5E: Corporations 4, 5, 12, 13, 16, 26, and 43.

Other

1J 288: *Formulaire*

2. Archives Municipales de Nantes

BB22–43: Déliberations et Assemblées du Conseil des Bourgeois, 1588–1660
CC86, 132, 340: Comptes de la Ville
EE30, 31, 32, 33: Affaires Militaires, Guet et Garde
EE62, 107: La Milice Bourgeoise
Série GG: Parish Registers for City Parishes, 1560–1660
GG701–3, 722, 725: Records of the Hôtel-Dieu

PUBLISHED PRIMARY SOURCES

Bernard, Maurice. *Divers Observations du Droit . . . contient plusieurs notables recherches
    des offices des Notaires et Tabellions Royaux, Protonotaires, Secretaires du Roy, Greffiers
    et autres Semblables.* Bordeaux, 1717.
Bodin, Jean. *Les Six Livres de la République.* Paris, 1576; reprinted Paris, 1986.
Chenu, Jean. *Cent Notables et Singuliers Questions du Droict décidées par Arrests Memo-
    rables des Cours Soveraines de France.* 4th ed., Paris, 1611.
Croset, Jean de. *C'est la Remonstrance au Roy Pour le resoudre à oster aux faux Notaires
    Les Moyens qu'ils ont d'antidatter et de varier, d'altérer et de supporser les feuillets de
    leurs livres.* Lyons, 1610.
"Description de la Ville de Nantes au dix-septième siècle, le vingt-troisième jour de
    mars, en l'an 1646 par un habitant de la ville." In Camille Mellinet, *La Com-
    mune et la milice de Nantes.* 3 vols., Nantes, 1841.
Dubuisson-Aubénay. *Itinéraire en Bretagne en 1636.* Nantes, 1902.
Ferrière, Claude Joseph de. *La Science Parfaite des Notaires ou le Parfait Notaire.* Paris,
    1681; rev. ed. Paris, 1741.
*La Coustume de Bretagne avec les Commentaires et Observations . . . par Maître Michel
    Sauvageau.* Nantes, 1710.

Isambert, François. *Recueil général des anciennes lois françaises depuis l'an 420 jusqu'à la Révolution de 1789.* Paris, 1829.

Loyseau, Charles. *Les Cinq Livres du Droict.* In Claude Joly, ed., *Les Oeuvres de Maistre Charles Loyseau.* Rev. ed. Paris, 1666.

SECONDARY SOURCES

Accampo, Elinor. "Gender Relations in the City: A Response." *French Historical Studies* 18 (Spring 1993).

Amussen, Susan. *An Ordered Society: Class and Gender in Early Modern England.* London, 1988.

Ariès, Philipe. *L'Enfant et la vie familiale sous l'Ancien Régime.* Paris, 1960.

Baron, Romain. "La Bourgeoisie de Varzy au dix-septième siècle." *Annales de Bourgogne* 36 (July–September 1964).

Baulant, Michèle. "La Famille en miettes: Sur un aspect de la démographie du dix-septième siècle." *Annales E.S.C.* 27 (July–October 1972).

———. "Niveaux de vie paysanne autour de Meaux en 1700 et 1750." *Annales E.S.C.* 30 (May–June 1975).

Beik, William. *Absolutism and Society in Seventeenth-Century France: State Power and Provincial Aristocracy in Languedoc.* Cambridge, 1985.

———. *Urban Protest in Seventeenth-Century France: The Culture of Retribution.* Cambridge, 1997.

Benedict, Philip, ed. *Cities and Social Change in Early Modern France.* London, 1989.

———. *Rouen During the Wars of Religion.* Cambridge, 1981.

Bennett, Judith. *Ale, Beer, and Brewsters in England: Women's Work in a Changing World, 1300–1600.* Oxford, 1996.

———. "The Tie That Binds: Peasant Marriages and Families in Late Medieval England." *Journal of Interdisciplinary History* 15 (Summer 1984).

———. *Women in the Medieval English Countryside: Gender and Household in Brigstock Before the Plague.* Oxford, 1987.

Bossy, John. "Blood and Baptism: Kinship, Community, and Christianity in Western Europe, from the Fourteenth to the Seventeenth Centuries." In Derek Baker, ed., *Sanctity and Secularity: The Church and the World.* Oxford, 1973.

———. "Godparenthood: The Fortunes of a Social Institution in Early Modern Christianity." In Kaspar von Greyerz, ed., *Religion and Society in Early Modern Europe, 1500–1800.* London, 1984.

Bottigheimer, Ruth. "Tale Spinners: Submerged Voices in Grimms' Fairy Tales." *New German Critique* 27 (Fall 1982).

Boulton, Matthew. *Neighbourhood and Society: A London Suburb in the Seventeenth Century.* Cambridge, 1987.

Bourdieu, Pierre. *Outline of a Theory of Practice.* Cambridge, 1977.

Brennan, Thomas. *Public Drinking and Popular Culture in Eighteenth-Century Paris.* Princeton, 1988.

Brodsky, Vivian. "Widows in Late Elizabethan London: Remarriage, Economic Opportunity, and Family Orientations." In Lloyd Bonfield, ed., *The World We Have Gained: Histories of Population and Social Structure.* London, 1986.

Brunelle, Gayle. *The New World Merchants of Rouen, 1559–1630.* Kirksville, Mo., 1991.

Bynum, Caroline. *Fragmentation and Redemption: Essays on Gender and the Human Body in Medieval Religion.* New York, 1991.

Chartier, Roger. *Cultural History: Between Practices and Representations.* Cambridge, 1988.

———. *The Cultural Uses of Print in Early Modern France.* Princeton, 1987.

———, ed. *The Culture of Print: Power and the Uses of Print in Early Modern Europe.* Princeton, 1987.

Chaytor, Miranda. "Household and Kinship: Ryton in the Late Sixteenth and Early Seventeenth Centuries." *History Workshop* 10 (Fall 1980).

Chevalier, Bernard. *Les Bonnes Villes de France, du quatorzième au seizième siècles.* Paris, 1982.

Clark, Alice. *Working Life of Women in the Seventeenth Century.* London, 1919.

Cole, John, and Eric Wolf. *The Hidden Frontier: Ecology and Ethnicity in an Alpine Valley.* New York, 1974.

Colley, Linda. *Britons: Forging the Nation, 1707–1837.* New Haven, Conn., 1992.

Collier, Jane Fishburne, and Sylvia Junko Yanagisako, eds. *Gender and Kinship: Essays Towards a Unified Analysis.* Stanford, 1987.

Collins, James B. *Classes, Estates, and Order in Early Modern Brittany.* Cambridge, 1994.

———. "The Economic Role of Women in Seventeenth-Century France." *French Historical Studies* 16 (Fall 1989).

———. "Geographic and Social Mobility in Early Modern France." *Journal of Social History* 24 (Spring 1991).

Collomp, Allain. *La Maison du père: Famille et village en Haute-Provence aux dix-septième et dix-huitième siècles.* Paris, 1983.

Couturier, Marcel. *Recherches sur les structures sociales de Châteaudun, 1525–1789.* Paris, 1969.

Cressy, David. "Kinship and Kin Interaction in Early Modern England." *Past and Present* 113 (November 1986).

———. "Thanksgiving and the Churching of Women in Post-Reformation England." *Past and Present* 141 (November 1993).

Croix, Alain. *La Bretagne aux seizième et dix-septième siècles: La Vie, la mort, la foi.* 2 vols., Paris, 1981.

———. *Nantes et le pays Nantais au seizième siècle: Etude démographique.* Paris, 1974.

Darrow, Margaret. *Revolution in the House: Family, Class, and Inheritance in Southern France, 1775–1825.* Princeton, 1989.

Davidoff, Leonore, and Catherine Hall. *Family Fortunes: Men and Women of the English Middle Class, 1780–1850.* London, 1987.

Davis, Natalie Zemon. *Fiction in the Archives: Pardon Tales and Their Telling in Sixteenth-Century France.* Stanford, 1987.

———. "Ghosts, Kin, and Progeny: Some Features of Family Life in Early Modern France." *Daedalus* (Spring 1977).

———. *Society and Culture in Early Modern France.* Stanford, 1975.

Dessert, Daniel. *Argent, pouvoir, et société au Grand Siècle.* Paris, 1984.

Dewald, Jonathan. *Aristocratic Experience and the Origins of Modern Culture, France, 1570–1715.* Berkeley and Los Angeles, 1993.

———. *The Formation of a Provincial Nobility: The Magistrates of the Parlement of Rouen, 1499–1610.* Princeton, 1980.

Diefendorf, Barbara. *Paris City Councillors in the Sixteenth Century: The Politics of Patrimony.* Princeton, 1983.

———. "Widowhood and Remarriage in Sixteenth-Century Paris." *Journal of Family History* 7 (Winter 1982).

Ditz, Toby M. *Property and Kinship: Inheritance in Early Connecticut, 1750–1820.* Princeton, 1986.

Doyle, William. *Venality: The Sale of Office in Eighteenth-Century France.* Oxford, 1996.
Dupaquier, Jacques, ed. *Marriage and Remarriage in Populations of the Past.* New York, 1981.
Fairchilds, Cissie. *Domestic Enemies: Servants and Their Masters in Old Regime France.* Baltimore, 1984.
———. "Women and Family." In Samia Spencer, *French Women and the Age of the Enlightenment.* Bloomington, Ind., 1984.
Farr, James R. *Authority and Sexuality in Early Modern Burgundy, 1550–1730.* Oxford, 1995.
———. *Hands of Honor: Artisans and Their World in Dijon, 1550–1650.* Ithaca, N.Y., 1988.
———. "The Pure and Disciplined Body: Hierarchy, Mortality, and Symbolism in France During the Catholic Reformation." *Journal of Interdisciplinary History* 21 (Winter 1991).
Fine, Agnès. "A propos du trousseau: Une Culture féminine?" In Michelle Perrot, ed., *Une Histoire de femmes est-elle possible?* Paris, 1984.
Flandrin, Jean-Louis. *Families in Former Times: Kinship, Household, and Sexuality.* Cambridge, 1977.
Ford, Caroline. "Private Lives and Public Order in Restoration France: The Seduction of Emily Loveday." *American Historical Review* 99 (February 1994).
Foucault, Michel. *History of Sexuality.* New York, 1980.
Gager, Kristen Elizabeth. *Blood Ties and Fictive Ties: Adoption and Family Life in Early Modern France.* Princeton, 1996.
Garrioch, David. *The Formation of the Parisian Bourgeoisie, 1690–1830.* Cambridge, Mass., 1996.
———. *Neighbourhood and Community in Paris, 1740–1790.* Cambridge, 1986.
Gaston, Jean. *La Communauté des notaires de Bordeaux, 1520–1791.* Bordeaux, 1913; reprinted Toulouse, 1991.
Gay, J.-L. *Les Effets pécuniaires du mariage en Nivernais, du quatorzième au dix-huitième siècles.* Paris, 1953.
Giesey, Ralph. "Rules of Inheritance and Strategies of Mobility in Prerevolutionary France." *American Historical Review* 82 (April 1977).
Goldthwaite, Richard. "The Florentine Palace As Domestic Architecture." *American Historical Review* 77 (October 1972).
Gresset, Maurice. *Gens de justice à Besancon, de la conquête par Louis XIV à la Révolution Française, 1674–1789.* 2 vols., Paris, 1978.
Gullickson, Gay. *Spinners and Weavers of Auffray: Rural Industry and the Sexual Division of Labor in a French Village, 1750–1850.* Cambridge, 1986.
Hamscher, Albert. *The Conseil Privé and the Parlements in the Age of Louis XIV: A Study in French Absolutism.* Philadelphia, 1987.
Hanley, Sarah. "Engendering the State: Family Formation and State Building in Early Modern France." *French Historical Studies* 16 (Spring 1989).
———. "Family and State in Early Modern France: The Marriage Pact." In Marilyn J. Boxer and Jean H. Quataert, eds., *Connecting Spheres: Women in the Western World, 1500 to the Present.* Oxford, 1987.
———. "The Monarchic State in Early Modern France: Marital Regime Government and Male Right." In Adrianna Bakos, ed., *Politics, Ideology, and the Law in Early Modern Europe: Essays in Honor of J. H. M. Salmon.* Rochester, N.Y., 1994.
Hareven, Tamara. *Family Time, Industrial Time: The Relationship Between Family and Work in a New England Industrial Community.* Cambridge, 1982.

———. "The History of the Family and the Complexity of Social Change." *American Historical Review* 96 (February 1991).

Harris, Barbara. "Property, Power, and Personal Relations: Elite Mothers and Sons in Yorkist and Early Tudor England." *Signs* 15 (Spring 1990).

Havard, Henry. *Dictionnaire de l'ameublement et de la décoration, depuis le treizième siècle jusqu'à nos jours.* Paris, 1894.

Hirschon, Renée, ed. *Women and Property, Women As Property.* London and New York, 1984.

Hoffman, Philip. *Church and Community in the Diocese of Lyon, 1500–1789.* New Haven, Conn., 1984.

Hoffman, Philip, Gilles Postel-Vinay, and Jean-Laurent Rosenthal. "Private Credit Markets in Paris, 1690–1840." *Journal of Economic History* 52 (June 1992).

Howell, Martha. "Marriage, Property, and Patriarchy: Recent Contributions to a Literature." *Feminist Studies* 13 (Spring 1987).

Hufton, Olwyn. "Women Without Men: Widows and Spinsters in Britain and France in the Eighteenth Century." *Journal of Family History* 9 (Winter 1984).

Hunt, Lynn. *The Family Romance of the French Revolution.* Berkeley and Los Angeles, 1992.

Hunt, Margaret. *The Middling Sort: Commerce, Gender, and the Family in England, 1680–1780.* Berkeley and Los Angeles, 1996.

Jurgens, Madelaine, and Pierre Coupperie. "Le Logement à Paris aux seizième et dix-septième siècles." *Annales E.S.C.* 17 (May–June 1962).

Kettering, Sharon. "Patronage and Kinship in Early Modern France." *French Historical Studies* 16 (Fall 1989).

Klapisch-Zuber, Christiane. *Women, Family, and Ritual in Renaissance Italy.* Chicago, 1985.

Ladurie, Emmanuel Leroy. "A System of Customary Law: Family Structures and Inheritance Customs in Sixteeenth-Century France." In Robert Forster and Orest Ranum, eds., *Family and Society: Selections from the Annales Economies, Sociétés, Civilisations.* Baltimore, 1976.

Larminat, Hervé de. "La Compagnie des notaires de Nantes, des origines à la Révolution." Thèse pour le doctorat en droit, Université de Rennes, 1955.

Langlois, Ludovic. *La Communauté des notaires de Tours, de 1512 à 1791.* Paris, 1911.

Lehoux, Françoise. *Le Cadre de vie des médecins parisiens aux seizième et dix-septième siècles.* Paris, 1976.

Lelièvre, Jacques. *La Pratique des contrats de mariage chez les notaires au Châtelet de Paris, de 1789 à 1804.* Paris, 1959.

Leonardo, Micaela di. "The Female World of Cards and Holidays: Women, Families, and the Work of Kinship." *Signs* 12 (Spring 1987).

Limon, Monique. *Les Notaires au Châtelet de Paris sous le règne de Louis XIV: Etude institutionelle et sociale.* Toulouse, 1992.

Litchfield, R. Burr. "Demographic Characteristics of Florentine Patrician Families: Sixteenth to Eighteenth Centuries." *Journal of Economic History* 29 (June 1969).

Lottin, Alain. "Vie et mort du couple: Difficultés conjugales et divorces dans le nord de la France aux dix-septième et dix-huitième siècles." *Dix-septième siècle* 102, 103 (1974).

Lynch, Katherine A. "The Family and the History of Public Life." *Journal of Interdisciplinary History* 24 (Spring 1994).

Macfarlane, Alan. *The Family Life of Ralph Josselin.* Cambridge, 1970.

Martin, Xavier. *Le Principe d'égalité dans les successions roturières en Anjou et dans le Maine.* Paris, 1972.

Martines, Lauro. *Lawyers and Statecraft in Renaissance Florence.* Princeton, 1968.

Maza, Sarah. *Private Lives and Public Affairs: The Causes Célèbres of Prerevolutionary France.* Berkeley and Los Angeles, 1993.

———. *Servants and Masters in Eighteenth-Century France: The Uses of Loyalty.* Princeton, 1983.

Medick, Hans, and David Warren Sabean, eds. *Interest and Emotion: Essays on the Study of Family and Kinship.* Cambridge, 1984.

Merrick, Jeffrey. "The Cardinal and the Queen: Sexual and Political Disorders in the Mazarinades." *French Historical Studies* 18 (Spring 1994).

———. "Fathers and Kings: Patriarchalism and Absolutism in Eighteenth-Century French Politics." *Studies on Voltaire and the Eighteenth Century* 308 (1993).

Merwick, Donna. "Archives and Cultural Formation: The World of Signs and the Construction of Colonial New Netherland Society." Paper presented to the Davis Center Seminar, Princeton University, 10 February 1989.

———. "The House of the Notary: Local Theatres for the Negotiation of Power." Paper presented at the Eleventh Conference of Australasian Historians of Medieval and Early Modern Europe, University of Adelaide, 28 September 1991.

———. "The Suicide of a Notary: Language, Personal Identity, and Conquest in Colonial New York," in Ronald Hoffman, Mechal Sobel, and Fredricka J. Teute, eds., *Through a Glass Darkly: Reflections on Personal Identity in Early America* (Chapel Hill, 1997).

Michaud, Claude. "Notariat et sociologie de la rente à Paris au dix-septième siècle: L'Emprunt du clergé de 1690." *Annales E.S.C.* (November–December 1977).

Mitchell, J. Clyde, ed. *Social Networks in Urban Situations.* Manchester, 1969.

Mousnier, Roland. *The Institutions of France Under the Absolute Monarchy, 1598–1789: Society and the State.* Chicago, 1979.

Neuschel, Kristen B. "Noble Households in the Sixteenth Century: Material Settings and Human Communities." *French Historical Studies* 15 (Fall 1988).

Nussdorfer, Laurie. "Notarial Inscription and Artisan Collectivities in Seventeenth-Century Rome." Paper presented to the Annual Meeting of the American Historical Association, San Francisco, 1994.

———. "Writing and the Power of Speech: Notaries and Artisans in Baroque Rome." In Carla Hesse and Barbara Diefendorf, eds., *Culture and Identity in Early Modern Europe, 1500–1800: Essays in Honor of Natalie Davis.* Ann Arbor, Mich., 1993.

Pardailhé-Galabrun, Annik. *La Naissance de l'intime: 3,000 foyers parisiens, dix-septième–dix-huitième siècles.* Paris, 1988.

Pateman, Carol. *The Sexual Contract.* Stanford, 1988.

Perry, Mary Elizabeth. *Gender and Disorder in Early Modern Seville.* Princeton, 1990.

Poisson, Jean-Paul. *Notaires et société: Travaux d'histoire et de sociologies notariales.* 2 vols., Paris, 1985, 1990.

Phillips, Roderick. *Family Breakdown in Late Eighteenth-Century France: Divorces in Rouen, 1792–1803.* Oxford, 1980.

Ranum, Orest. *The Fronde: A French Revolution.* New York, 1993.

———. "Vers une histoire de l'esthétique sociale: Le Contrat de mariage du Comte de Grignan et de Marie Angélique du Puy du Fou et de Champagne." In Wolfgang Leiner and Pierre Ronzeaud, eds., *Correspondances: Mélanges offerts à Roger Duchêne.* Aix-en-Provence, 1992.

Rapp, Rayna, Ellen Ross, and Renata Bridenthal. "Examining Family History." *Feminist Studies* 5 (Spring 1979).

Rappaport, Steve. *World Within Worlds: Structures of Life in Sixteenth-Century London.* Cambridge, 1987.

Reiter, Rayna. "Men and Women in the South of France: Public and Private Domains." In Rayna Reiter, ed., *Toward an Anthropology of Women.* New York, 1975.

Revel, Jacques. "The Uses of Civility." In Roger Chartier, ed., *Passions of the Renaissance: A History of Private Life.* Cambridge, Mass., 1989.

Robbins, Kevin. "Families and Politics in La Rochelle, 1550–1650." Ph.D. dissertation, Johns Hopkins University, 1990.

Roche, Daniel. *Le Peuple de Paris: Essai sur la culture populaire au dix-huitième siècle.* Paris, 1981.

Roper, Lyndal. "Discipline and Respectability: Prostitution and the Reformation in Augsburg." *History Workshop* 19 (Spring 1985).

———. *The Holy Household: Women and Morals in Reformation Augsburg.* Oxford, 1989.

Roth-Lochner, Barbara. "L'Evolution de l'activité notariale à Genève aux dix-septième et dix-huitième siècles." *Revue d'histoire moderne et contemporaine* 33 (January–March 1986).

Rouzeau, Louis. *Repertoire numérique des archives notariales: Minutes des notaires Nantais.* Nantes, 1988.

Ryan, Mary. *Cradle of the Middle Class: The Family in Oneida County, New York, 1790–1865.* Cambridge, 1981.

Sabean, David Warren. "Aspects of Kinship Behaviour and Property in Rural Western Europe before 1800." In Jack Goody, Joan Thirsk, and E. P. Thompson, eds., *Family and Inheritance: Rural Society in Western Europe, 1200–1800.* Cambridge, 1976.

———. *Power in the Blood: Popular Culture and Village Discourse in Early Modern Germany.* Cambridge, 1984.

Sacks, David Harris. *The Widening Gate: Bristol and the Atlantic Economy, 1450–1700.* Berkeley and Los Angeles, 1991.

Saupin, Guy. "La Vie municipale à Nantes sous l'Ancien Régime, 1565–1789." Thèse pour le doctorat de troisième cycle, 2 vols., Université de Nantes, 1981.

Schnapper, Bernard. *Les Rentes au seizième siècle: Histoire d'un instrument de crédit.* Paris, 1957.

Schneider, Jane. "Trousseau As Treasure: Some Contradictions of Late Nineteenth-Century Change in Sicily." In Marion Kaplan, ed., *The Marriage Bargain: Women and Dowries in European History.* New York, 1985.

Schneider, Robert. *Public Life in Toulouse, 1463–1789.* Ithaca, N.Y., 1989.

Schochet, Gordon J. *Patriarchalism in Political Thought: The Authoritarian Family and Political Speculation and Attitudes, Especially in Seventeenth-Century England.* New York, 1975.

Scott, Joan. "Gender: A Useful Category of Historical Analysis." *American Historical Review* 91 (December 1985).

Segalen, Martine. *Love and Power in the Peasant Family: Rural France in the Nineteenth Century.* Chicago, 1983.

Sewell, William. *Work and Revolution in France: The Language of Labor, from the Old Regime to 1848.* Cambridge, 1980.

Shammas, Carole. "The Domestic Environment in Early Modern England and America." *Journal of Social History* 4 (Fall 1980).

Smith, Bonnie. *Ladies of the Leisure Class: The Bourgeoises of Northern France in the Nineteenth Century.* Princeton, 1981.

Stone, Lawrence. *Family, Sex, and Marriage in England, 1500–1800.* Abridged ed., London, 1979.

Strocchia, Sharon. *Death and Ritual in Renaissance Florence.* Baltimore, 1992.

———. "Remembering the Family: Women, Kin, and Commemorative Masses in Renaissance Florence." *Renaissance Quarterly* 42 (Winter 1989).

Taylor, Larissa. *Soldiers of Christ: Preaching in Late Medieval and Reformation France.* Oxford, 1992.

Tilly, Louise. "Women's History and Family History: Fruitful Collaboration or Missed Connection?" *Journal of Family History* 12, nos. 1–3 (1987).

Trumbach, Randolph. *The Rise of the Egalitarian Family: Aristocratic Kinship and Domestic Relations in Eighteenth-Century England.* New York, 1978.

Turlan, J. M. "Amis et amis charnels d'après les actes du Parlement au quatorzième siecle." *Revue historique du droit français et étranger,* 4th ser., 47 (1969).

Ulrich, Laurel Thatcher. *Good Wives: Image and Reality in the Lives of Women in Northern New England, 1650–1750.* Oxford, 1980.

Vann, R. "Towards a New Lifestyle: Women in Preindustrial Capitalism." In Renata Bridenthal and Claudia Koonz, eds., *Becoming Visible: Women in European History.* Boston, 1977.

Wheaton, Robert. "Affinity and Descent in Seventeenth-Century Bordeaux." In Robert Wheaton and Tamara Hareven, eds., *Family and Sexuality in French History.* Philadelphia, 1980.

Wilson, Adrian. "The Ceremony of Childbirth and Its Interpretation." In Valerie Fildes, ed., *Women As Mothers in Pre-Industrial England.* New York, 1990.

Wrightson, Keith, and David Levine. *Poverty and Piety in an English Village: Terling, 1525–1700.* London, 1979.

Wyntjes, Sherrin Marshall. "Survivors and Status: Widowhood and Family in the Early Modern Netherlands." *Journal of Family History* 7 (Winter 1982).

Yver, Jean. *Egalité entre héritiers et exclusion des enfants dotés: Essai de géographie coutumière.* Paris, 1966.

Zonabend, Françoise. "La Parenté baptismale à Minot (Côte d'Or)." *Annales E.S.C.* 33 (May–June 1978).

Index

Accampo, Elinor, x
apothecaries, xiii, 11–12, 27, 30, 60, 122,
      133, 165, 169, 173, 178, 186, 189, 211,
      226
architects, 7, 67
artisans, xiii, 10–12, 26–30, 39, 59–60, 63,
      79, 90, 96, 101, 103, 132, 138, 171,
      173, 186, 203, 208, 214, 223

bakers, 1, 11–12, 101, 179, 189
baliffs (*sergents royaux*), 11–12, 14, 208
baptisms, xv, 159, 162, 167–81, 191, 193,
      228
   attendance at, 167, 171–79
   godparents at, 165, 167–71, 80
   kin at, 169–73, 175–78
   women at, 167, 172, 180–81
   See also parishes
barristers (*avocats*), 8, 10, 14, 59, 79, 127,
      165
basket makers, 7
books, ownership of, 29, 82
booksellers, 178
Bourdieu, Pierre, 161

candle makers, 12, 60
clerks, of notaries, 12, 28–29, 60, 67–68,
      85, 92, 95, 146, 177–78, 179
   assistant court clerks, 33, 178
   city clerks, 199–200
   court clerks (*greffiers*), 12, 34, 101, 173
clock makers, 214
Colbert, Jean-Baptiste, 51
contributions, 135

courts, xi, xiv–xv, 2–3, 6, 14–15, 113, 122,
      169, 186, 222. *See also* laws
court ushers (*huissiers*), 11, 106, 165, 178,
      179
credit, ix, 18, 34–41, 42, 46, 159, 162,
      181–93, 227
   borrowers and lenders, 34–41, 132, 162,
      185–93
   as *cedullas*, 187–88
   co-signers (*cautions*), 36–37, 159,
      182–87, 191
   kinship and, 36–37, 48, 159, 182–88,
      190–92
   notaries as credit brokers, 34–41
   as *rentes*, 18–19, 34–41, 43, 48, 138,
      154–55, 181–91, 217
   women and, 39–41, 48, 159, 183–84,
      189, 193
Croset, Jean de, 22–23, 41

Davis, Natalie Zemon, 42
doctors, 8, 165, 169, 171, 173, 177
domestic violence, 86–87, 102
donations, 110, 112, 115–20, 141
dowries, 7, 13, 48, 58–59, 62, 67–69, 71–74,
      116, 225
drapers, 11–12

elites, x, 11, 58, 63, 79, 132, 173, 186, 188,
      190, 204, 208, 211, 213, 215, 227
   nobles, 9–12, 36, 165
endogamy, 10, 60

families, ix, xi–xiv, xvi, 1, 4, 6–15, 18,

52–55, 60–75, 83, 91, 99, 142, 149,
160, 162, 167, 175, 221–23
middling, ix, 6–15, 58–60, 62, 67, 70,
77–78, 82, 84, 88, 94, 101, 104–8, 109,
113, 117, 123, 142, 157, 169, 181, 186,
188–90, 193, 195–97, 210, 205–7, 213,
217–18, 223, 225, 227–28
parents and children, 55, 63–75, 84, 92,
110, 117–20, 126, 128, 130, 135,
138–41, 145–46, 145–47, 157, 169–71
siblings, 55, 58, 66–72, 85, 115, 149–50,
153–58
stepparents and stepchildren, 87,
118–19, 133, 148–53
See also households; kinship; marriages;
women
Ferrière, Claude-Joseph de, 20
friends, 178–81
Fronde, 228
Furetière, Antoine, 19

gender, ix–xi, xvi, 4, 35, 84, 160, 179,
191–93, 210–11
and authority, xii, xvi, 19, 47–48, 52, 91,
107–8, 112–13, 124, 128, 141–42,
180–81, 193, 221, 223–28
See also households; *mesnagement*;
patriarchy; women
godparents. *See* baptisms
goldsmiths, 170
guardianships, 53, 62, 71, 109, 110,
120–29, 152, 177

haberdashers, 11
Hanley, Sarah, xi
heralds, 11–12
Hôtel-Dieu. See poor house
households, ix, x, xii–xiii, 4, 47–49, 51–54,
63–64, 72–74, 77–108, 157–58, 206,
210, 213, 222, 224–29
characteristics of, 78–84, 101–8, 110
sociability in, 101–7
See also mesnagement

inheritance, xii, 53–55, 66–70, 85, 140,
143–58. *See also* laws; women, as heirs

kinship, 4, 52–53, 55–58, 61–63, 74–75,
84–85, 91–92, 101, 109–42, 148–58,
159–93, 211, 222, 225–26

official, 161–62, 191
practical, 161, 164–67, 175, 177–79,
192–93
spiritual, 161, 165, 169–71, 179, 185–86,
211
women and, 48, 166–67, 176–77, 211,
226, 228
See also credit

laws, xi, 53-55
customary, xii, 29, 53–55, 63, 66, 69–70,
115–16, 120–21, 144, 156–58, 162, 225
Roman, xiv,
royal, xi, 51, 53–54, 225
lawyers (*procureurs*), 1, 2, 7–8, 10–11,
13–15, 28, 33, 40, 67, 101, 127, 146,
165, 171, 173, 201, 203, 208
linen, 97–100, 104–5
loans. *See* credit
locksmiths, 3, 58, 189
Loyseau, Claude, 23

marriage, 6–10, 51–75, 174
age at, 58–59
marriage contracts, 18, 30, 42, 60–75,
164–67, 228
See also dowries; households; women
Mazarin, Cardinal, 228
Medick, Hans, 150, 160
merchants, 8, 10–13, 33, 60, 66, 79, 101,
103, 110, 165, 178, 184, 186, 204, 208,
214, 215
Merrick, Jeffrey, 228
mesnagement, 78, 84–101, 103, 107–8,
110–20, 136, 142, 158, 190, 218, 225,
227
mesnagers, 84, 91, 117, 136
millia, xv, 193, 195–97, 218, 227–28
and parishes, 202
service in, 199, 202–7
millers, 11, 60, 187

Nantes, ix, xiv–xvi, 5–6, 32–33
city council, xvi, 199–200, 212–16
council assemblies, 196–97, 200–201, 227
See also militia; parishes; poor house
neighbors, 101–3, 178
notaries, ix, xiii, xv–xvi, 4–5, 17–49, 138, 193,
197–201, 205, 208, 213, 221–24, 226
attitudes toward, 20–24, 41

community of, xv, 4–5, 23, 24–27, 198
    as credit brokers, 34–41, 185, 205, 217,
        221–22, 224
    French state and, xv, 4, 18–19, 24–27, 42,
        46, 197–200, 221, 224
    manuals for, 17, 29–30
    Parisian, xiv, 6 n. 9, 12–13, 26, 59, 79
    purchase of office, 4, 7, 13–14, 33,
        65–66, 73, 159, 183–84, 185
    regulation of, 5, 25
    rural, xiv, 13
    socioeconomic character of, 6–15
    urban, 12, 15, 32–33, 34
    work of, 4–5, 28–48, 199–201, 221–22
    wrongdoing, 2–3
    See also credit; militia; Nantes; parishes;
        poor house

orange sellers, 101

parishes, 173–75, 177–79, 201–13, 226
    governance of, 209–10, 212, 218
    meetings (*chapitres*), xv, 30, 193, 202,
        207–12
    public life and, xvi, 201–12, 227
    St. Clement, 175
    St. Croix, 8, 14, 103, 173–75, 177–78,
        203, 205, 208, 209–11
    St. Denis, 8, 9, 14, 173–75, 178, 211
    St. Donatien, 7
    St. Laurent, 7, 14–15, 174
    St. Nicolas, 6, 8, 14, 58, 143, 174–75, 208
    St. Saturnin, 6, 14, 143, 174–75, 177–79,
        208, 210–11
    St. Similien, 8, 92, 175, 177, 179
    women and, 211
    See also baptisms; militia
patissiers, 60
patriarchy, ix–xi, xvi, 48, 87, 112 n. 8, 190,
    206, 223, 226–29. *See also* gender
patrimony. *See* property
peasants, 7, 12, 151
pewterers, 135
political culture, xii–xiv, xvi, 1, 3, 15, 49,
    196–97, 206, 217–19, 221–23,
    228–29

poor house (*Hôtel-Dieu*), xv, 196, 212–17
    women and, 213
prohibitions (*interdictions*), 110–11
property, 52–53, 70–75, 109–42, 143–58, 221
    community property, 62–63, 74, 115–20,
        130, 139
    lineage property (*propres*), 54, 62–63, 70,
        73–74, 110, 114–16, 130-31, 139, 183,
        191
    See also donations; inheritance;
        separations

rentes. See credit

Sabean, David, 52, 150, 160
saddlers, 104, 179, 189
separations, 86–87, 110–20, 141, 183, 188
servants, 85–92, 103
sharecroppers, 94, 105
shoemakers, 189
state, French, ix, xi, 3, 4–5, 18–19, 20,
    24–27, 46, 53, 198, 221, 224
    kings, xi, 77, 198, 227, 229
    monarchy, 4–5
    royal authority, x, 18
    sovereignty, x–xi, 228
    See also courts; laws; notaries
surgeons, xiii, 8, 11, 30, 169, 170, 173, 178,
    186, 208

tailors, 173, 189
tanners, 58

Wars of Religion, xii, 201, 205, 216
    Catholic League, 197
wills, 18, 42, 123, 143, 188, 215
women, xi, xiv, xvi, 47–48, 75, 78, 192–93,
    225–26, 228–29
    as heirs, 54, 66–70, 144, 147, 157
    as widows, 39–40, 47, 53, 63, 72, 84–85,
        120, 123–24, 126, 129–41
    as wives of notaries, 1–4, 7–10, 12, 29,
        55–60, 66–69, 72–74, 80, 84, 86, 87,
        89–91, 93–101, 105–7, 176–77
    See also credit; donations; households;
        kinship; marriages; separations